D0792919

School Prayer and Discrimination

American River College Library
4700 College Oak Drive
Sacramento, California 95841

School Prayer and Discrimination

The Civil Rights of
Religious Minorities and Dissenters

Frank S. Ravitch

Northeastern University Press
Boston

Northeastern University Press 1999

COPYRIGHT 1999 BY FRANK S. RAVITCH

All rights resesrved. Except for the quotation of short passages for the purposes of criticism and review, no part of this book may be reproduced in any form or by any means, electronic or mechanical, including photocopying, recording, or any information storage and retrieval system now known or to be invented, without written permission of the publisher.

Library of Congress Cataloging-in-Publication Data

Ravitch, Frank S., 1966–
  School prayer and discrimination : the civil rights of religious
minorities and dissenters / Frank S. Ravitch
    p. cm.
  Includes index.
  ISBN 1–55553–392–2 (cloth : acid-free paper);
  ISBN 1–55553–477–5 (pb : acid-free paper)
    1. Prayer in the public schools—Law and legislation—United
States. 2. Religious minorities—Legal status, laws, etc—United
States. 3. Freedom of religion—United States. I. Title.
KF4162.R38 1999
344.73´ 09796—dc21   98—48851

Designed by Janis Owens

Printed and bound by The Maple Press Company in York, Pennsylvania. The paper is Sebago Antique Cream, an acid-free sheet.

MANUFACTURED IN THE UNITED STATES OF AMERICA
05 04 03 02 01   6 5 4 3 2

To my wife Jamie and my daughter Elysha
with love,
Frank/Dad

Contents

Preface

Harassment, discrimination, beatings, death threats, bomb threats, bomb-ings, hate mail, destruction of property, and school prayer—what is out of place on this list? Ironically, a frequently correct answer would be "nothing." This is because public school religious exercises are divisive enough to give rise to any of the problems listed above. When organized school prayer or other religious exercises occur in public schools, those who are in the religious minority and those who oppose the religious activity frequently become the focus of discrimination, harassment, and even physical violence. Still, the debate over separation of church and state generally, and over public school religious exercises particularly, rarely focuses directly on this discrimination. Instead, the debate has been dominated by a conception of the parties and goals involved, which is overwhelmingly focused on civil liberties and the Constitution.

Considering the current legal discourse in this area, one cannot avoid noticing the almost single-minded devotion to constitutional norms in both framing and deciding the issues. In this regard, there are essentially two principles that fuel the debate. The first is protecting the "right" to the free exercise of religion and the second the "right" to be free from state establishment of religion. While I am fascinated by this debate, I am troubled by the fact that it ignores, or at least is not directly concerned with, the potentially harmful side effects of public school religious exercises, particularly the facilitation of discrimination aimed at religious minorities, a concern that may be properly termed a civil rights issue. This book is, in part, a response to the lack of attention paid directly to the discrimination public school religious exercises can facilitate.

This issue is certainly relevant to those who oppose school prayer on traditional constitutional bases, but it is not central or even necessary to their position—a position grounded in traditional conceptions of civil liberties and the constitutional prohibition against the establishment of religion. In this book, I advocate an alternative conception, one that does not require the abandonment of the traditional approach, but rather focuses more directly on an often unspoken, unanalyzed issue that is both separate from, and at the heart of, the larger debate, namely the discrimination that religious minorities and dissenters often suffer when religious exercises occur in the public schools.

The rise and power of the Christian Right in the United States and its obsession with religious exercises in the public schools are at the center of my concern regarding the facilitation of discrimination. Issues such as majoritarian "voluntary, student-initiated school prayer" and the willingness of some school officials to ignore constitutional mandates have gained momentum from a highly effective campaign to return religion in some form or another to the public schools. I hope that the ideas set forth in this book will at the very least lead to discourse that directly addresses the discrimination that can result from allowing religious exercises in the public schools whether or not those exercises are constitutional.

This book has at its core three purposes. The first is to point out the discrimination often facilitated when public school religious exercises occur, a problem that is rarely addressed separately from the broader constitutional issues associated with it and that is not generally discussed as a concern outside of the ultimate disposition of those issues. The second is to explain why, given the current legal, political, and social landscape relating to public school religious exercises, this kind of discrimination is becoming more widespread. The third is to provide a normative mechanism for dealing with such discrimination. In order to achieve this, I look to civil rights principles and antidiscrimination law, which are particularly well-suited for this issue. Moreover, I explain why current legal doctrines in this area are not effective tools for addressing the discrimination caused or facilitated by public school religious exercises.

The way I have viewed the issues addressed in this book, and thus much of the material contained here, has been influenced by the wonderful results of interdisciplinary research I have witnessed through participation in the Law and Society Association annual meetings over the last few years. While the legal issues and cases discussed in this book are perhaps its core, the more I researched the more I came to believe that it would be hard to properly address many of the issues raised without looking at their broader social context and possible historical parallels. This led me to discover an unfortunately rich history of discrimination and violence relating, at least in part, to public school religious exercises.

A stark example of this history, the one I focus on to show that the modern discrimination and violence facilitated by public school religious exercises are not unique, is the Philadelphia Bible Riots of 1844. I owe a debt to the scholars who have written about this sad chapter in United States history. Moreover, the work by social scientists who have studied the relationships between religious orientation and prejudice, as well as more general in-group/out-group dynamics, particularly among younger people, has been invaluable.

Yet, I would be remiss if I implied that I was being exhaustive in these fields that have enriched my work so much. I am not an historian, sociologist, or psychologist. Thus, while I use and have learned a great deal from the relevant scholarship generated by those disciplines, I believe it essential to note that this book is not exhaustive. It could stand on its own as a legal piece addressing the often-ignored discrimination that is facilitated by public school religious exercises, the climate in which such issues currently arise, and the usefulness of using civil rights principles to deal more directly with this discrimination. However, the work from other disciplines that influenced this project has enriched me, and I hope the perspective it adds will enrich those who read this book.

There are many people to whom I owe a great debt, both personally and professionally. First on the list is my wife Jamie, without whose support and encouragement this book could have never been written. She has been patient, supportive, and caring throughout this process. Moreover, her comments on earlier drafts of the book were quite helpful, and she constantly gives me a fresh perspective. Next comes my daughter Elysha, who was born during the writing of this book, and whose unconditional love always brightens me up even on the busiest days. Her smile has a way of both warming my heart and giving me perspective.

My parents, Arline and Carl Ravitch, who are the best and most supportive parents any child could ever hope to have and who have taught me the value of respecting others, have made this book possible in the truest sense by supporting me in my quest for knowledge and the hope for a brighter future. They are amazing human beings, and their faith in me has been a constant source of inspiration.

My Bubby and Pop-Pop, Edith and Albert Karp, did not live to see this book published, but their wisdom, inspiration, and love live on through it and me. My sisters Sharon and Elizabeth have been both a resource and a source of great support. My uncle Gary Karp has been both friend and relative, and the Grosslicht and Schwartz families have been supportive of all I do.

There are three scholars to whom I owe a special debt, and for whose guidance, inspiration, and support, "thank you" is hardly adequate. These scholars have taken time on numerous occasions to share their wisdom with me and I am forever grateful. They have been wonderful mentors and role models. First is Charles Abernathy who also provided valuable comments on both the proposal for this book and parts of the manuscript. Next is Gary Gildin who likewise provided valuable comments on the proposal for this book. Last, but certainly not least, is Lucinda Finley who gave me my first opportunity to teach and write for a living.

Thanks also go to Carl Stychin and Didi Herman for their helpful comments as chair/discussants on panels at the 1996 and 1997 Law and Society Association annual meetings and to Audrey McFarlane who served as chair/discussant for my panel at the 1998 meeting. Portions of the papers I presented at those meetings were integrated into this book. I also must thank the Law and Society Association for teaching me that legal issues should be explored within broader social context where possible. I especially thank David Engel and Frank Munger for introducing me to the Law and Society Association.

I am indebted to Randy Fisher, Amy Tobol, and Larry Manekin for their helpful comments on some of the material that ultimately became part of this book. I would also like to thank Kate Pomper, Maurice Hued, and Christine Klepak for their able research assistance at various times during the writing of this book. Additionally, I am grateful to People for the American Way, which opened its library to me while I was researching portions of this book, enabling me to get materials that I might otherwise have never found. Additionally, Americans United for Separation of Church and State was quite helpful in providing me with materials from the Christian Coalition 1997 "Road to Victory" conference.

The staff at Northeastern University Press has been incredibly helpful in bringing this book to publication. I want to particularly thank John Weingartner, Emily McKeigue, Jill Bahcall, and Scott Brassart, who have helped to make this book possible, and whose professionalism and courtesy was most appreciated. Moreover, Emily and John were unfailingly helpful in getting this book to press and providing excellent suggestions and advice during the editing process. Finally, I would like to thank my colleagues at the State University of New York at Buffalo Law School and the University of Central Florida for their support and inspiration.

School Prayer and Discrimination

chapter one
From Riots to Harassment

F O R   T H E   G R E A T E R   P A R T of this century, controversy has raged over the separation of church and state in the United States. Perhaps no issue has so fueled this controversy as religion in the public schools. Today, fifty years after *Everson v. Board of Education*,[1] which brought Thomas Jefferson's famous phrase "a wall of separation between church and state" into modern Establishment Clause jurisprudence,[2] the debate rages on. Despite the passage of more than thirty years since the *School District of Abington Township v. Schempp*[3] and *Engel v. Vitale*[4] decisions, which held that school-sponsored bible reading and prayer, respectively, are unconstitutional, public school religious exercises still breed controversy.

Virtually all of the discourse addressing the legal issues driving the church–state debate has focused on the Constitution. Yet the Constitution has often proven ineffective in protecting the rights of religious minorities and others who object to religious exercises in the public schools. Many school districts simply ignore constitutional mandates, and these mandates themselves have recently become less clear as a result of the legal tactics of school prayer advocates. This is occurring at a time when factions from the Christian Right are engaged in an organized campaign to influence public school policy, making great strides in influencing school boards and, in some instances, winning a majority of seats on such boards.

United States history is replete with examples of religious exercises in public schools facilitating discrimination and intolerance against religious minorities and dissenters. In some cases, the discrimination has been an unintended byproduct of the exercises. At other times, it has been a significant purpose behind them. Regardless, a disturbing trend of discrimination results when public schools engage in religious exercises. From the earliest days of such exercises, they have called attention to difference. In particular, they have pointed out those students, families, or groups who do not believe in the faith of the majority or its position on public school religious exercises. As will be demonstrated below, this has led to mistreatment, discrimination, violence, and even death.

It would be wonderful if such discrimination was limited to the past—an interesting historical anomaly. Unfortunately, today we see terrible instances of discrimination occurring as the result of public school religious exercises and the divisiveness those exercises breed. Later in this chapter, modern instances of discrimination will be addressed, but first discussion of incidents from early in the history of public school religious exercises is useful to provide historical context for the role these exercises have had in the clash between religious-political conservatism and religious pluralism.

Not long after the foundation of American public schools,[5] over fifty people were killed, and many more injured, in two riots that became known as the Philadelphia Bible Riots of 1844.[6] These riots were part of the reaction to Catholic immigration and participation in the public schools. They were fueled by a fear of increasing religious and cultural pluralism as well as by anti-immigrant zeal. In the period preceding the riots, the first quarter of the nineteenth century, parts of the United States experienced something of a religious enlightenment, which had created a more tolerant attitude toward Catholics, who were relatively few in number at that time. Mainstream Protestant sects dominated American society, and Universalism and Unitarianism were becoming popular in New England.[7] At this time, there was not a great deal of religious pluralism in the United States. With few exceptions, religious pluralism was limited to the differences between various Protestant sects.[8]

By 1840, the country was in the midst of an evangelical revival known as the "Second Great Awakening," as well as growing nationalist fervor, which was later reflected in the anti-immigrant and reactionary Know Nothing Party.[9] Around this time, non-Protestant religious diversity began to grow, as large numbers of Catholics immigrated to North America and less mainstream denominations such as the Mormons grew in strength.[10] This new religious pluralism and the immigrant status of many of those who gave rise to it created tensions with the Protestant majority who saw it as a threat to their values and dominant status. This situation was aggravated by another strain of anti-immigrant sentiment, which was fueled by economic competition.[11]

Unfortunately, the evangelical revival rekindled Protestant animosity toward Catholics as did nationalist sympathies, which pitted "natives" against immigrants.[12] One result was the strict enforcement of laws, school board policies, and unofficial practices throughout the country that required, or were interpreted as requiring, the reading of the King James version of the bible and the recitation of Protestant-oriented prayers and hymns in the recently formed public schools.[13] Such practices were not uncommon even when the public schools were primarily attended by Protestants. These laws and practices were sometimes created, however, and often enforced, to discriminate against Catholics, who were forbidden by canon law to read the King James version of the bible, which they viewed as an affront since its dedicatory preface "refers to the pope as the 'man of sin.'"[14] These attempts to introduce or enforce sectarian religious exercises in the increasingly pluralistic public schools were the flashpoint for intolerance and violence. They exacerbated tensions between the religious majority and minorities throughout the country and demonstrated Madison's fear of uncontrolled factionalism as a danger to tolerance and democracy.[15] Ultimately, the situation, which was also aggravated by the use of anti-Catholic materials in the public schools, contributed to the founding of the Catholic school system—the only practical means available in many areas to avoid the bias and persecution prevalent in the public schools.[16]

During the mid-nineteenth century, Catholic children were sometimes whipped and beaten in public schools for refusing to engage in school-sanctioned religious exercises;[17] a priest in Maine was tarred, feathered, and ridden on a rail as the result of a dispute over bible reading in the public schools;[18] and other incidents occurred throughout the country. However, the Philadelphia Bible Riots of 1844 brought a new level of hatred, violence, and persecution relating to public school religious exercises. As the result of riots in May and July of 1844, which were initially sparked by a dispute over public school bible reading, at least fifty-eight people were killed; over one hundred and forty others were wounded; and property damage in the city has been estimated at hundreds of millions of dollars.[19] While the May rioting was directly sparked by tensions over the bible reading issue, the July rioting was also fueled by the discovery that firearms were being stored in St. Philip's church in response to fears that it might be attacked as other churches had been in the May rioting.[20] Regardless, the issue of bible reading in school was the catalyst for the riots. It exacerbated the tensions which gave rise to them and served as a flashpoint.[21]

Sadly, all of this death and destruction was the result of a school board resolution complying with a reasonable request by the local bishop that Catholic children not be required to read from the King James bible. Neither the request nor the resolution took any rights away from the Protestant children within the district, since they were still allowed to read from the King James version.[22] However, the facts were irrelevant to the majority, and the resulting riots devastated Philadelphia. Unfortunately, as will be discussed below, when it comes to public school religious exercises today, the facts are often irrelevant to those who lash out at religious minorities and dissenters.

While the Bible Riots of 1844 were sparked by the dispute over the bible in public schools, other factors contributed as well, especially the growing nationalist and anti-immigrant movements.[23] Moreover, the evangelical revival that had been sweeping the country during the Second Great Awakening widened religious differences between Protestants and non-Protestants, lowered religious tolerance, and fueled the nationalist movement,[24] for as immigration increased, so too did religious and cultural pluralism. In response, those who had traditionally held power and dominated American society felt threatened and began to use the mechanisms of government, such as the public schools, to enforce their dominance.[25] Decreased tolerance toward non-Protestants, facilitated by the evangelical revival, ensured that there was a majoritarian religious flavor to this process.

In modern times, we see similar phenomena, although there are significant historical differences between the Second Great Awakening and the current evangelical revival. Society is becoming increasingly pluralistic, but at the same time the country is witnessing the immense growth in power of the Christian Coalition and other evangelical organizations with similar agendas.[26] In addition, large numbers of citizens identify themselves as "born again." Much of this group sees increasing religious and cultural pluralism as a threat to its values and beliefs.[27] This powerful segment of society actively seeks to use the mechanisms of government, and particularly the public schools, to back its beliefs and political views.[28]

This is quite similar to the reaction of the dominant Protestant majority to the influx of Catholics in the nineteenth century, although, as will be discussed below, the passage of time has altered the strategies and language utilized. In the nineteenth century, it was often proclaimed that the United States was a "Protestant nation" founded on Protestant values.[29] Now, it is being said that the country is a "Christian nation," founded on Christian values and traditions.[30] The implication in both statements is that those values and traditions should be followed or enforced and that people who oppose such enforcement are outsiders. This has serious ramifications.

These ramifications are reflected in several recent cases that provide examples of the discrimination and persecution facilitated by public school religious exercises. Despite the Supreme Court's prohibition against organized school prayer,[31] some school districts still engage in practices the Court has specifically prohibited. Others try to work within the parameters the Court has laid down, but still allow religious exercises, usually through moments of silence sanctioned by state legislation or under the theory that organized "voluntary, student-initiated prayer" at school events is somehow constitutional.[32] When this has occurred, the result is an unfortunate trend of discrimination aimed at religious minorities and dissenters.

I am not suggesting that every time such religious exercises occur they automatically facilitate discrimination. However, the following cases demonstrate that it occurs too often to be ignored. As will be discussed later in this book, discrimination under these circumstances is predictable, since the exercises call attention to differences, which are frequently perceived negatively and have a tendency to create an ingroup and outgroups.

The case descriptions that follow provide excellent examples of the traumas often inflicted on religious minorities by public school religious exercises. Moreover, the cases provide consistent, vivid, and troubling anecdotal evidence regarding the abuse and discrimination so often associated with public school religious exercises. Since these examples do not exist in a vacuum, they will be followed throughout this book by broader discussions of the phenomena underlying them, especially the highly successful campaign to increase public school religious exercises in the 1980s and 1990s. It is important to remember that many people who experience the type of discrimination described below do not file lawsuits, for fear of worse discrimination, and that few lawsuits actually progress to the point where a written opinion is issued.[33] Moreover, many of the published cases dealing with school prayer issues do not address the incidents of discrimination involved,[34] because as will be discussed in later chapters, current legal doctrines in this area are not equipped to address that problem. Thus, the cases that follow are simply "the tip of the iceberg."[35]

In 1993, the Herdahl family moved from Wisconsin to Mississippi for work-related reasons.[36] The Herdahl children were baptized Lutheran and attended a Pentecostal church. The area to which they moved is heavily Southern Baptist.[37] Mrs. Herdahl was shocked to learn that the North Pontotoc Attendance Center, the local K–12 public school in her new home, Ecru, Mississippi, practiced public prayer over the public address system and conducted religious bible study thirty years after such practices had been outlawed by the Supreme Court.[38] These activities had a decidedly Southern Baptist bent.[39] Her children were ridiculed and harassed because they did not share the majority faith. They were referred to as devil worshipers and atheists, and were accused of not believing in God.[40] Both teachers and students took part in the harassment. A teacher made one child wear headphones to avoid hearing the offending prayers and the child was taunted as a result.[41] Friends of the children stopped playing with them for fear of being beaten up. One of the Herdahl children tried to avoid going to school, and another asked whether the people who were making things so hard for them were Christian. When his mother responded in the affirmative, the child replied that he did not want to be Christian because he did not want to be like them. This upset Mrs. Herdahl, who is herself Christian, albeit of a different denomination from the persecutors.[42]

When the practices did not stop, Mrs. Herdahl filed a lawsuit, and the harassment got even worse. Her family received bomb threats. She received a death threat, and the name calling and ridicule worsened.[43] Ultimately, the Herdahls won their lawsuit and got an order enjoining the religious exercises,[44] but Mrs. Herdahl stated that others who felt the way she did, even in her own school district, were afraid to say so in public.[45] This fear of opposing practices that facilitate discrimination against one's family or that are patently offensive to one's beliefs is common because of the even harsher response that often results.[46]

The pain the Herdahls endured as the result of the situation facilitated by the Pontotoc County School District's disregard for constitutional mandates might seem to be an isolated case. Sadly, this is far from the truth. In fact, the Herdahl case is not even the worst example of the willingness of school districts, overcome by religious zeal, to ignore constitutional requirements regarding religious exercises.

In August 1997, a lawsuit was filed against the Pike County, Alabama, School District by the Herrings, a Jewish family whose children had been subjected to severe religious discrimination and harassment in school. Many of the alleged incidents of discrimination were tied to a variety of religious exercises sponsored or condoned by the schools on school property.[47] The harassment, discrimination, and ridicule were intense.[48]

The Herring children were forced to participate in or witness a plethora of religious activities at school. Among the allegations in the case were the following incidents. The Herring children were required to bow their heads during Christian prayers. David Herring, a seventh grade student, was physically forced to do so. A minister spoke at a school assembly and told the students that those who do not accept Jesus as their savior were doomed to hell. When Sarah Herring, a sixth grade student who was present for that assembly, got up to leave, she was taunted by her classmates. The incident caused her to have serious nightmares. Sarah endured a similar incident when the school invited the Gideons to distribute bibles at school. Because she was Jewish, Sarah was sent to wait in the hall. The other children called her names as she left the classroom. In the hallway, a Gideon representative tried to persuade Sarah to take a bible. When she explained she did not want it because of her faith, he held a cross in front of her face. She began screaming and ran back into the classroom for help, but her teacher did nothing.

The Pike County schools regularly engaged in Christian activities in classes and religious assemblies, such as "Birth of Jesus" plays and "Happy Birthday, Jesus" parties. On one occasion, a vice principal disciplined Paul Herring, an eighth grade student, for a class disruption by requiring him to compose an essay on the subject of "why Jesus loves me." Additionally, Paul and David Herring were prevented from participating in gym class while wearing their yarmulkes; they were physically assaulted by classmates because of their religion; swastikas were drawn on their lockers, bookbags, and jackets; and they were regularly taunted by the other children. The verbal assaults were especially intense after religious activities at school.

The children were sometimes excused from the religious activities, and sometimes they were not. Mrs. Willis, the children's mother, in a sworn statement submitted to the court, addressed the ineffectiveness of allowing the children to leave to avoid the offending religious exercises: "Even when they have been given permission to leave by a teacher, however, their leaving makes them a target for name-calling, ostracism and harassment by their classmates."[49] She also stated: "[I]njection of Christian religion into these school events provokes the expression of religious bigotry toward my children."[50]

Like Mrs. Herdahl, Mrs. Willis was unable to effect any significant improvement by contacting school officials. In her sworn statement to the court, she stated:

Every day that I send my children to Pike County schools, I wonder if I am sending them into a war zone. The moment one event is over, a worse one follows on its heels. Every day that I send my children to Pike County schools, I feel that the environment threatens every value that my husband and I have tried to teach them at home. I have asked school officials how they expect me to train my sons to respect other people's property when their own property is vandalized at school and no one is punished. I have asked school officials how I can teach my children to be tolerant human beings and not bigots when they are subjected to outright religious persecution and bigotry in school. The consequences of the school environment on my children's psyches are devastating. My children are growing up believing that America is a caste society and they are untouchables—except for the purpose of getting beaten up.[51]

Several of the activities described above were characterized by school officials as "student-initiated religious exercises," a concept that is being used increasingly by those who wish to return such exercises to the public schools, but is still controversial from a legal perspective. That concept will be discussed in great detail in Chapter Three. However, if even a small percentage of the allegations in the *Herring* case are proven, it is doubtful that individuals who advocate the "student-initiated religious exercises" concept would claim that most of the religious activities occurring at Pike County schools were "student-initiated."

While the *Herdahl* and *Herring* cases might seem a bit extreme, they are not the only examples of the intolerance and hatred often aimed at religious minorities and dissenters when public school religious exercises occur. Another example of the pain facilitated by public school involvement with religious exercises arose in a school district in Utah where, in a bit of irony, the persecutors were Mormons—a denomination that has itself been the target of a great deal of discrimination.[52]

Rachel Bauchman, a Jewish high school student, objected to overtly religious songs, which were sung at high school graduations by the high school choir of which she was a member.[53] The same public school choir also performed at churches and performed religious songs on numerous occasions.[54] Most of this activity was organized by the school's choir teacher.[55] When Rachel protested against the songs, she was harassed and called names. The teacher noted that she was Jewish to other students.[56] Rachel obtained a court order prohibiting the graduation songs. However, at the urging of parents and some students, the choir performed one of the religious songs anyway, while nearly the entire audience joined in—a blatant disregard of the court order.[57] When Rachel and her mother got up to leave—Rachel in tears—parents and students in the audience jeered and spat on them.[58] Of course, if the religious songs and performances had never been promoted by the choir teacher in the first place, it is likely that what Rachel endured would never have happened. In a meeting with other Jewish youth in Washington shortly after the experience, Rachel said that she is "now more determined than ever not to give up. . . . Nobody should be put through what I was put through in their own public school."[59]

Despite serious allegations that the choir teacher had engaged in such religious practices for over twenty years, implying on an earlier occasion that the choir was somehow connected to the Mormon church, and that he had even been cautioned by school officials about such activities, a panel of the Tenth Circuit Court of Appeals, over a vigorous dissent, refused to reverse a trial court's holding that the practices alleged in the *Bauchman* case were constitutional.[60] This decision is discussed in greater detail in Chapter Seven. However, it is significant that in addition to its decision regarding the constitutional issues, the court held that Rachel Bauchman could not obtain redress for the discrimination she suffered as a result of the negative attention called to her by her teacher's practices, because such conduct, while insensitive, does not "rise to the level of a constitutional violation."[61]

Perhaps the worst example of the discrimination and hatred resulting from public school religious exercises in recent years occurred in a quiet town in Oklahoma. From 1980 until 1982, the Little Axe Independent School District in Oklahoma was divided by a controversy revolving around religious meetings held before class at the Little Axe primary school. The meetings were openly religious, often conducted by teachers, and held during school hours after students arrived on school premises.[62]

Two families, one belonging to the Nazarene denomination and the other to the Church of Christ, complained to the superintendent of schools when their children were confronted and harassed by other students because they did not attend the meetings. The other children asserted that the children of the two families "must not believe in God" since they did not attend the meetings.[63] On another occasion, the son of one of the families was refused entry to school to work on his class project because only those who had the purpose of attending the prayer sessions could be admitted at that time.[64]

Initially, the superintendent of schools suspended the meetings to enable the school board to make a determination. Ultimately, the school board decided to allow the meetings to continue until they were declared unlawful—the board president apparently yelled "bring on the ACLU."[65] That is exactly what the two families, the Bells and McCords, did. After the lawsuit was filed, the board adopted an "equal access policy" in an attempt to enable the meetings to continue, but the court found that both this policy and the district's original policies violated the Establishment Clause.[66]

Unfortunately, the initiation of the lawsuit brought even more persecution. The Bell and McCord children were called "devil worshipers";[67] Joann Bell received her own obituary in the mail, and her children received constant threats on their lives.[68] Both families received numerous threatening telephone calls and mail;[69] an inverted cross was hung on one of the McCord children's locker at school;[70] Mrs. Bell had her hair pulled by a school employee;[71] at a school sports banquet, the only school athletes not recognized were the McCords' two sons, who played three sports each;[72] there were threats that the Bells' house would be burned; and it was later burned to the ground under suspicious circumstances.[73] The persecution continued and was so extreme that it forced both families to move out of the school district for the following school year.[74] After the McCords moved out of their home it was vandalized (of course, the Bells' home could not be vandalized since it had already been burned down).[75]

In this case, it appears that the Bells were in the religious minority in the area, but that the McCords were not. Regardless, the families' position on the issue, arising from sincere beliefs that it is their right to determine their own children's exposure to religious doctrine, placed them clearly in the minority.[76] In this regard, they were treated with the same disdain as the individuals belonging to religious minorities discussed elsewhere in this chapter.[77]

Mrs. Bell later said:

> The threats [sic] to burn my home was the one that I probably should have taken the most seriously. I just couldn't see in an [sic] civilized area— I considered that these people would not ever do that. But my home was firebombed. Unless you've ever had a fire—the devastation is something you can not ever begin to describe. To lose everything you've ever had. And with four children you really accumulate a lot of things—the trophies . . . Everything that you saved, your baby pictures, the little things— your marriage license. You lose everything. . . . One of the things, the very few things that survived the fire was the christening dress of my daughter. We have three sons and we have a daughter that we are very proud of and this was her christening dress and that little hat was melted. It's one of the things that you'd like to pass on and let them use it for their children. This is just an example of the things that were ruined and what our family lost in the fire. Because we essentially lost everything we had.[78]

Mrs. McCord stated:

> Every day something happens that brings back the memories, something that happens, something the kids will say, something they do, something that I see. It was a devastating experience. For anyone. And I can understand why people don't want to get involved with it.[79]

Ironically, the Tenth Circuit Court of Appeals held that the school district could not be held liable for the discrimination and persecution perpetrated by the citizens in the district, despite the fact that board policy facilitated the entire incident.[80] The court held instead that the district was liable only for those harms flowing from its own violation of the Bells' and McCords' constitutional rights.[81]

The incidents that Sarah Herring faced, discussed above, demonstrate that the intolerance and discrimination demonstrated in the *Herdahl, Herring, Bauchman,* and *Bell* cases are not limited to children in high school and middle school. Even young children have utilized the religious differences brought into focus by public school religious exercises as a basis upon which to discriminate. In fact, studies have shown that children act out against, and can be more overtly negative toward, those perceived as different.[82] The following case provides yet another example of such behavior.

Sally was an eleven-year-old Jewish girl attending elementary school in West Virginia in 1984. At that time, West Virginia had a moment of silence statute, which required a period to be set aside each day for "private contemplation, meditation or prayer."[83] The statute acknowledged that no student could be denied the right to engage in such activity or be forced to do so, but its legislative history demonstrated it was religiously motivated.[84] Sally dealt with this rule by quietly reading a book during the period set aside in homeroom each day for the moment of silence. Later, in a different class, a student who had noticed her reading during the moment of silence informed her that she would go to hell with the other Jews.[85] Another student added that Jews were not worth saving because they killed Christ.[86] The incident was facilitated by the moment of silence. Sally felt hurt, angry, and uncomfortable because she felt the students should not have been able to "say things like that during the school day and get away with it."[87]

Sally didn't complain or protest to her teacher because she thought the teacher would not listen to her or that she would be made the center of negative attention in the school.[88] Sally's fears were probably justified. This is demonstrated by the cases where students and their parents stood up to fight religious practices in the public schools.[89] Many people are afraid to oppose such practices, even when those practices are facilitating discrimination against them. Many people fear that they will be treated even worse if they stand up for their constitutional rights.[90] In a sense, this victimizes them twice and gives them a Hobson's choice.

Significantly, this is not an isolated story. In fact, even in regard to legislative measures as seemingly innocuous as moments of silence, the harm inflicted on minorities and dissenters can leave lasting scars. The following statement by Debbie Wasserman Schultz, a Florida state representative who opposed a proposed school prayer bill in that state, is indicative of this. Her opposition to the bill resulted from her experiences in eighth grade, when her homeroom teacher used a moment of silence to pray to "a god I wasn't familiar with . . . I would really, literally, squirm in my chair."[91]

The cases discussed above are some of the better-documented and serious examples. However, there are others. In fact, some of the most famous Supreme Court cases dealing with religion in the public schools were accompanied by allegations of discrimination aimed at those who opposed the religious practices in question or who were in the religious minority. These allegations were likely not addressed in the Supreme Court opinions because, as the *Bauchman* and *Bell* cases demonstrate, they are generally not actionable or relevant to the constitutional claims that are the focus of such cases. Much of the discrimination in these cases was in response to the challenges to the offending religious exercises.

In response to their complaint in the famous 1948 case of *Illinois ex rel. McCollum v. Board of Education*,[92] in which James Terry McCollum challenged a Christian release time program, the McCollum family was subjected to vitriolic harassment.[93] While the suit was pending the family received thousands of hostile letters using phrases such as "you slimy bastard" and "[y]our filthy rotten body produced three children so that you can pilot them all safely to hell."[94] The family's child involved in the case was regularly beaten up and called a "godless communist."[95]

During the pendancy of the now-famous *Lee v. Weisman* case,[96] the Weismans received hate mail and death threats.[97] In another well-known case, which ultimately went before the Fifth Circuit Court of Appeals, involving a challenge to a high school coach's policy requiring the team to say the Lord's Prayer, the complaining student was taunted by fellow students and spectators and was called a "little atheist" by a teacher during a lecture.[98] In fact, the divisiveness and strife that can be facilitated by government-sanctioned religious activity in the public schools were addressed by Justice Blackmun in his concurring opinion in *Lee v. Weisman*.[99] In a significant footnote in that concurrence, he quotes James

Madison's Memorial and Remonstrance against Religious Assessments and a recent statement by an ACLU official in Utah who noted that the organization's position on school prayer "elicits death threats." In particular, Justice Blackmun was concerned with the "'anguish, hardship and bitter strife' [that] result 'when zealous religious groups struggle with one another to obtain the Government's stamp of approval.'"[100] That portion of the relevant note in the concurring opinion reads as follows:

James Madison stated the theory even more strongly in his "Memorial and Remonstrance" against a bill providing tax funds to religious teachers: "it degrades from the equal rank of Citizens all those whose opinions on Religion do not bend to those of the Legislative authority. Distant as it may be in its present, from the Inquisition it differs from it only in degree. The one is the first step, the other the last in the career of intolerance." The Complete Madison, at 303. Religion has not lost its power to engender divisiveness. "Of all the issues the ACLU takes on—reproductive rights, discrimination, jail and prison conditions, abuse of kids in the public schools, police brutality, to name a few—by far the most volatile issue is that of school prayer. Aside from our efforts to abolish the death penalty, it is the only issue that elicits death threats." Parish Graduation Prayer Violates the Bill of Rights, 4 Utah Bar J. 19 (June/July 1991).[101]

Finally, consider the statements of the Reverend Dr. James Forbes, an African-American minister who is currently the senior minister at Riverside Church in New York City.[102] Reverend Forbes testified against a proposed constitutional amendment regarding school prayer in September 1995.[103] During that testimony, he recalled from his youth in North Carolina "the pain and the damage to one's religious consciousness that the majority can inflict." He equated his minority racial status with his minority religious status, noting that as a Pentecostal growing up he belonged to a minority in a town where mainline Protestant denominations far outnumbered Pentecostals. He was also in the minority among Pentecostals because he did not speak in tongues.[104] Reverend Forbes testified:

When you feel affirmed by God in your spirit, but the community in which you live, in promoting its own religious practices, rejects your personal affirmation, you are led to question the authenticity of your own spiritual relationship with God. Having suffered doubly from the suspicion of those of other religions and those of my own, I have a sense of the suffering of Lisa Herdahl and her children. *I believe that no government should ever inflict such suffering upon the religious minority.* As a religious leader, I am self-critical enough to know how easy it is in the passion of the moment to promote one's own faith in a manner which is oppressive and intolerant of the religious views of others [emphasis added].[105]

These are some examples of the discrimination that dissenters and religious minorities are subject to when religion and the public schools mix in the United States. The examples indicate a pattern linking public school religious exercises to discrimination and intolerance, though not one that will necessarily occur at every school. The types of religious exercises vary, but each is organized, public, and calls attention to religious differences. Additionally, as the next chapter demonstrates, there is currently a highly organized and well-funded campaign aimed at bringing school prayer and other religious exercises back into the public schools. Thus, the likelihood of incidents such as those described in this chapter occurring and the potential for religious divisiveness in public schools and their surrounding communities are increasing. As will be discussed in Chapters Six, Seven, and Ten, there is currently no legal mechanism available that is able to directly address this discrimination and harassment effectively.

chapter two

The Christian Right
and the Public Schools

INITIALLY, MANY PEOPLE will likely point to the Supreme Court decisions that greatly limit public school religious exercises and assume that situations like those discussed in Chapter One are extremely rare, since few public schools would allow religious activities to occur. At this moment, however, numerous school districts across the country are violating Supreme Court mandates or pushing the envelope testing what may or may not be constitutional. The number of school districts engaging in such activities is likely to continue to grow as the result of the large-scale campaign currently being waged by the Christian Right to return religious exercises to the public schools. Those behind this campaign see public school board and other local elections as the new battleground for promoting their beliefs and political agenda.

Before discussing that campaign in greater depth, it is essential to clarify what is meant by "Christian Right." Essentially, I am referring to what most Americans understand the term or its related term "Religious Right" to mean—i.e., the politically active facets of fundamentalist or like-minded Christian organizations and similarly inclined individuals generally associated with a conservative religious and political agenda as embodied by groups like the Christian Coalition. The term does not refer to all "born again" or fundamentalist Christians, some of whom do not share the Christian Right's political agenda. It is important to point this out to avoid engaging in the kind of religious stereotyping that can support the type of discrimination addressed in this book. Moreover, nothing in this chapter, or this book as a whole, should be taken as an attack on the religion or theology of the Christian Right. Still, much of the information contained herein does demonstrate that the Christian Right political agenda is a threat to religious pluralism and tolerance in public schools across the United States.

The purpose of this chapter is not to provide a comprehensive discussion of the Christian Right's political activities and religious beliefs or of the vast network of organizations and individuals who support its agenda. Rather, this chapter elucidates the Christian Right's highly effective campaign to influence school policy. References in this book to the Christian Right's "agenda" for the public schools do not imply that everyone in the Christian Right agrees on every issue relating to the public schools. When it comes to religious exercises in the public schools, however, as will be seen below, the major players in the Christian Right generally share the same agenda. Since the focus of this chapter is on political activity within the Christian Right, theology will be addressed only to the limited extent that it is relevant to this discussion. In this regard, perhaps the most significant theological focus within this group, for present purposes at least, is the strong belief in proselytizing and spreading "Christian" values and beliefs.

It is tempting to write this group off as a bunch of extremists or closed-minded sheep following their tunnel-visioned leaders, but this would be a huge error. Make no mistake, this is a well-organized, intelligently run political movement that effectively uses religious doctrine and the attendant social values to reinforce its political agenda. Underestimating the influence of this group, particularly in regard to public school policy at the local level, could cause painful repercussions for public school children who are in the religious minority in their communities and for those who object to public school religious exercises. This is particularly so since many Americans who do not share much of the Christian Right political agenda support school prayer.[1] Most of these people are unaware of or unoffended by the totality of the Christian Right agenda for the public schools and by the discrimination issues raised in this book.

Significantly, the types of discrimination discussed in this book can occur wherever public school religious exercises take place, even in areas where the Christian Right is not strong. The reason for focusing so much on the Christian Right here is that their campaign regarding school issues and their involvement in national and local legal and policy issues is increasing the number of school districts willing to permit unconstitutional religious exercises or to experiment with exercises in the hope that they will prove constitutional. Additionally, the rhetoric of the Christian Right can lower tolerance toward religious minorities and dissenters.

The Christian Right's efforts to influence public school policy are extremely well organized and well funded. Their goal is to put individuals on school boards who favor school prayer and other religious exercises and who consider religious interpretations that are consistent with Christian Right beliefs, not the Constitution, as dispositive of what is appropriate in the public schools.[2] Many of these individuals also dislike the public school system and would like to see it either eliminated or completely revamped in a manner consistent with their beliefs.[3]

Even when the Christian Right's candidates are not elected to school boards, grassroots organizations seek to influence school boards through organized support for policies favoring their views.[4] Organizations within the Christian Right have broadcast how-to advice on skirting the Supreme Court's mandates regarding school prayer and have become highly efficient in their efforts to take over or influence local school boards.[5] These organizations and their members have been highly successful and, given their funding and organization, will likely continue to be so.[6]

Some of the key Christian Right organizations involved in the battle over public school religious exercises are the following: Citizens for Excellence in Education (hereinafter referred to as CEE) and its affiliate group, the National Association for Christian Educators, the American Family Association, Concerned Women for America, the Eagle Forum, Focus on the Family, the Family Research Council, the Free Congress Foundation, and the Traditional Values Coalition. Of course, the Christian Coalition is central to the movement and a key ally and resource for these organizations.

Most of these national (or international) organizations help local chapters organize grassroots campaigns outside the national media spotlight. Moreover, there are also smaller organizations, which are in turn often aided by more massive organizations like the Christian Coalition, which as will be explained below has backed grassroots campaigns to take over school board and other local government positions.[7] The Christian Coalition and other Christian Right organizations sponsor leadership-training seminars and teach members how to become effective participants in grassroots campaigns across the country or to enter the political arena.[8] These training seminars enable the Christian Coalition to spread information on successful tactics to the local level—where it can be used to influence local elections.[9]

Many people believe that the ultimate goal of this campaign is to have nonproselytizing, nonsectarian religious exercises in schools. The following statement by Jay Sekulow, the chief counsel for the American Center for Law and Justice, an organization involved in the legal battle to return prayer and other religious exercises to the public schools illustrates that its goals are much more ambitious: "Our purpose must be to spread the gospel on the new mission field the Lord has opened—public high schools."[10] Mr. Sekulow is a leading legal advocate in Christian Right legal causes, and his statement is indicative of the underlying attitudes shared by many school prayer advocates within the Christian Right. These attitudes are reflected by numerous Christian Right leaders. Their statements have served as rallying cries for the movement and illustrate the type of rhetoric that has successfully mobilized the Right's grassroots efforts.

The following statements—derived from public speeches, organization literature, and interviews—shed light on the power, tactics, and beliefs of this movement. They are but a few examples of the numerous similar statements made by Christian Right leaders. Naturally, given the focus of this book, the statements included here deal with church-state and school-related issues. Understanding how these leaders view such issues helps to explain their intense focus on public school policy. In this regard, Pat Robertson said in a 1993 address: "They have kept us in submission because they have talked about separation of church and state. There is no such thing in the Constitution. It's a lie of the left, and we're not going to take it anymore."[11] Robertson has also compared the current situation of evangelical Christians to the persecution of Jews in Nazi Germany:

> Just like what Nazi Germany did to the Jews, so liberal America is now doing to the evangelical Christians. It's no different. It is the same thing. It is happening all over again. It is the Democratic Congress, the liberal-biased media and the homosexuals who want to destroy all Christians. Wholesale abuse and discrimination and the worst bigotry directed toward any group in America today. More terrible than anything suffered by any minority in our history.[12]

The theme that judicial interpretation and enforcement of the Establishment Clause is an attack on evangelical Christians is often repeated, usually accompanied by assertions that "Christians" (meaning Christians who share the same religious doctrines as the Christian Right) are frequently the victims of intentional bigotry and discrimination. This idea of Christianity under assault is reflected in a March 1993 sermon by Jerry Falwell:

> Modern U.S. Supreme Courts have raped the Constitution and raped the Christian faith and raped the churches by misinterpreting what the founders had in mind in the First Amendment of the Constitution. . . . [W]e must fight against those radical minorities who are trying to remove God from our textbooks, Christ from our nation. We must never allow our children to forget that this is a Christian nation. We must take back what is rightfully ours.[13]

Similarly, Robert L. Simonds, the founder and president of Citizens for Excellence in Education, has written: "As the church watches from the sidelines, the ungodly elect atheists and homosexuals to school boards and legislatures to enact policies and laws that destroy our Christian children and discriminate against Christian families."[14] Simonds delineates the type of politicians acceptable to his group in the following credo, which echoes his statements and writings over the years: "We need strong school board members who know right from wrong. The

Bible, being the only true source of right and wrong, should be the guide of board members. Only godly Christians can truly qualify for this critically important position."[15] Simonds sees the battle over church and state in the public schools as a battle to save innocent school children from a list of "horribles," which he cites frequently in his newsletters. He has written, for example:

> CEE is still the only Christian ministry I know of that devotes all of their time and energies to saving our 52,000,000 American school children from atheism, agnosticism, dialectic materialism, evolutionary thought, immorality, new-age spiritism, false religions and a host of psychological, affective, and political brainwashing programs in our schools' curriculum.[16]

Simonds wrote recently: "Hiding behind false legalities and misinterpretations of the Constitution, God's true enemies would destroy religious freedom, and Christian students' right to pray or meet for reasons of faith in Christ."[17]

In a 1995 article in the *William and Mary Bill of Rights Journal* based on a symposium presentation, a more measured Pat Robertson addressed in detail his concerns regarding the courts' interpretations of the Establishment Clause in regard to the public schools. In that presentation, he stated:

> I will not enumerate the many Court cases from 1962 which did violence to our history or to the clear understanding of the "Establishment of Religion" Clause of the First Amendment to the Constitution. I protest with all my being the judicial distortions which have forbidden little children to pray or read the bible in school; which have taken the Ten Commandments from classroom walls; which have denied a Christian teacher the right to have a bible on his desk; which have implied that religion is a dangerous infection which must be confined, if possible, within the walls of a church; that have struck down laws of sovereign states merely because their authors may have entertained a religious motive in the drafting process of the legislation.[18]

As will be seen later in this book, much of this statement is a mischaracterization of what the law does and does not allow. Similarly, Beverly LaHaye, another leading figure in the Christian Right and the founder of Concerned Women of America, has written:

> Today instead of protecting our right to freely exercise our religious faith in public places, publicly honoring our God and Creator as our forefathers did, we are forbidden to speak, to pray aloud, to read the Bible, to even teach Judeo-Christian values in our public schools and other public places because of an imaginary "wall of separation" conjured by non-believers.[19]

Likewise, Lou Sheldon, the chairman of the Traditional Values Coalition has declared: "Unless we learn in a spiritual manner to kick butt, they'll ruin us."[20] He also said: "We were here first. You don't take our shared common values and say they are biased or bigoted."[21]

Another common theme relating to church-state issues among Christian Right leaders is the idea that the First Amendment and the Constitution as a whole reflect a Christian order and values. This claim is often mentioned in statements that demonstrate a highly ethnocentric religious view. John Whitehead, the head of the Rutherford Institute, has written: "The Court by seeking to equate Christianity with other religions merely assaults the one faith. The Court is in essence assailing the true God by democratizing the Christian religion."[22] While Whitehead's more recent writings evince a more "toned down" discourse,[23] this statement displays explicitly what much of the Christian Right discourse and activity in this area implies: that the goal of the movement is not so much a proper legal interpretation of relevant issues, but rather one that meets with their religious and political beliefs.

Of course, this may simply be a question of semantics, because Whitehead and others would likely assert that their interpretation of the Constitution is "proper" and that any interpretation that does not maintain Christianity's supremacy in American life is incorrect. Whitehead has written: "It is of little surprise then that the First Amendment (as well as the entire Constitution) was written to promote a Christian order."[24] In a recent book, Whitehead equates the current state of affairs regarding the role of religion in the public sphere with apartheid. In a chapter entitled "The End of Public Religion," he writes:

> While debating the theoretical and small points between "civil liberties" and "civil rights," the American Civil Liberties Union and other organizations are using the courts and threats of litigation to cleanse Christian religious expression from American public life. Their subterfuge is the so-called wall of separation between church and state—a phrase that is not even found in the United States Constitution. The wall of separation is, therefore, fast becoming the wall of religious apartheid.[25]

While Whitehead, a leading legal advocate for Christian Right causes, makes the argument that America is a "Christian" nation in the legal context, other Christian Right leaders have done so in the political context. Paul Weyrich, a leading figure in the Christian Right and the president of the Free Congress Foundation, has said: "We are talking about Christianizing America. We are talking about simply spreading the gospel in a political context."[26] Pat Robertson has echoed the positions of both Whitehead and Weyrich:

> The Constitution of the United States, for instance, is a marvelous document for self-government by Christian People. But the minute you turn the document into the hands of non-Christian people and atheistic people they can use it to destroy the very foundation of our society. And that's what's been happening.[27]

Reverend Donald Wildmon, the president of the American Family Association, also clearly states the important implications the Christian Right sees in political races: "Christianity and politics not only do mix, but for democracy as we have known it to survive, they must mix."[28] Beverly LaHaye has also directly touched upon this:

> Yes, religion and politics do mix. . . . America is a nation based on biblical principles. Christian values dominate our government. The test of those

values is the Bible. Politicians who do not use the Bible to guide their public and private lives do not belong in office.[29]

The language quoted above suggests that to understand the political climate influencing the Christian Right's policy relating to public school religious exercises, it is essential to have a basic understanding of the major organizations engaged in the battle over religion in the public schools along with their strategies and successes. It is also necessary to be aware of the rhetoric and deeply felt beliefs that drive these organizations and their supporters. Much of the work these organizations do is influenced by a relatively small number of politically active and astute leaders who are closely affiliated with one or more of these organizations. Their charisma and power as speakers and leaders facilitate the movement's success.

The genesis for the current effort to influence school board policy arose from the tactics of the Christian Coalition and their allies, who began in the late 1980s and early 1990s to focus increasingly on local politics as a means for influencing policy. This focus grew into a well-funded grassroots campaign to win local government elections, especially for school boards, and to influence local policy. Much of the machinery for this effort was in place by the late 1980s as a result of Pat Robertson's failed presidential campaign, which provided a ready-made volunteer force, mailing lists, and infrastructure for the burgeoning Christian Coalition. The greatest ally the Christian Right currently has in this grassroots campaign is voter apathy. Low voter turnouts for local elections enable the Christian Right to have significant impact in local elections, even in areas where they are not a majority. Ralph Reed, the former leader of the Christian Coalition and arguably a political visionary (whether one likes his politics or not), had a major influence on this grassroots campaign. In 1990 he laid out his strategy:

What Christians have got to do is to take back this country, one precinct at a time, one neighborhood at a time and one state at a time. . . . I honestly believe that in my lifetime we will see a country once again governed by Christians . . . and Christian values.[30]

He echoed that sentiment again in a statement quoted in the *Washington Post:* "We tried to change Washington when we should have been focusing on the states. The real battles of concern to Christians are in neighborhoods, school boards, city councils and state legislatures."[31]

Pat Robertson, the patriarch of the Christian Coalition and a powerful speaker himself, who reaches millions of viewers daily through his television program, *The 700 Club,* also supports this grassroots campaign. Robertson may be the single most important figure in the Christian Right in the 1990s. In a 1997 address that Robertson delivered to state leaders at the Christian Coalition's "Road to Victory" conference in Atlanta, which dealt mostly with state and national politics, Robertson made some telling, troubling, and potentially accurate statements about the effectiveness a grassroots campaign can have at the local level:

> Now you know the old thing, there are 175,000 precincts in the country and we wanted 10 trained workers in each of them. That's about enough to pretty much take the nation. But we're talking about a very simple thing. When you get it down to the school board races and the city council races and the legislative races, it is amazing. A few thousand votes make the difference. Sometimes the total vote in a state legislative race won't be more than four or five thousand. . . . So if you have a couple thousand people, you can do wonderful things. But it means executing the basic plan, where you have organizational structure, where people are trained and they've got to be kept motivated because they get tired in service.[32]

Similarly, in regard to local politics Paul Weyrich has stated: "We need to get active at the local level. We will never control the situation in Washington until we control the situation back home."[33] Reverend Louis Sheldon made an almost prophetic boast in a 1990 interview with CNN: "Give us a few more years under the belt and we will learn how to replace many of the school board members. Give us more time to understand how the system works, and we'll work the system even better than one could ever imagine."[34]

These Christian Right leaders see themselves as fighting for the soul of America. Their political activity is aimed at restoring what they see as the traditional American institutions, which they believe have been degraded or destroyed during the latter half of the twentieth century. The grassroots effort to influence local governments and school boards is key to their success.

Many Christian Right organizations and their leaders are forthright about their goals when addressing members or those with similar agendas. For example, Robert L. Simonds, the founder of CEE, one of the most important of the groups concerned with school issues, makes the purpose of his organization clear:

> Reclaim our public schools to a Christian morality and elect Christians to public school boards (and all other government offices). A big job? Sure. Impossible? Absolutely not. . . . We're not talking about a petty church dispute. . . . Forty-four million innocent children are at stake along with our entire nation and our form of government.
>
> Proverbs tells us "with good men (the righteous) in authority the people rejoice; but with the wicked in power they groan" (Proverbs 29:2, L.B.). God's instructions are clear—those who know the living God and possess eternal truth (Bible) must be in authority (run for office) if a nation is to be happy. . . . Removing anti-God, anti-Christian forces from office (secular humanists) will only be done by Christians becoming responsible citizens and *voting* them out. . . . We have the truth. [footnotes deleted].[35]

Like the Christian Coalition, organizations such as CEE have become highly organized, effectively using technology and public relations to increase their support. Many of these groups, including CEE, have been known to support covert tactics to take over school boards and influence school decisions.[36] In a sense, the names of some of these organizations reflect the image they want to present to the general public. For instance, most people would not object to Citizens for Excellence in Education, unless they knew more about the group. One has to dig beneath the name and facade of most of these organizations to learn what they are really about. Of course, CEE is simply part of a much larger network of organizations working toward the same goals, and Robert Simonds has recently acknowledged that these organizations do work together.[37]

However, CEE is particularly relevant to the present discussion because it is primarily focused on public education, while some of the other organizations are involved in numerous other issues as well.

These organizations are not simply small groups of fringe "yahoos," as many people assume. They are well-funded, well-organized, national and grassroots organizations with an agenda in which they deeply believe. There is little doubt that they can have, and have had, significant impact on public education. H. L. Mencken's references to right-wing fundamentalists as "half-wits" and "gaping primates" could not be farther from the truth when it comes to this new breed of fundamentalist.[38] One need only watch Ralph Reed, Pat Robertson, or some of the other highly literate and publicity-savvy members of the Christian Right to see that Mencken's view is simply a stereotype from the past, which has little connection to today's reality. While some of their statements may seem extreme to those of us who do not share their agenda, to underestimate them or assume they are only a small group of "right wingers" would be foolhardy. Moreover, to castigate them based on a stereotype is to engage in the same type of behavior that gives rise to the discrimination discussed throughout this book. They have as much right to take part in the political process as any other individual or group, and should be dealt with on that level. They are a formidable political force. Respecting their power has proven to be the best starting point for those who oppose them, such as People for the American Way and Americans United for Separation of Church and State, which have enjoyed great successes in fighting against the Christian Right agenda.[39]

Many groups that face the daunting task of opposing the Christian Right political-religious machine would be envious of their support and funding. For example, CEE claims to have 325,000 members, approximately 1,700 chapters, and an annual budget of approximately $610,000.[40] The American Family Association claims to have over 1,700,000 members, over 450 local affiliates, and an annual budget of over $10,000,000.[41] Concerned Women for America reported 600,000 members in 1996 and 1,200 chapters in the United States. In 1994, it reported over $14,000,000 in income.[42] The Eagle Forum had a membership of 80,000 in 1996 and chapters in all fifty states.[43] The Family

Research Council claims 250,000 supporters and a $10,000,000 annual budget.[44] Focus on the Family has a staggering $110,000,000 annual budget, an international staff of about 1,300 people, and 3,500,000 people on its mailing list.[45] The Free Congress Foundation, which broadcasts *National Empowerment Television* or *NET,* has over $9,000,000 in income.[46] The Traditional Values Coalition claims 31,000 churches as members nationwide and a $2,000,000 annual budget.[47] The Christian Coalition, which works with many of these groups, has at least 1,700,000 members, 2,000 local chapters, and an annual budget of about $26,000,000.[48]

In addition to these national groups, there are numerous local groups, several legal think tanks, and a well-oiled legal machine supporting some or all of the Christian Right agenda regarding the public schools. Thus, there is a significant likelihood that more and more school boards will be influenced by the national grassroots campaign being promoted by many of these groups. As a result, the possibility is quite real that more public school religious exercises will occur around the United States, thus facilitating the kind of discrimination discussed in this book. The focus of much of the rest of this chapter is the political tactics and some of the specific successes Christian Right and other school prayer advocates have enjoyed. Their legal tactics will be mentioned later in this chapter, but discussed in greater detail in Chapter Three.

One tactic these groups have used in the past is to run a stealth campaign.[49] In the early 1990s, these campaigns were used successfully to win local government and school board positions around the country.[50] Essentially, a stealth campaign uses lack of information and misinformation. For instance, candidates who hold Christian Right views do not reveal their alliances to the Christian Right or their views on potentially controversial issues. Such candidates do their best to avoid the spotlight and ideally avoid voicing their positions to the general public.[51]

At the same time, many stealth campaigns target rival candidates and officials with negative information and misinformation, such as inflammatory distortions of school programs and candidates' records and positions on issues.[52] Additionally, Christian Right groups (often affiliates of national organizations such as CEE or loosely connected local groups) may send individuals to public forums where an opponent is speaking to attack that opponent. The candidate that the CEE or similar group favors does not show up for such functions, and many voters know very little about that candidate when election day arrives. However, given the negative attention focused on rival candidates and programs they have supported, the stealth candidate has a serious chance to win.[53] As a Christian Coalition member said in regard to local election strategy in 1995: "We are told not to identify ourselves as Christian Coalition members, just as John Q. Public."[54]

In 1992, this type of campaign was used with great effectiveness in Vista, California, a community near San Diego, to take over a local school board.[55] The community is conservative, but not demographically dominated by those sympathetic to the Christian Right. The Christian Right orientation and agenda of the new school board members came as a surprise to many in the community. Organizations such as the Christian Coalition and CEE touted the election, along with earlier successes in local government and school board races in San Diego in 1990,[56] as great victories and began to use them as models for other school board and local government campaigns across the country.[57] In fact, the Vista election was a great political victory, given the demographics of the area—although it was somewhat short-lived.

Almost immediately after winning a majority on the Vista Unified School District school board, the new members began to foster a controversial agenda involving such things as the teaching of creationism, censorship of curriculum materials, and sectarian prayers at public school board meetings.[58] The policies of the board divided the community, as church-state issues in the public schools so often do, and pitted neighbor against neighbor in heated battles. Ultimately, the Christian Right lost its majority, after a group of concerned citizens successfully effectuated a recall campaign, but only after significant damage was done to community solidarity and to the more mundane but vitally important educational issues, to which the district had not devoted as much time during the controversy.[59]

However, the success in Vista and San Diego served as a model for other local elections across the country, and the Christian Right achieved greater success in such elections than most people would have thought possible. In regard to the San Diego election, Ralph Reed said:

> It's like guerilla warfare. If you reveal your location, all it does is allow your opponent to improve his artillery bearings. It's better to move quietly, with stealth, under cover of night. You've got two choices: You can wear cammies and shimmy along on your belly, or you can put on a red coat and stand up for everyone to see. It comes down to whether you want to be the British army in the Revolutionary War or the Viet Cong. History tells us which tactic was more effective.[60]

Similarly, in 1991, Reed said in regard to election strategy: "I want to be invisible. I do guerilla warfare. I paint my face and travel at night. You don't know it's over until you're in a body bag. You don't know until election night."[61]

Since then the use of stealth tactics has been discovered by the media and opponents of the Christian Right, and the Christian Coalition and its allies claim to have given up such tactics.[62] Instead, they have realized that low voter turnout (which, along with get-out-the-vote campaigns, was essential to the success of stealth campaigns) and creative rhetoric can achieve similar results. Despite these protestations, however, stealth campaign tactics are still a threat across the country.

With and without the use of stealth tactics, school boards, mayors' offices, and other local political offices have seen those sympathetic to the Christian Right agenda take office with the support of the Right. Others have been influenced in policymaking by the active voice many of these organizations and their local counterparts have applied to issues important to them. CEE has claimed that it helped 10,111 Christian Right candidates get elected to school boards in 1994,[63] and the Christian Coalition claimed in 1993 that there were 4,000 religious conservatives serving on school boards across the country.[64] In fact, Ralph Reed has said: "I would exchange the Presidency for 2,000 school board seats in the United States."[65] In 1993, People for the American Way, which monitored 500 elections involving the Christian Right, said that the Christian Right candidates won about 40 percent of the races monitored and that thousands more ran in other races.[66] In the 1993 New York

City school board election, the Christian Coalition joined forces with others who shared similar views on moral and family issues (though not necessarily on religious doctrine) to win 56 seats, approximately 20 percent of the total in New York City. They also took control of six of New York City's districts.[67]

The rhetoric of the Christian Right—a subject far beyond this author's expertise—is also a significant issue. Thus despite its complexity, it is important to briefly address the issue here. The current tactics of the Christian Right in influencing school policy involve a highly evolved rhetoric, some might say doublespeak, which hides the essential meaning or underlying basis of the issues being discussed. For example, teaching biblical creationism is called "intelligent design theory" or "creation science"; the *Impressions* reading series used in many public schools is called "new-age occultic"; a constitutional amendment that would eviscerate the Establishment Clause and allow organized prayer in the public schools is labeled a "Religious Freedom Amendment"; the teaching of many mainstream subjects that do not fit well with the Right's agenda is called "secular humanism"; and those who oppose school prayer or other important Christian Right positions may be called "godless," "demonic," "atheistic," or "satanic." Finally, the plight of Christians who are not allowed to engage in organized religious exercises during instructional time or at school-sponsored events is equated with the persecution inflicted by Hitler and Stalin.[68] The quotes throughout this chapter provide many examples of this rhetoric.

The list of examples could go on for pages. The questions of how this rhetoric is developed and of its general properties are best left to linguists and communication experts. For present purposes, the key is that the language hides the full meaning of what is being discussed or distorts reality with vitriolic terms meant to demonize persons, programs, or ideas that do not fit with the Christian Right agenda. The former type of rhetoric can make a Christian Right candidate or issue seem less threatening to mainstream Americans. After all, who would oppose "religious freedom" or support teaching children "occultic" materials? As noted above, few parents would have a problem with a group called Citizens for Excellence in Education or Focus on the Family, unless they were able to see behind the name.

To see this rhetoric in action, one need only watch *The 700 Club* or *NET* (*National Empowerment Television*) when school issues are being discussed and then check the facts brought forth in the discussion. One will often find that the rhetoric distorts the facts and issues. This rhetoric can also "sanitize" some of the more radical aspects of a candidate's or organization's agenda. Significantly, for those who oppose the Christian Right agenda or who are in the religious minority, this can have serious ramifications if school board elections are affected.

This rhetoric can be quite ominous. For example, in the October–November 1992 *Pat Robertson's Perspective,* Robertson stated:

> If Christian people work together, they can succeed during this decade in winning back control of the institutions that have been taken from them over the past 70 years. Expect confrontations that will be not only unpleasant but at times physically bloody. . . . This decade will not be for the faint of heart, but the resolute. Institutions will be plunged into wrenching change. We will be living through one of the most tumultuous periods of human history. When it is over, I am convinced God's people will emerge victorious. But no victory ever comes without a battle.[69]

Unfortunately, while I doubt Robertson intended to arouse the type of behavior addressed in Chapter One, his prediction that the battle would get bloody has come all too true for families like the Herdahls, Herrings, and Bauchmans. Whether intended or not, this type of rhetoric, combined with the religious justifications behind it, can incite brazenness and intolerance toward those who do not share in the Christian Right agenda. How this intolerance can flourish among "religious" people will be discussed in Chapter Four. For purposes of this chapter, the key is that the confrontational or violent implications of this quote from Robertson are reflected in thousands of similar statements made by Christian Right leaders and other school prayer advocates across the country every year. The rhetoric presented here is but a small sampling. In fact, there are far more inflammatory statements and leaders than those discussed here. The ones mentioned in this book are included for their direct relevance to the present discussion.

The rhetoric quoted in this chapter is not simply a list of statements by Christian Right leaders provided to generate fear among readers. When this language filters down to those directly involved in school prayer disputes, the alleged "victimization" of Christians by the prohibition against organized school prayer can become a rallying point for negative attention aimed at religious minorities and objectors. Moreover, as will be seen in Chapter Four, such rhetoric creates a clear characterization of an ingroup, with superior moral, political, and religious norms, and an outgroup that is characterized as anything from "unbelievers" to "the ungodly" to the "enemies of God." This is a dynamic ripe for discriminatory behavior. Of course, ingroup-outgroup social dynamics have been facilitated by any number of religious and nonreligious factions throughout history. Still, the dynamic created by the Christian Right's rhetoric is highly relevant to the discrimination discussed in this book and to the success of their grassroots efforts.

As noted above, in addition to effective rhetoric, low voter turnout has been integral to the great success of the Christian Right in local elections over the last few years. Moreover, on some issues, such as school prayer, they enjoy widespread public support.[70] Therefore, a more mainstream image and political focus has essentially enabled the Christian Right to continue to influence local politics in some areas, despite the exposure and condemnation of stealth tactics. Naturally, the excellent organization and funding of national, state, and local organizations is key to this effort. Significantly, the focus on grassroots efforts has been recently reaffirmed by Randy Tate, the executive director of the Christian Coalition, who, along with Donald Hodel, the new president, leads the post–Ralph Reed organization (Reed is still a board member).[71]

While this chapter focuses primarily on school board elections, the Christian Right has had success in other types of local government races as well. Melbourne, Florida, and Truth or Consequences, New Mexico, provide two recent examples of local governments that have come under Christian Right influence and illustrate the kinds of political and legal tactics currently being used to bring sectarian practices into government. In each case, the mayor of the city (and in Truth or Consequences, a neighboring mayor and a county commissioner) made a "proclamation" with serious religious connotations.

In Melbourne, the mayor declared a month of prayer and fasting in opposition to abortion. This offended many citizens who are pro-choice and also those who object to the church-state problems that arise from a government official's declaring a religiously oriented practice to protest what many consider a religious issue.[72] The mayor made the proclamation with the consent of the city council, although three council members objected.[73] While this proclamation more directly concerned the abortion issue and was particularly offensive to those who are pro-choice, the Establishment Clause implications of the incident, due to the "prayer and fasting" aspects of the proclamation and the religious undertone of the abortion issue, were significant.

In Truth or Consequences, at the behest of local clergy, the mayor, the county commissioner, and the mayor of neighboring Williamsburg proclaimed 1998 to be "the year of the Bible" and encouraged everyone to read from a New Testament for at least five minutes a day.[74] The key segments of the proclamation read as follows:

> [T]he bible, the Word of God, has made a unique contribution in shaping the United States as a distinctive and blessed nation and people. . . . All citizens are encouraged to read the New Testament at least five minutes daily.[75]

Almost immediately a number of Jewish, Native American, Catholic, and other concerned citizens, including a retired Episcopalian priest protested against the proclamation. Some called the ACLU in, and those who are Jewish almost immediately began getting late night anti-Semitic telephone calls.[76] Likewise, a Catholic man and his business partner, who own a local frozen yogurt shop, were boycotted and those supporting the proclamation flooded the town with five thousand New Testaments.[77] A Jewish woman who wore a Star of David pendant was spat on and given "the finger" while waiting to cross the street.[78] The executive director of the ACLU in New Mexico said in reference to a public meeting held in the town by the ACLU on the issue, "It was a little more vitriolic than anything I've ever been in front of, and we have all kinds of problems with church and state in New Mexico."[79]

From a legal perspective, the likely argument on behalf of the city officials is that a proclamation does not have the same effect as a law and thus cannot violate the Establishment Clause. This is a weak argument, given the current state of Establishment Clause jurisprudence, which frequently looks at whether the government is endorsing religion through a particular practice—an issue discussed in greater depth, along with other Establishment Clause standards, in Chapter Three. Under any current standard, the proclamations would likely be seen as unconstitutional government action. Still, if such proclamations were ever found to be constitutional, government officials, including school board members, could conceivably make such proclamations with impunity, and perhaps without legal liability.

Significantly, in the New Mexico case, the city and county will be backed in any lawsuit by the Rutherford Institute, a Christian Right legal organization and think tank, which acknowledges it is involved "in a number of cases like" the one in New Mexico.[80] Given the similarities between the Melbourne and Truth or Consequences situations, and the Rutherford Institute's admission that it is involved in other similar cases, it is likely that this is a new legal tactic of the Christian Right, which is being disseminated through its grassroots network. Without outside influence, it is highly unlikely that local officials, like those involved in these cases, would be legally sophisticated enough to understand the possible legal distinction between a proclamation and other government action or the way such proclamations might be viewed under the Establishment Clause. Such legal tactics on the part of the Christian Right are not new, and legal creativity has become the forte of some of their advocates in an effort to get around the Establishment Clause. As the above-mentioned incidents show, divisiveness is often the result.

Thus, school prayer advocates, whether members of organizations such as CEE or simply individuals who desire to see some form of religious exercises returned to the public schools, have a powerful ally in their fight. This ally is the well-organized, well-funded, legal support network of which the Rutherford Institute is a part. Perhaps the most significant organization in this network, at least on the issue of public school religious exercises, is the American Center for Law and Justice (ACLJ), which has received tremendous support from the Christian Coalition and Pat Robertson, and which has consistently pushed the envelope in regard to religious practices in the public schools.

The organization involves itself in issues of significance to the Christian Right, including cases relating to school prayer and abortion. While the ACLJ, like similar organizations, is careful about the cases it chooses to become involved with, it serves a function for the Christian Right similar to that which the ACLU serves for society in general. It becomes involved in cases on behalf of plaintiffs that otherwise might not be able to afford legal representation, or at least significant legal representation, when those cases involve rights or issues that are important to the organization's religious or political agenda. It also represents defendants, such as school boards, in lawsuits relating to these issues. Other major legal organizations supportive of the Christian Right agenda such as the Rutherford Institute and the Christian Legal Society serve similar functions. There are also hosts of smaller legal organizations or "ministries" that do the same.

These legal advocates for the Christian Right, while suffering some significant defeats,[81] have been quite successful in promoting their legal agenda. In regard to public school religious exercises, they have succeeded in significantly blurring the line between constitutional private action and unconstitutional state action. Even when they have lost, they have been somewhat successful in reframing issues in such a way as to breathe new life into them. Frequently, however, their legal tactics, along with some of the statements made about certain cases and their relative value, have been of questionable legal merit.

Perhaps the best example of this, one which will be discussed in much greater depth in Chapter Three, is the use of organized "voluntary, student-initiated" prayer to enable school districts to have graduation prayer after the Supreme Court found such prayers unconstitutional in *Lee v. Weisman*.[82] The ACLJ and other school prayer advocates have attempted to resuscitate graduation prayer by asserting that voluntary, student-initiated prayer is constitutional even after *Lee*, since *Lee* dealt with a prayer and speaker chosen by school officials. There are serious legal problems with this argument, but it is not wholly without support, and at least two courts have accepted it.[83] The most significant of these cases was the decision of a panel of the United States Court of Appeals for the Fifth Circuit in *Jones v. Clear Creek Independent School District,* which found organized "voluntary, student-initiated prayer" at school-sponsored graduations to be constitutional so long as it is nonsectarian and nonproselytizing.[84] While the *Jones II* decision is highly questionable, it has become a rallying point for the ACLJ and other school prayer advocates throughout the country. They have used the holding in literature and information mailed to school districts in an effort to facilitate student-initiated prayer.[85]

Through this very clever legal position, the ACLJ and its allies have succeeded in facilitating religious observances at school events in some districts. In fact, the voluntary, student-initiated prayer idea has taken on a life of its own. Throughout the country, even in jurisdictions that have not found voluntary, student-initiated prayer to be constitutional, such exercises are occurring at graduation ceremonies. This is in addition to those school districts that knowingly, or through ignorance of the law, violate constitutional mandates through non-student-initiated graduation prayer.

In a recent survey of school superintendents, conducted by the *Phi Delta Kappan* and the Gallup organization regarding 1993 graduation ceremonies (over a year after the *Lee* decision), more than 45 percent of those responding indicated that student- or adult-led prayers were part of their district's official commencement exercises.[86] In the South, 76 percent of school districts reported having graduation prayer, and of those 86 percent reported that it was delivered by students.[87] In the East, where 34 percent of school districts reported having prayers at commencement, 65 percent of those districts reported the prayer was delivered by students.[88] A 1995 issue of the *American Bar Association Journal* cited a Gallup poll that found 76 percent of public high schools in the South were planning prayers delivered by students at their commencement ceremonies.[89] The journal acknowledged the efforts of Christian Right legal advocates in supporting the spread of voluntary, student-initiated prayer:

> Religious organizations, including the American Center for Law and Justice in Virginia Beach, Va., however, have seized *Jones* as ammunition in

the battle for public opinion. Its representatives even have suggested that the Supreme Court's denial of certiorari was the same as upholding the appeals court case on its merits.[90]

While a first-year law student, well versed in the precedential value of a denial of certiorari by the Supreme Court, should know that this suggestion by ACLJ representatives is blatantly incorrect, this claim demonstrates the types of legal distortions that are sometimes used by organizations like the ACLJ to support their positions on issues such as school prayer. This is reminiscent of the distorting rhetoric discussed above. Still, one cannot deny the success these groups have had in influencing school policies throughout the country on issues such as voluntary, student-initiated prayer. Nor can one deny that their legal and political tactics are creative and astute, even when they stand on a shaky legal basis, as will be discussed in Chapter Three. Legal advocacy groups are a major aspect of the Christian Right effort to facilitate more religious exercises in the public schools, and, as the student-initiated prayer issue demonstrates, they can be successful, both in reshaping the issues and in effecting practices that comport with that reshaping on a large scale. This, of course, can lead to more religious exercises in the public schools and thus more of the discrimination that is the subject of this book.

This is supported by the *ABA Journal* article mentioned above, which acknowledges the success the student-initiated prayer movement has been able to garner after the *Jones* case:

> In the south school districts have been energized by the news that voluntary, student-led prayers will pass muster. . . . Throughout the United States, the magic language, "student-initiated, non-sectarian, nonproselytizing school prayer," has been replicated in resolutions and laws.[91]

In fact, several state governments have gotten involved by passing student-initiated school prayer statutes. A Mississippi statute was recently struck down as unconstitutional, however, and a similar Alabama statute is likely to meet the same fate.[92] Still, high-ranking politicians with alleged ties to the Christian Right, such as a recent governor of Alabama, have vowed to keep fighting for school prayer in their states.[93] In fact,

Fob James, who lost his bid for re-election as governor of Alabama, in language reminiscent of former Governor George Wallace, stated that the Bill of Rights does not apply to the state of Alabama.[94] The focus of James's comment, which was contained in a thirty-four-page letter to federal Judge Ira DeMent, who had recently struck down the Alabama school prayer statute as unconstitutional, was on the Establishment Clause and school prayer.[95] Alabama has also enlisted the help of Jay Sekulow in the case involving its school prayer statute, making him a deputy attorney general for the case, despite his role with the highly partisan ACLJ.[96]

The tactics and heavy funding of groups like the ACLJ and CEE, as well as their great success in moving toward their goals, make a mechanism for protecting religious minorities and dissenters from abuse and discrimination a necessity. School districts that are dominated or influenced by members of Christian Right organizations or that share their agenda, especially those following advice from the ACLJ or similar groups, may have little to fear if they know that these groups or ones like them will cover most of their legal expenses if they engage in questionable behavior. Nor are they likely to care a great deal about the feelings of religious minorities and dissenters.[97]

What do the frequent success of these tactics and the increasing willingness of some school boards to ignore constitutional mandates regarding separation of church and state signal for religious minorities and dissenters subject to the discrimination often facilitated by religious exercises in the public schools? As the Herrings and Herdahls learned, one's freedoms and the well-being of one's children in school may be harmed as the result of one's religion and the need or desire to move to a new community. As the residents of Vista, California, learned, even when one lives in a mainstream community, a few votes in a school board election can alter the fate of one's children and community.

Since discrimination may be facilitated both by unconstitutional and by arguably constitutional public school religious exercises, and since what is constitutional in this regard is in a state of flux, it makes sense to address such discrimination directly and not simply as a by-product of the broader constitutional debate. This can best be done by applying civil rights principles. As the incidents described in Chapter One demonstrate, many school districts see the Constitution simply as a barrier to be ignored or gotten around. Even in regard to issues where the Constitution clearly prohibits a specific activity, there can be no guarantee that a given school or school district will heed that prohibition. The activity of the Christian Right makes this an even greater concern.

chapter three

The Current Legal Status of
Public School Religious Exercises

THE LAW DEALING with school prayer and other religious exercises in the public schools is important in regard to the discrimination that can be facilitated by such exercises. As will be discussed in later chapters, this law is significant, not so much because of its success in combating discrimination when it occurs, but rather because of its failure. Still, an outline of the current state of the law in this area is essential to place in context both the need for new legal protections and the likelihood that an increasing number of public schools will engage in religious exercises.

The Establishment and Free Exercise Clauses of the First Amendment, which have given rise to the legal concept of separation of church and state, and the judicial interpretations that follow from them can sometimes prevent school-facilitated religious discrimination, at least in districts that are inclined to follow constitutional mandates. However, as demonstrated in Chapters One and Two, many school districts are ignoring constitutional mandates, and there are organized efforts to blur the lines between what is constitutional and what is not—efforts that can cause school districts that would otherwise not have organized religious exercises to believe that it is now constitutionally acceptable to have them under certain conditions.

Although this chapter will give some background on the state of the law in this area, it will not provide an exhaustive study of First Amendment jurisprudence relating to religion. Moreover, there is an excellent scholarly discourse addressing the Religion Clauses that is beyond the scope of this book, although some of that scholarship is referenced in this book. The cases and issues addressed were selected because of their direct relevance to public school religious exercises. The primary focus of this chapter will be on the line-blurring concept of voluntary, student-initiated prayer, which has become a significant legal issue and which exacerbates the potential tension between the Establishment and the Free Speech Clauses of the First Amendment. This chapter will also discuss the successful efforts to pass legislation, such as the Equal Access Act, to protect the rights of religious students to engage in organized religious activities at school under appropriate circumstances.[1]

The vast majority of cases dealing with public school religious exercises arise under the United States Constitution.[2] The Establishment Clause of the First Amendment is usually the constitutional provision that is focused upon in such cases, although increasingly Free Exercise Clause issues are also being raised. As a general matter, these clauses taken together have been interpreted to require government neutrality toward religion.[3] Given the focus of this book, the Establishment Clause is particularly relevant here because of its frequent application to public school religious exercises. To evaluate whether or not a public school religious exercise is an unconstitutional establishment of religion, courts generally look to one, or a combination, of three tests: (1) the *Lemon* test, (2) the Endorsement test, and (3) the Coercion test. Under any of these tests, one thing is abundantly clear: individual students have the right to pray before tests, to say grace before meals, and to engage in other individual private religious speech, so long as it does not infringe on the rights of other students and does not "substantially interfere" with school functioning—for example, a student praying loudly in the middle of class.[4] Any violation of these rights would raise Free Exercise Clause questions. In regard to religious exercises in the public schools, constitutional concerns generally arise when public group prayer or religious exercises are involved. This is where the tests mentioned above are most relevant for purposes of the discussion here.

The *Lemon* test has been used for many years, but has come under increased scrutiny recently, both from the judicial and the scholarly communities. The Endorsement and Coercion tests are more recent developments, but both have strong antecedents in earlier Establishment Clause cases, including *Lemon v. Kurtzman*,[5] the case that gave rise to the *Lemon* test. These tests will be briefly set forth and elucidated in the discussion of student-initiated prayer. Even before the development of the *Lemon* test, the Supreme Court had found, in the historic *School District of Abington Township v. Schempp* and *Engel v. Vitale* decisions, that school-sponsored bible reading and prayer in public school classes are unconstitutional.[6] Before addressing the *Lemon* test and other modern Establishment Clause standards, a brief discussion of the legal concepts that arose from the *Schempp* and *Vitale* decisions is important, because they set the stage for later cases dealing with public school religious exercises.

In the *Vitale* case, the Court dealt with a constitutional challenge to the "Regents Prayer," a prayer developed by the Board of Regents of the New York state public schools.[7] The prayer was to be said in every classroom as part of the opening exercises for the school day. It was nondenominational, at least in regard to monotheistic religions, but did acknowledge dependance upon God and ask for God's blessing.[8] There were procedures in place so that students could be excused from the ceremony with parental consent—although these procedures were also questioned in the case.[9] The Supreme Court found the prayer to be unconstitutional because it violated the Establishment Clause of the First Amendment.[10]

The Court did not create a specific test to be applied in Establishment Clause cases, but rather made a broad statement that government can not prescribe any particular form of prayer, nor can it control, support, or influence the kind of prayer citizens can say.[11] The Court was clear that government action need not overtly coerce nonobserving individuals to engage in such activities in order to be unconstitutional, but the Court noted that there is an inherent coercive force whenever government places its power or support behind a specific religious belief.[12] The Court also held that in order to be unconstitutional government action need not totally establish one particular religious sect or doctrine.[13] The Court looked at the tortured history of government-established prayers and their divisive effect. Perhaps most significant in the present context, the Court stated that the Establishment Clause was based on awareness of the "historical fact that governmentally established religions and religious persecutions go hand in hand."[14]

In *Schempp,* the Supreme Court was faced with another constitutional challenge to a religious exercise in the public schools. *Schempp* actually involved two separate challenges—one to a Pennsylvania statute and the other to a Baltimore school board rule—both of which required bible reading and the recitation of the Lord's Prayer in the public schools at the beginning of each school day.[15] Both the statute and rule were found to be unconstitutional.[16] The Court held that under the facts presented the bible reading and prayer exercises were inherently religious. It then applied a test that is strikingly similar to the *Lemon* test. In order to determine whether the statute and rule violated the Establishment Clause, the Court held that if either had the purpose or primary effect of advancing or inhibiting religion, the Establishment Clause would be violated.[17] To survive scrutiny under the Establishment Clause, the enactments had to have a secular legislative purpose and a primary effect that neither advanced nor inhibited religion.[18]

The Court found that neither the statute or the rule could survive this test. Students were required to attend school; the exercises occurred in school buildings and were supervised by school employees; and teachers participated as well—all these facts were significant to the holding.[19] The Court also reiterated aspects of its decision in *Vitale,* including the holding that coercion is unnecessary for government action to violate the Establishment Clause.[20] The schools argued that the bible reading and prayer had several secular purposes, including the promotion of moral values and the teaching of literature. However, the Court was not persuaded by these arguments, since the schools chose a religious means to achieve these purposes. It also held that the purpose of the exercises need not be strictly religious to violate the Establishment Clause.[21] The Court also rejected the schools' argument that since the students could be excused from the exercises and the exercises were only minor en-

croachments on the Establishment Clause, they could survive constitutional scrutiny.[22] Significantly, the Court stressed that the majority of
citizens cannot consent to a violation of the Establishment Clause, nor
can it use the "machinery of state to practice its beliefs." Furthermore,
the majority's inability to do so does not conflict with the Free Exercise
Clause of the First Amendment, which "prohibits the use of state action
to deny the rights of free exercise to *anyone*." [23]

In 1971, the Supreme Court applied a three-pronged test to determine whether government action violates the Establishment Clause. Because the test was set forth in *Lemon v. Kurtzman,* it became known as
the *Lemon* test. However, much of its substance had been espoused in
earlier cases, most notably in the present context, *School District of Abington Township v. Schempp.*[24] Pursuant to the *Lemon* test, a government
practice does not violate the Establishment Clause if: (1) it has a secular
purpose; (2) its primary effect neither advances nor inhibits religion; and
(3) it does not create an excessive entanglement of government with
religion.[25] After the *Lemon* case was decided, courts began applying this
test to cases brought under the Establishment Clause, including those
arising from public school religious exercises. The *Lemon* test is still used
in Establishment Clause cases today, but it has been increasingly criticized. In addition, the Endorsement and Coercion tests are frequently
applied in Establishment Clause cases along with the *Lemon* test.

The Endorsement test was set forth in *County of Allegheny v. ACLU,*[26]
a 1989 case involving Christmas displays on public property. The Court
quoted an earlier case involving similar issues, *Lynch v. Donnelly,* in setting forth the test.[27] The Endorsement test is sometimes characterized as
part of the *Lemon* test and sometimes as a separate test.[28] In her concurring opinion in *Allegheny,* Justice O'Connor championed the use of the
Endorsement test as a separate test. After that case, many lower courts
followed Justice O'Connor's lead, since there has been no clear pronouncement by the Supreme Court in this regard. However, when one
considers the *Lemon* test as augmented by the Endorsement language
from *Lynch* and *Allegheny,* it appears that whether the Endorsement test
is indeed a separate test may be an interesting question, but as long as
Lemon is still valid, the issue is not a practically significant one. The

reason for this is that the Endorsement test fits nicely into *Lemon* test analysis, and thus as long as *Lemon* is good law, courts would be wise to consider *Lemon* in light of the Endorsement language of *Allegheny* and *Lynch*. Whether courts essentially repeat or expound on this language in a separate discussion of the Endorsement test is really an issue of organization, since the substance of that test should be considered in some form.

That substance is essentially the following: a government entity unconstitutionally endorses religion when it appears to "take a position on issues of religious belief, or makes adherence to a religion relevant in any way to a person's standing in the political community." [29] Such an appearance is created when government sends the message that religion in general, or any particular religion, is "favored," "preferred," or "promoted" over irreligion or other religious beliefs. [30] In her concurrence in *Allegheny*, Justice O'Connor suggested that this inquiry should be made by considering the totality of the circumstances from the viewpoint of a reasonable observer—that is, would a "reasonable observer" view the government action in question as a "disapproval of his or her particular religious choices"? [31] This "reasonable observer" standard has been followed recently by at least one court applying Endorsement analysis in a context involving school prayer. [32]

The Coercion test is not really a broad-based test but rather a set of criteria that were applied to a fact-sensitive question in *Lee v. Weisman*, a case involving prayer at middle school and high school graduation ceremonies. [33] The Court held that it did not need to apply the *Lemon* test since under the facts in *Lee* the school district in question had placed nonbelievers and dissenters in an untenable position by requiring them either to miss their own graduation or to participate, directly or indirectly, in a religious exercise sponsored by the school. [34] Thus, the government action in that case coerced students to participate in a religious exercise, and that was more than enough to make it unconstitutional. Of course, as explained above, both the *Vitale* and *Schempp* cases were quite clear that coercion is not necessary for an Establishment Clause claim to be successful, but this does not conflict with the holding in *Lee*, a holding that did not presume to set forth the parameters of unconstitutional activity.

The legal analysis in *Lee* is set against the backdrop of the following statement:

> These dominant facts mark and control the confines of our decision: State officials direct the performance of a formal religious exercise at promotional and graduation ceremonies for secondary schools. Even for those students who object to the religious exercise, their attendance and participation in the state-sponsored religious activity are in a fair and real sense obligatory, though the school district does not require attendance as a condition for receipt of the diploma.[35]

The role of the state officials, the school principals in this case, was to determine that an invocation and benediction should be given at graduation, to select a local member of the clergy to deliver those prayers, to instruct the speaker that the prayers must be nonsectarian, and to provide a pamphlet on guidelines for prayer at civic occasions, which recommended that such prayers be nonsectarian and composed with "inclusiveness and sensitivity."[36] However, the school district's supervision and control over the graduation ceremonies was also a very significant factor.[37]

The Court held that the "principle that government may accommodate the free exercise of religion does not supersede the fundamental limitation imposed by the Establishment Clause" and that "at a minimum" the government cannot coerce anyone to participate in or support a religious exercise.[38] Moreover, citing *Lynch v. Donnelly,* the Court held that the government may not "otherwise act in a way which 'establishes a [state] religion or religious faith, or tends to do so.'"[39] The state's involvement in the prayers in *Lee* was found to violate these principles.

Much of the Court's decision focused on the "subtle coercive pressures" present when such prayer occurs in the public schools, since an objecting student has no "real alternative which would" allow that student "to avoid the fact or appearance of participation."[40] In this regard, the Court noted that the Establishment Clause was "inspired by the lesson that in the hands of government what might begin as a tolerant expression of religious views may end in a policy to indoctrinate or coerce. Prayer exercises in elementary or secondary schools carry a particular risk of indirect coercion."[41] This aspect of the *Lee* holding is particularly significant in light of the discrimination against religious minorities and dissenters these exercises often facilitate. Perhaps the core of the *Lee* decision is best summed up by the following statements from that opinion:

> The undeniable fact is that the school district's supervision and control of a high school graduation ceremony places public pressure, as well as peer pressure, on attending students to stand as a group or, at least, maintain respectful silence during the invocation and benediction. This pressure, though subtle and indirect, can be as real as any overt compulsion. . . . There can be no doubt that for many, if not most, of the students at the graduation the act of standing or remaining silent was an act of participation in the . . . prayer. . . . What matters is that, given our social conventions a reasonable dissenter in this milieu could believe that the group exercises signified her own participation or approval of it.
>
> Finding no violation under these circumstances would place objectors in the dilemma of participating, with all that implies, or protesting. . . . [T]he State may not, consistent with the Establishment Clause, place primary and secondary school children in this position. Research in psychology supports the common assumption that adolescents are often susceptible to pressure from their peers towards conformity, and that influence is strongest in matters of social convention. . . . [T]he government may no more use social pressure to enforce orthodoxy than it may use more direct means [citations omitted].[42]

The Court then elaborated:

> [T]he embarrassment and the intrusion of the religious exercise cannot be refuted by arguing that the prayers, and similar ones to be said in the future, are of a de minimis character. To do so would be an affront to the rabbi who offered them and to all those for whom the prayers were an essential and profound recognition of divine authority. . . . That the intrusion was in the course of promulgating religion that sought to be civic or

nonsectarian rather than pertaining to one sect does not lessen the offense or isolation to the objectors. At best it narrows their number, at worst increases their sense of isolation and affront [citation omitted].[43]

In 1993, shortly after the Supreme Court decided *Lee,*[44] school boards all across the country received a letter from the American Center for Law and Justice,[45] which purported "to address the questions and concerns of school officials regarding the issues of prayer at graduation ceremonies."[46] However, the letter did so in a one-sided way. Essentially, *Lee* was portrayed as a very limited decision, not as the sound defeat for school prayer advocates that it appeared to be.[47] The letter suggested that organized "student-initiated" prayer would still be acceptable at school sponsored graduations if it were voluntary and if a majority of the graduating class voted for it.[48] As will be discussed below, this concept of student-initiated prayer has become a hotly debated legal issue and a major rallying point for school prayer advocates.

For those who understand American constitutional theory and practice, the majoritarian student-initiated prayer concept may seem odd. After all, public school functions are still sponsored by the public schools, and organized prayer at such functions has all the indicia of government sponsorship. The fact that a majority of students supported it would be irrelevant to a dissenter, because the majority could only enforce its will through mechanisms within the public school. Beyond that, it is an old and strong constitutional principle that fundamental constitutional rights are not subject to a majority vote.[49]

It is likely that the ACLJ letter was based on an interpretation of *Lee* that focused heavily on the Court's reliance on the role of the school principals in influencing the prayer involved in that case. However, it is significant that the *Lee* Court was also very concerned about the school district's role in sponsoring and controlling the graduation ceremonies and that *Lee* did not presume to set the boundaries of unconstitutional public school religious exercises. Thus, the law set forth in *Schempp* and *Vitale,* including the holdings that constitutional rights are not subject to the whims of the majority, remains intact after *Lee.* In fact, *Lee* reinforced significant aspects of those cases.[50]

Moreover, a salient aspect to the student-initiated prayer concept is the requirement that it be voluntary. Given the language in *Lee,* which states that a dissenter is essentially forced to protest or participate in the prayer ceremony, by at the very least remaining respectfully silent, and given the *Lee* Court's focus on the inherent psychological and social pressure for children and adolescents to participate in religious exercises at public school functions, such prayer is not likely to be considered truly voluntary. Of course, as is discussed below, the student-initiated prayer concept attempts to vitiate this concern by suggesting that such prayer is not state action. Still, since the school district inevitably controls the forum for graduation ceremonies, one could argue that even if student-initiated prayer were not state action, the audience hearing it is still under the control of the state. This is discussed further below.

As the ACLJ letter pointed out, however, in *Jones v. Clear Creek Independent School District,*[51] the Fifth Circuit Court of Appeals accepted the student-initiated prayer argument, so long as that prayer is voluntary, nonsectarian, and nonproselytizing. The *Jones* case originally arose before *Lee* was decided. Before the Supreme Court decided *Lee,* a panel of the Fifth Circuit Court of Appeals upheld a school policy created by the Clear Creek Independent School District in Texas that allowed prayer at high school graduations so long as a majority of the senior class voted to have it, a student delivered the prayer, and the prayer was "non-proselytizing and non-sectarian."[52] The court based this holding on its application of the *Lemon* test to the policy in question.[53] That decision has since become known as *Jones I.*[54]

While the court's application of the *Lemon* test in *Jones I* was questionable, this soon appeared to be a moot point because the Supreme Court decided *Lee v. Weisman,* granted certiorari in *Jones,* vacated the *Jones* court's judgment, and remanded the case back to the Fifth Circuit for further consideration in light of *Lee.*[55] On remand, in *Jones II,* the Fifth Circuit panel again upheld the school policy, holding that it did not violate the test set forth in *Lee* or the Endorsement test, and that the earlier *Lemon* analysis was still applicable, since the school board policy did not violate *Lee.*[56] The court applied all three tests, since the Supreme Court has not clearly stated which test should apply when the *Lee* test is not violated by government action.[57]

The opinion has a highly critical tone in several places, and the court most definitely gives the impression that it disapproves of the Supreme Court's Establishment Clause jurisprudence—at least as it is applied to the public schools. The *Jones II* court's analysis seems geared toward finding a way to uphold the graduation prayer in question despite serious questions raised by all three tests the court applies, which has led scholars and other courts to criticize the opinion.[58]

The *Jones II* court held that under the facts of that case the prayer in question did not violate the *Lemon* test because the solemnization of the ceremony was a legitimate secular interest that supported ceremonial prayer. It held that since the prayer was nonsectarian, its primary effect was solemnization of the ceremony and not the advancement of religion. The court also held that there was no entanglement problem, even though the policy required the school to review the prayer to be sure it was nonsectarian, because there was no precedent holding that such yearly review was unconstitutional entanglement.[59] The court did not give much explanation as to why a religious observance, prayer, was necessary to solemnize a graduation ceremony. Nor did the court discuss why the ceremony would not be solemn without the prayer.

In stating that the nonsectarian nature of the prayer precluded the advancement of religion, the court failed to address the long line of Supreme Court precedent that holds that advancing religion in general over irreligion or vice versa can create an Establishment Clause violation. To an atheist or someone from a faith that finds public prayer offensive, the nonsectarian nature of the prayer would be irrelevant. In addressing the entanglement issue, the court only addressed the potential entanglement created by school board review of the prayer (an issue discussed in more detail later in this chapter). The court did not even attempt to address the potential entanglement created by the fact that the board empowered the students to vote on the prayer through a formal policy or that the school controlled the graduation ceremony.

The prayer did not violate the Endorsement test, according to the court, because the policy let students decide whether there would be prayer. Since the students made the decision whether to have prayer, the reasoning suggests they would not perceive government endorsement.[60] In this regard, the court essentially relied on *Board of Education v. Mer-*

gens.[61] That case involved the constitutionality of the Equal Access Act (discussed below), which allows religious student groups to meet at secondary schools during non-instructional time if other non-curriculum-related student groups can do so.[62] In finding that statute constitutional, the Supreme Court, in *Mergens,* distinguished government speech from private speech and held that secondary school students "are likely to understand that a school does not endorse or support student speech that it merely permits on a non-discriminatory basis."[63] In finding no endorsement, the *Jones II* court analogized the school prayer in that case to the student group meetings, which the *Mergens* Court found did not endorse religion.[64]

Of course, there are significant factual differences between *Jones* and *Mergens.* Most significant is the fact that the student groups involved in *Mergens* were extracurricular and voluntary. Thus, no student was required to go to any meeting, and the case did not involve a once-in-a-lifetime event such as graduation. Moreover, the Equal Access Act specifically limits the participation of school officials in events allowed under the Act—a stark contrast to a graduation ceremony, which is run by school officials in a formal manner. The *Jones II* court did not even address such factors as the *Lee* Court's analysis regarding peer pressure or the likelihood that secondary school students would perceive state compulsion at a graduation ceremony. *Lee* was much more germane factually than *Mergens* in this regard.

Still, the key issue the *Jones II* court had to face was whether the prayer in that case violated the Coercion test set forth in *Lee.* In doing so, the *Jones II* court gleaned three requirements that must be met to establish a violation pursuant to *Lee:* (1) the government must direct; (2) a formal religious exercise; (3) in a manner that obliges the participation of objectors.[65] The court went on to hold that the school board did not "direct" the religious exercise because its policy permitted the graduating class to determine whether prayer would occur and allowed only a student to conduct such prayer.[66] Moreover, the court found there was no formal religious exercise because the policy simply tolerated the prayer without requiring or favoring it.[67] Finally, the court found the policy did not coerce objectors to participate in the prayer because it allowed student participation in the prayer decision, and thus objecting students would be aware that such prayer represented the will of their peers and not the state, especially since high school students are less impressionable than younger students.[68]

In a staggering and, given the tenor of the opinion, probably intentional oversight, the court did not address the following facts: the school board policy empowered the students to vote on the prayer; the prayer occurred at a school-controlled graduation; and the minority of students who opposed the prayer were subject to the religious will of the majority as empowered by the state—factors certainly relevant to the "state direction" and "Coercion" issues. Nor did the court analyze in detail the fact that the *Lee* Court held that high school students are subject to a great deal of peer pressure. Instead, the court simply stated that *Lee* applied to "state initiated clergy prayers," and thus that case did not vitiate the *Mergens* holding that "seniors are less impressionable than younger students."[69] While this makes some sense in the context of *Mergens,* the court never dealt with the implication in *Lee* that secondary school students are more impressionable when it comes to graduation prayer nor with the very significant factual differences (discussed above) between *Lee* and *Mergens*. Moreover, the court did not adequately explain why the prayer at Clear Creek was not a formal religious exercise. The opinion devoted only six lines to this issue and cited nothing to support its conclusion.[70]

The *Jones II* court rejected the idea that the prayer under the facts in that case was coercive but did not address any of the studies regarding peer pressure and ingroup–outgroup dynamics mentioned in *Lee* or the wealth of other social science data on these subjects. Chapter Four of this book does look at this social scientific data, which are directly at odds with the *Jones II* court's holding that such pressure is less attenuated when a majority of one's peers vote to have prayer at a school function. This is one of the biggest weaknesses throughout the *Jones II* opinion. The court makes sweeping statements without analysis or support regarding issues such as peer pressure under the facts of that case and ignores the plethora of data that contradict its holding, even though some of this research was actually cited by the *Lee* Court.

When one looks at *Jones II* in light of *Lee, Schempp, Vitale,* and the data discussed in Chapter Four of this book, the best justification for the *Jones II* decision is that the prayer in question there was simply not state action. The court did imply this in several places, but did not deal with it directly.[71] The court seemed hell-bent, if you will pardon the term, on finding the prayer to be constitutional and to voice its support of such religious exercises in the public schools, albeit indirectly if not subtly. Though the *Jones II* decision waxed poetic in much greater detail than it engaged in much of its constitutional analysis, the court did raise the valid issue of state action (in a somewhat vague fashion)—an issue that courts that have criticized *Jones II* have ultimately analyzed in greater depth.

Yet, the *Jones II* decision was, and is, an important victory for school prayer advocates. For now, at least in the Fifth Circuit, it is legal for a school policy to enable the majority of a senior high school class to vote to have prayer at graduations, if the prayer is nonproselytizing and nonsectarian.[72] Moreover, as will be discussed below, when one looks at the reasoning underlying *Jones* through the lens of free speech, an argument can be made that the prayer need not be nonsectarian or nonproselytizing.

Surprisingly however, the ACLJ letter implied that *Jones* was controlling elsewhere.[73] At that time, I was working as an associate in a practice in the Mid-Atlantic region that represented several school districts. One of the school superintendents who received the ACLJ letter was informed enough to realize that something was fishy and asked for a legal opinion. I was asked by a partner in the firm to research the issue. My conclusion was that the ACLJ letter was at the least an overstatement and at the worst intellectual dishonesty or outright malpractice. The ACLJ letter did not clearly state that theirs was only one possible interpretation of *Lee,* that *Jones* only governed in the Fifth Circuit, or that it would likely take a large sum of money and long, divisive litigation to determine if the ACLJ's interpretation was correct.

Within a year, the Loudoun County, Virginia, school district decided to follow the ACLJ's advice.[74] That district was soon embroiled in a divisive lawsuit over its new graduation prayer policy. In 1993, in *Gearon v. Loudoun County School Board,* the district's policy, which was based on the ACLJ's letter, was found unconstitutional by the United States District Court for the Eastern District of Virginia.[75] In that case, the court specifically rejected the reasoning from *Jones II* and found that the delegation of the prayer decision to the senior class did not save the school board's prayer policy under *Lemon* or *Lee* because the school board was still the sponsor of the graduation ceremony and because the same coercive pressures present in *Lee* are present any time prayer occurs at a public school graduation.[76] Similarly, the Ninth Circuit Court of Appeals seriously questioned *Jones II* and came to the opposite conclusion under similar facts in *Harris v. Joint School District No. 241.*[77] *Harris* was vacated as moot, since the complaining students had graduated, but its reasoning was reflected in the approach taken two years later in *American Civil Liberties Union of New Jersey v. Black Horse Pike Regional Board of Education.*[78]

In *Black Horse Pike,* the Court of Appeals for the Third Circuit followed and expanded on the reasoning set forth in *Harris* and *Gearon.* The case involved facts strikingly similar to those in *Jones* but like the *Gearon* and *Harris* courts, the *Black Horse Pike* court rejected the reasoning from *Jones.*[79] The *Black Horse Pike* decision is significant not only because it is the most recent case to address this issue in depth, but because it was carefully reasoned, addressed many of the issues ignored by the court in *Jones II,* and was decided by the Third Circuit sitting *en banc.*[80]

In that case, the Black Horse Pike Regional Board of Education directed the superintendent of schools to develop a policy that paralleled the holding in *Jones II*—i.e., a policy that permitted voluntary, student-initiated prayer at high school graduation ceremonies if a majority of the graduating class voted for it.[81] The policy required that the voting process be conducted by "duly elected class officers" and that the balloting provide students with three choices: prayer, a moment of reflection, or nothing at all. The students were to determine the form of any prayer to be given at graduation, and a disclaimer stating that any presentation given at commencement did not reflect the views of the school board was to be included in the printed programs for graduation.[82] The most significant difference between the policy here and the one in *Jones* is that the Black Horse Pike policy did not require the prayer to be nonsectarian or nonproselytizing.

However, as will be discussed below, that limitation in *Jones* is likely problematic, since the underlying principle in *Jones* is that student-initiated prayer is not really attributable to the state. Thus, any content-based censorship of such prayer would likely be a free speech violation—an issue the *Jones II* court basically overlooked in what some might call its rush to find a basis to allow graduation prayer. Thus, this difference between the policy in *Jones II* and the one in *Black Horse Pike* is basically irrelevant to any application of the *Jones II* holding to the policy involved in *Black Horse Pike*. In fact, one might argue that the policy involved in *Black Horse Pike* is more consistent with the underlying reasoning in *Jones II*. Of course, one could also argue that the *Jones II* court did believe that the prayer involved in *Jones* was state action, since it applied the *Lee, Lemon,* and Endorsement tests, and did not simply hold that the prayer was not state action. However, given the language and reasoning of *Lee,* were it state action the coercion would be at least as great, and perhaps greater than in *Lee,* since the peer pressure referred to in *Lee* might be worse when a majority of one's peers selects the prayer. Ultimately the *Jones II* decision is most supportable when the question it raises is not whether coercion exists, but whether it is coercion by the state. *Black Horse Pike* demonstrates that even this argument is not enough to overcome the flaws in the *Jones II* decision.

The results of the voting in the first year of the new Black Horse Pike policy were as follows: 128 students voted for prayer; 120 for a moment of silence or reflection; and 20 voted for neither. A student was selected to deliver the prayer by the senior class officers.[83] Soon afterward, a student asked the principal if a representative from the ACLU could also discuss safe sex at graduation. This was likely done because the prayer policy claimed to be "in the spirit of protected speech." However, the principal denied the request because of the time restraints relating to commencement and because the topic requested was "not generally one discussed at graduation ceremonies."[84] The complaint giving rise to the lawsuit was filed soon after that. The United States District Court for

the District of New Jersey ultimately found the prayer policy to be unconstitutional and enjoined the school board from conducting any
school-sponsored graduation ceremony that included prayer.

In rejecting the school board's arguments on appeal, the Third Circuit
Court of Appeals applied the *Lee* (Coercion), *Lemon,* and Endorsement
tests, although it discussed the Endorsement test in the context of its
Lemon analysis. The court held that the school board policy failed all
three tests. In regard to the Coercion test set forth in *Lee,* the court held
that although the prayer was put to a student referendum rather than
simply being decided upon by a school official, this measure did not
render the exercise constitutional. Echoing themes elucidated in the
Harris and *Gearon* decisions, the court noted that simply delegating one
aspect of the ceremony, the prayer, to the students did not negate the
school officials' control over the ceremony or the fact that students were
only empowered to vote on the question because school officials agreed
to let them make that choice.[85] The court also held that there was no
difference between the coercion in *Lee* and that in the Black Horse Pike
schools. In doing so, it followed the reasoning in *Lee,* specifically rejected the reasoning in *Jones II,* and pointed out that the reasoning in
Jones II was inconsistent with *Lee.*[86]

The court also rejected the school board's claim that the policy was
constitutional because to hold otherwise would violate the free speech
rights of students. The court held that high school commencement ceremonies have not been considered, "either by law or tradition, as public
fora where a multiplicity of views" on any topic can be expressed,[87] and
it further held:

> An impermissible practice can not be transformed into a constitutionally
> acceptable one by putting a democratic process to an improper use. There
> should be no question "that the electorate as a whole, whether by referen-
> dum or otherwise, could not order [governmental] action violative of the
> [Constitution], and the [government] may not avoid the strictures of [the
> Constitution] by deferring to the wishes or objections of some fraction of
> the body politic." A policy that does this can not be legitimized by arguing
> that it promotes free speech [citation omitted].[88]

Moreover, the court acknowledged what the *Vitale* and *Schempp* cases had previously stated in regard to a majoritarian view of the First Amendment: "The First Amendment does not allow the state to erect a policy that only respects religious views that are popular because the largest majority can not be licensed to impose its religious preferences upon the smallest minority."[89]

The court also found that the school board policy violated the first two prongs of the *Lemon* test, and thus it held that there was no need to address the third prong. The board had argued that the first prong was not violated because the policy had the secular purposes of recognizing the students' free speech rights and their desire to use the prayer to solemnize the graduation ceremony—a basis that the *Jones II* court accepted as valid. However, the *Black Horse Pike* court held that graduation was not a forum for public speech and debate since, as the refusal to include the ACLU speaker demonstrated, prior approval by school officials was required to speak at commencement.[90] Additionally, the court held that solemnization is not a viable secular purpose because graduation would be no less solemn in years when students voted to have no prayer. Furthermore, even if solemnization were a secular purpose of the policy, students who did not believe that prayer should be put to a vote would be placed in an impossible situation because the policy would require them either to "refuse to vote out of religious conviction," or to vote in order to avoid the risk that "their forbearance may provide the margin of victory" for those who favor having prayer or a particular type of prayer.[91]

The court also found that the policy advanced and endorsed religion in violation of the Endorsement test and the second prong of the *Lemon* test—the court essentially analyzed the two together. It acknowledged that the policy might not lead to the same outcome every year but held that "the effect of the particular prayer that is offered in any given year will be to advance religion and coerce dissenters."[92] The disclaimer was of no avail, since the policy still gave an advantage to religious speech over nonreligious speech and a reasonable observer would conclude that the school board favored the inclusion of prayer in the graduation ceremony.[93] Reiterating Supreme Court decisions holding that the government must remain neutral toward religion, the court explained why the policy could not be justified as an accommodation of religion rather than an endorsement:

> The Supreme Court has never countenanced a practice that requires some members of the community to subordinate their religious preferences to those of a majority. Rather, "[t]he Establishment Clause, at the very least, prohibits government from appearing to take a position on questions of religious belief or from 'making adherence to a religion relevant in any way to a person's standing in the political community.'" Although the Supreme Court has allowed certain accommodations to religion, "accommodation is not a principle without its limits." The Supreme Court has never hinted that an unconstitutional delegation of political power to a religious group could be saved as a religious accommodation [citation omitted].[94]

In an interesting connection to the subject of this book, the court noted that one of the students who objected to the prayer policy had received threatening letters at school and threatening telephone calls at home.[95] Such actions are quite common when public school religious exercises occur. The court did not go into great detail regarding these incidents, and even though the school policy facilitated them, the student would likely have had no recourse against the school for the acts of the persons who harassed him, because there is no law, including the Constitution, that clearly provides redress for such actions. Chapters Five, Six, Seven, and Ten discuss this issue in greater detail.

Significantly, despite the *Black Horse Pike* and *Gearon* decisions, *Jones II* and the reasoning underlying it are still frequently relied upon by school boards and legislatures and are not nearly as limited as they might seem.[96] The *Jones II* case could be used as a jumping-off point for majority-initiated sectarian prayer at public school events. Since a large part of its reasoning is that a majority of students can do what the school cannot, the implication is that the students' action is not state action. Otherwise, the reasoning would almost certainly run afoul of *Lee*. As will be discussed below, if such prayer is not state action, free speech rights may attach to it. At least one court has followed *Jones II* under similar facts. That case, *Adler v. Duval County School Board,* was decided by a federal district court in Florida and involved a policy that was quite similar to that in *Jones* but with some significant differences.[97] The reasoning in *Adler* is more problematic for opponents of student-initiated prayer because the court addressed the free speech issue that arises if it is presumed that such prayer is private rather than state action. It also raises the public forum issue, which *Jones II* did not address in any depth.

Adler, however, does not answer, and in some cases simply ignores, some of the key questions raised later by *Black Horse Pike* and its more detailed analysis. Despite this, a discussion of the *Adler* case is useful to understand the real implications of *Jones II,* especially the possibility that at least some of its reasoning may be used to increase the frequency of public school religious exercises in areas where this issue is still undecided. *Adler* relies on *Jones II,* particularly in dealing with *Lee.* Yet there are significant differences as well. In *Adler,* the policy in question arose from a letter from a school board attorney, which was meant to address the possibilities for graduation prayer after *Lee* and in light of *Jones II.*[98] Pursuant to the policy suggested in the letter, the high school principals determined how to present the issue to the senior class. The phrase "opening, or closing, message" was used instead of prayer; there was no explicit requirement that a vote be taken, but the policy was clear that the senior class should decide whether to have opening/closing messages and the content of such messages; and most significantly, other than the requirement that a student should deliver the message, no censorship of the message by school officials was allowed.[99] It is not clear whether the senior classes at the seventeen high schools involved in the case voted on the prayer as a class or whether senior class representatives made the decision, but it is clear that the high school principals delegated the issue to senior class members.

The court in *Adler* applied the *Lemon* and Coercion tests, but not the Endorsement test. The court's *Lee* analysis relied heavily on *Jones II* regarding the coercive effect of the prayer involved and on the factual differences between the government action involved in *Lee* and the policy in the Duval County schools in addressing the state-direction issue.[100] However, in interesting and somewhat persuasive dicta toward the end of the opinion, the *Adler* court stated that since *Lee* was so factually limited, it would be "an unwarranted extension of *Lee*" to hold that all graduation prayer places unconstitutional psychological pressure on students to participate in the prayer.[101] In doing so, the *Adler* court explained that the *Lee* Court could have chosen to hold that any graduation prayer at public school graduations is unconstitutional, but chose not to do so.[102]

This is a potentially compelling argument, although it remains to be seen whether the decision not to explicitly find all graduation prayer unconstitutional was a result of the judicial politics involved in getting a majority of the court to agree on an opinion; the facts of that case in light of the rule that on constitutional matters the Court should generally address the issue before it in the narrowest way possible or as the *Adler* court implied, an intent to leave open the possibility of organized student-initiated prayer at such ceremonies. Moreover, as was the case in *Jones II,* the *Adler* court ignored the issues raised by the state's delegating to others responsibility for an act at a state-controlled event, an act that the state could not do on its own. Nor did the court address the *Schempp* and *Vitale* cases and their holdings regarding the inappropriateness of ceding constitutional rights or duties to the will of the majority.

Still, the key to the *Adler* case is its discussion of the free speech issue and the attendant implications regarding whether student-initiated prayer is state or private action. Central to this issue is the way the court characterizes the nature of the speech in regard to the relative government involvement and the nature of the forum in which the speech occurs. The court essentially holds that the prayer involved is not attributable to the state, both in regard to its *Lemon* analysis and its Coercion analysis.[103] Thus, the fact that the prayer was not to be monitored by the school for content was consistent with the free speech rights attendant on private speech. As mentioned above, despite the *Jones II* court's failure to address it, the possibility of sectarian, proselytizing prayer is perfectly consistent with the underlying philosophy of student-initiated prayer as accepted in *Jones II* and *Adler,* since if the prayer is not state action, free speech rights may attach to it. If the prayer is subject to free speech protection, the government (school officials) would not generally be able to censor the prayer content, and thus proselytizing, sectarian prayer could be allowed.[104] This has serious implications for the nature of permissible prayer if the concept of voluntary student-initiated prayer at school events takes hold. If it is state action, it likely violates *Lee* and *Lemon*.

The nature of the forum involved is relevant to this issue as well, because if the graduation ceremony is not a traditional public or limited public forum for speech, any speech that occurs there is more easily attributed to the state. In *Adler*, the court found the graduation ceremony to be a limited public forum because "virtually the entire program is given over to public speech making by the valedictorian and other leaders of the senior class, and by community leaders who are invited to give the principal commencement address."[105] By so holding, the court essentially declared the ceremony to be a venue for expressing free speech rights, a holding that may conflict with its position implying that the ceremony is a solemn occasion that the prayer can serve to solemnize. This holding also raises the issue of what should be done when free speech is brought forth as a justification for an alleged Establishment Clause violation. Despite the fact that it based much of its decision on the schools' deference to the will of the senior class, the court ignored the fact that the government cannot get around the Constitution by deferring to some portion of the body politic and that any policy that does so cannot be legitimized by arguing that it promotes free speech rights.[106]

Instead, to address the potential conflict between the Establishment Clause and the Free Speech Clause, the court relied heavily on cases that involve the placing of religious symbols on public grounds.[107] In doing so, it ignored the fundamental differences between such cases and those involving graduations and other public school settings. In the former situations, the state maintains a public forum that, according to the cases cited in *Adler*, would provide an arena for private groups and citizens to exercise their free speech rights, a secular purpose.[108] State officials do not preside over any ceremony where this occurs; school-aged people are not the primary focus of the display; and people are free to walk by the displays in such a forum. Of course, quite the opposite is true of graduation ceremonies. In fact, the *Black Horse Pike* court was rather blunt about this: "[H]igh school graduation ceremonies have not been regarded, either by law or tradition, as public fora where a multiplicity of views on any given topic . . . can be expressed or exchanged."[109] In this regard, the *Adler* court never dealt with the fact that the schools would not likely allow students or members of the audience to come up on stage and address those gathered or that the school would not allow the students to determine whether to give a message in the middle of the ceremony as opposed to the beginning or end. In other words, the state still had ultimate control over the ceremony, its content, and its general sequence. At least a basic analysis of this would help determine whether the court's declaration that Duval County High School gradua-tion ceremonies are "limited public fora" is in keeping with reality. If it is, the ceremonies are quite different from the rather controlled fora that most of us picture when we think of commencement exercises.

One wonders, if the principals in Duval County would have allowed a student to speak on "safe sex" or the "wonders of satanism" (as counter-speech or for any reason at all) after a senior class had decided to allow prayer. The *Black Horse Pike* court was able to address this more squarely because of the safe sex issue it discussed, but the *Adler* court did not have such facts before it. Thus, we do not know exactly how "public" the forum was. However, given common knowledge regarding graduation ceremonies, we must assume it was unusually public or that the court has found some new way to view closed fora as traditional public, or limited public, fora for free speech purposes.

An excellent example of this tension between "free speech" and the *Jones II/Adler* conception of student-initiated prayer would arise in the following situation. A school policy allows the senior class to vote on whether or not to allow a message or prayer to be delivered by a class member at graduation under a "free speech" oriented policy such as the one in *Adler*. A class member delivers a sectarian message that not only praises Jesus, but also condemns homosexuality as immoral and unnatu-ral. Several students are disturbed by the message for a variety of reasons. If the ceremony were truly a "limited public forum" it would be appro-priate for these individuals to have an opportunity to respond to the speech during the ceremony.

While a limited public forum may be limited to entities of a similar character (i.e., students, unions, and teachers), once the forum is opened the school can not engage in viewpoint discrimination unless any content-based restriction is "narrowly drawn to effectuate a compelling state interest." [110] Thus, if the school opens its graduation forum to student speech, it cannot allow the majority, or anyone else, to pick a speaker or type of speech without allowing students who oppose that speech equal access to the forum to exercise their free speech rights. Time, place, and manner restrictions would not likely justify limiting the rights of students to respond to the religious message. This is so because such a justification would essentially be based on the character of the graduation ceremony (i.e., the need for decorum, control, and solemnity), which could be disrupted by the counterspeech. Of course, this essentially demonstrates that the forum is not truly a public forum, and thus it proves too much. The school has two choices: let those who oppose the majoritarian speech also speak or don't pretend the forum is open.

If a policy like the one in *Adler,* which does not specifically require a vote on prayer, is involved, it might be argued that the school is only opening the "slot" in the graduation ceremony (not the entire ceremony) to free speech, and that the students through a democratic process essentially decide how to fill the open slot. Of course, this raises significant problems, because the government still must open the slot to free speech, and to do so in a fashion that allows the speech wishes of the majority to prevail while subordinating the speech rights of others would hardly be consistent with free speech or the public forum doctrine.

If the ceremony is not a public forum and the school allows or accommodates student-initiated public prayer in the closed graduation forum and does not allow or accommodate other student speech on similar terms, it is quite arguable that the school is favoring religious speech over nonreligious speech. Thus, in addition to a possible claim of viewpoint discrimination, the Establishment Clause would likely be violated. Some of these free speech issues are discussed in greater detail in Chapter Nine.

Significantly, if it is not state action to have graduation prayer delivered by a student pursuant to a majority vote of students, what is to keep a majority of students from voting for prayer or other religious exercises at other school events?[111] The issue of whether certain school events are considered limited public fora could have a significant impact in this regard, but as *Adler* demonstrated, what is and is not considered a public forum may not be predictable, especially when courts with the orientation of the *Jones II* and *Adler* courts make that determination. One can envision a situation in which a school district dominated by a particular faith, as in the *Herdahl* and *Herring* cases, decides to declare homeroom and school assemblies to be limited public fora and allow student-initiated prayer at those times. Perhaps courts like those in the *Adler* or *Jones II* cases would uphold this without looking in depth at exactly how "public" the forum really is in regard to all views.[112] Given the number of school boards who are likely to favor prayer at public school functions, as described in Chapters One and Two, some districts will likely choose to have, or at least not to restrict, voluntary student-initiated prayer at such times. If even a small percentage of districts across the country choose to do this, the ramifications for religious minorities and dissenters could be significant.

What does this mean for purposes of this discussion? It means that at least for now graduation prayer is constitutional in some jurisdictions if it complies with *Jones II.* It could conceivably be upheld even on the national level.[113] Moreover, the student-initiated, majority rule idea has taken hold in the language and literature of the Christian Right, and organizations like the ACLJ are pushing the envelope on such issues.[114] For example, without regard for the discomfort it will cause, the ACLJ has written to schools that even in graduation speeches other than invocations and benedictions, speakers may initiate Christian prayers and other types of religious speech.[115] This advice has apparently been followed in some school districts.[116] Given the cases discussed above and the increasing influence of the Christian Right on local school boards, the possibility is significant that the reasoning from *Jones II* and *Adler* will be used to justify sectarian prayer and other religious exercises at graduations and other school events or activities.[117]

As noted in Chapter Two, the student-initiated prayer issue is taking on a life of its own. Three examples that demonstrate the levels it has reached are the Alabama and Mississippi student-initiated prayer statutes, which have both been the subject of litigation, and the Religious Freedom Amendment that recently went before Congress. The Mississippi statute allowed "nonsectarian, nonproselytizing student-initiated voluntary prayer" at virtually all "school-related events," whether compulsory or noncompulsory.[118] The statute was challenged and found to be unconstitutional by a federal district court in Mississippi, except to the extent that it applied to graduation ceremonies as in *Jones II*.[119] The Fifth Circuit Court of Appeals (a different panel from the one that decided *Jones II*) affirmed the district court opinion, finding that the statute violated the *Lemon,* Coercion, and Endorsement tests.[120] This holding might serve to limit the use of the *Jones II* reasoning, but as Chapter Two demonstrates, that is unlikely in many areas.

About the same time that the Mississippi statute was enacted, the Alabama legislature passed a similar law.[121] There is an uncanny similarity between the two. Like the Mississippi law, the Alabama prayer statute was challenged in federal court on the basis that it violated the Establishment Clause. As in Mississippi, a federal district court held that the statute was unconstitutional.[122] However, the Alabama court, which was not bound by the *Jones II* decision, found it to be unconstitutional as to graduation prayer as well.[123] As of this writing, the case is on appeal to the United States Court of Appeals for the Eleventh Circuit, and it may ultimately be appealed to the Supreme Court. However, given existing precedents, commonly understood constitutional principles, the breadth of the statute, and its legislative history, it is unlikely to be upheld by any court. Still, other states have enacted, or are considering enacting, similar statutes. This is yet another sign of the success of the Religious Right's political efforts in regard to public school religious exercises.

At the national level, the House of Representatives recently voted on a proposed constitutional amendment called the Religious Freedom Amendment, the "Istook Amendment," named after Representative Ernest Istook, the Republican from Oklahoma who introduced it. That amendment, as voted upon (after modification by a House Resolution recommended by the House Committee on the Judiciary), read:

To secure the people's right to acknowledge God according to the dictates of conscience: Neither the United States nor any State shall establish any official religion, but the people's right to pray and recognize their religious beliefs, heritage, or traditions on public property, including schools, shall not be infringed. Neither the United States nor any State shall require any person to join in prayer or other religious activity, prescribe school prayers, discriminate against religion, or deny equal access to a benefit on account of religion.[124]

A majority of House members voted in favor of the amendment, but it failed to garner the two thirds majority needed to move forward.[125] Still, the fact that a proposed constitutional amendment that would amend the Bill of Rights and eviscerate the Establishment Clause was able to gain the votes of a majority of the House of Representatives demonstrates the risk that public school religious exercises, and the discrimination they can facilitate, will become more widespread. Thus, it is even more important that we acknowledge and address this discrimination.

The "Istook Amendment" is simply the latest in a long line of proposed constitutional amendments aimed at altering or vitiating the Establishment Clause. Earlier attempts to amend the religion clauses of the Constitution, such as those proposed by Senator Orrin Hatch, have failed in Congress (if they had passed, they would have gone to the states for ratification). However, with the recent shift of power to the right in Congress and the strong lobbying of well-funded groups supporting school prayer and other public school religious exercises, it is possible that a reintroduced "Istook Amendment" or some later version of it could get through Congress, although it is doubtful that enough state legislatures would ratify such an amendment. Still, the fact that the "Istook Amendment" won a majority in the House is sobering.

When one reads the Religious Freedom Amendment or its predecessors, such as the Religious Equality Amendment, it is clear that a significant purpose for these amendments is the institution or facilitation of organized prayer in the public schools and other government facilities. The Religion Clauses of the First Amendment, which are an already existing "Religious Freedom Amendment," do not prohibit individual citizens or students from engaging in religious exercises and prayers in the schools so long as they are not disruptive. Thus, a significant purpose for such an amendment would be to facilitate or permit organized group prayer or other religious exercises. Otherwise, much of the substance of these proposed amendments would be redundant.

The fact that the "Istook Amendment" is couched in terms that very much resemble the concept of voluntary student-initiated prayer is no coincidence, and this makes the amendment seem less threatening. However, as was discussed in Chapter One and earlier in this chapter, even under the existing Religion Clauses of the Constitution, this concept, if accepted, is not nearly as limited as it seems and can be used to justify all kinds of practices, even those that are exclusive and divisive. Considering the success school prayer advocates have had in evading the Constitution or blurring its mandates with the existing Religion Clauses in place, one can hardly imagine what would occur were the Establishment Clause essentially replaced by such an amendment. I point out these attempts to amend the Constitution because they demonstrate the level that the campaign to restore public school religious exercises has reached. From school board policies to constitutional amendments, the battle to roll back the separation of church and state is being waged. As much of this book demonstrates, when school prayer advocates win this battle, even at the local level, the results for religious minorities and dissenters can be devastating.

Even if these efforts to support student-initiated prayer at the state and national level fail, individual school boards, influenced by groups like the ACLJ or perhaps fearing litigation initiated by such groups, will continue to keep the issue alive. Moreover, as the response to *Lee* by groups like the ACLJ demonstrates, barring a clear pronouncement from the Supreme Court that all organized religious exercises in the public schools are unconstitutional, there will be no closure on this issue, because new tactics will be forged by school prayer advocates to roll back the effects of any limiting cases. Given the fact-sensitive way in which the Supreme Court often decides practices challenged under the Establishment Clause, such a clear pronouncement is unlikely.

It is useful in any discussion of the current state of the law relating to public school religious exercises to mention that in addition to the constitutional questions discussed above, there are also some recently enacted statutes that have some bearing on public school religious exercises. In recent years, amidst an outcry that religious expression is being stamped out of the public schools and that religious people are suffering discrimination on account of that expression, legislation has been passed in an attempt to protect those individuals from discrimination based on such expression. Perhaps the most successful example of this legislation is the Equal Access Act, which was passed in 1984.[126] That act allows religious clubs to meet in public schools during non-instructional time when other non-curriculum-related student groups are also permitted to meet.[127]

While this Act is not nearly as relevant to the discrimination addressed in this book as school prayer is, it is relevant nonetheless. At some schools, groups meeting pursuant to the Act can contribute to the ingroup-outgroup dynamics discussed in later chapters. Some schools also push the Act to its limits, creating an environment in which Christian or bible study groups may appear to be favored by the administration (of course, in such situations the Act itself might be violated). Despite these concerns, this author has no intention of questioning the relative merits of the Act in this book. Rather, I believe the Equal Access Act is an example of what can be accomplished by shifting focus and pursuing legislation or other nonconstitutional alternatives in the quest to protect the rights of religious minorities and dissenters who are subject to discrimination facilitated by public school religious exercises. Just as the Christian Right (along with a diverse coalition of other leaders and scholars) was able to lobby successfully for the Equal Access Act, to ensure that student religious and political groups would not suffer discrimination, similar tactics might help provide redress for the victims of discrimination facilitated by public school religious exercises and perhaps serve as a prophylactic measure against such discrimination. The Equal Access Act will be discussed in more detail in Chapter Eight.

In 1993, the Religious Freedom Restoration Act (RFRA)[128] was passed in response to *Employment Division v. Smith*,[129] a decision that criminalized the ritual use of peyote by Native Americans in Oregon. *Smith* was a highly questionable decision based on the Free Exercise Clause of the First Amendment, and RFRA had support from both sides of the church-state debate. RFRA prohibited government at all levels from "substantially burdening" an individual's free exercise of religion even through laws of general applicability unless the government can show that the burden on free exercise furthers a "compelling governmental interest" and "is the least restrictive means of furthering that . . . interest."[130]

While RFRA was certainly laudable in the context of the *Smith* decision, it became a rallying point for those arguing that religious exercises in the public schools, particularly those that are student-initiated, should be protected. In 1997, RFRA was found unconstitutional by the Supreme Court in *City of Boerne v. P. F. Flores, Archbishop of San Antonio*.[131] The *Boerne* Court held that Congress had exceeded its power in enacting RFRA, but left open the possibility that individual states could enact state RFRAs.[132] Several states are in the process of doing so, and others are being urged to do so by a surprisingly broad coalition of individuals and groups. While state RFRAs may certainly help avoid situations like that in the *Smith* case, they will also provide more legal ammunition for school prayer advocates and others who wish to use the public schools to further their beliefs.

The legal battle over the constitutionality of public school religious exercises is far from over. Moreover, the recent battle over prayer at secondary school graduations demonstrates the willingness of school districts to find ways to have religious exercises and of the Christian Right to facilitate that process. The attempts by state legislatures and members of Congress to facilitate religious exercises in the public schools will continue as well. As Chapters One and Two demonstrate, even when something is clearly unconstitutional, there are numerous school districts influenced or run by individuals belonging to groups like CEE and the Christian Coalition that simply ignore constitutional mandates. Thus, incidents like those faced by the Herdahl, Herring, Bauchman, and Bell families are likely to increase in frequency.

chapter four
The Social Context

CHAPTER ONE PROVIDED several recent cases and some historical incidents that demonstrate the discrimination that dissenters and religious minorities can suffer when religion and the public schools mix in
the United States. These are only a few examples, and similar incidents
are alluded to even in cases that do not directly address this discrimination and harassment, such as the *Black Horse Pike* case.[1] Moreover, as will
be explained in Chapters Six, Seven, Eight, and Ten, there is currently
no legal mechanism available to directly address discrimination and harassment perpetrated by nongovernmental parties such as students, parents, and others, even when that conduct is facilitated by public school
religious exercises. The cases discussed in Chapter One represent only
those incidents that are reported by the courts or the media. Since discrimination is not directly relevant to the constitutional issues that are
generally raised in school prayer cases, acts of discrimination reported in
court proceedings represent only a small percentage of such incidents
nationwide.[2] The current legal approach to this discrimination, essentially treating it as a nasty byproduct of constitutional violations, ignores
the social dynamics underlying it. By ignoring the discrimination as a
discrete issue, the law does not treat it for what it is.

The examples in Chapter One are indicative of a pattern linking public school religious exercises to discrimination and intolerance, although

this pattern will not necessarily occur at every school that allows or sponsors religious exercises. Because of its anecdotal nature and the paradox that increased religion in an environment can lead to increased intolerance and prejudice, this evidence seems to beg the question of how likely religious exercises in the public schools are to facilitate prejudice and discrimination on a larger scale. Existing research in the social sciences, however, is helpful in answering this question, although more research needs to be done.

This chapter is not meant to explain the social dynamics of religious discrimination and intolerance generally. That is a complex subject far beyond the scope of this book. Nor is it meant to explain the ways in which prejudice and discrimination come into being generally. While much has been written on these subjects in a variety of disciplines,[3] the existence and perpetuation of discrimination are complex phenomena that cannot be explained by any one theory in all of the contexts in which they occur. For purposes of this book, these issues need not be explored, because it does not propose a solution to prejudice or religious prejudice generally, nor do I believe any legal mechanism can create such profound change in regard to these issues. However, I do intend to make a connection between religiosity or, more specifically, certain religious orientations and the type of discrimination and prejudice that occur in school prayer situations. Thus, in discussing the way in which religious orientation can facilitate discrimination under some circumstances, I do not attempt to explain religious bias and discrimination in all its complexities. Likewise, in mentioning the concept of ingroup-outgroup dynamics rather briefly I do not mean to imply that such dynamics are simplistic or unidimensional. I simply point out certain connections that have serious implications, given the material contained in earlier chapters.

Of course, many people may say that the dynamics involved here are obvious. After all, it could be argued, "everyone knows that religious zealots and religious exercises are likely to facilitate this type of conduct, particularly when supported by the power of government and majoritarian factionalism. We have learned this is true throughout human history." While such generalizations may satisfy this question for some, they do not answer the question for many others and cannot do so for purposes of academic discourse, which requires more than simple generalizations.

Yet there is a significant body of social science research that supports this historical "reality." Although this research cannot demonstrate absolute connections between religious exercises, religiosity, and discrimination, and much of it does not focus on public school religious exercises, it does support the conclusions that discrimination is predictable when public school religious exercises occur in areas with certain social dynamics and that even in other areas there is a significant chance that discrimination will be facilitated by public school religious exercises, given the right circumstances.

Early on, social scientists began to explore the seemingly contradictory assertion that religiosity is related to increased prejudice. In 1967, Gordon Allport and J. M. Ross published a seminal study that attempted to explain this paradox with the concepts of "intrinsic" and "extrinsic" religious orientation, that Allport had developed in earlier research.[4] Prior to that J. R. Feagin had published a less-known, but perhaps more compelling study, pointing toward the same phenomenon.[5] More recently, researchers have focused on the relationship between fundamentalist religious orientation and increased prejudice, and the converse relationship between "quest" religious orientation and lower levels of prejudice.[6] Moreover, there is a rich literature on more general ingroup-outgroup dynamics.

In this chapter, I will explore this research along with research on peer pressure among children and adolescents. I will also explore the way in which public school religious exercises can tag religious minorities and dissenters as "other" and the ramifications of this labeling. I am not a sociologist or social psychologist, and my aim is not to answer the questions raised by the current debates in those fields. What is significant to me and this book is that three claims can be supported in regard to public school religious exercises, regardless of the perspective one chooses from the social science literature: (1) when religious exercises occur in the public schools, there is significant potential for discrimination against religious minorities and those who object to such exercises; (2) discrimination is more likely to occur in areas where the majority faith has a fundamentalist-authoritarian orientation; and (3) more re-search needs to be done by social scientists to explore the extent to which such discrimination is likely to occur in a variety of social and demographic settings. For present purposes, the key is that regardless of which theory one finds most convincing, the social science data provide support for the concern that public school religious exercises in our in-creasingly pluralistic and mobile society are likely to facilitate many more incidents such as those the Herdahls, Bells, Herrings, and Bauchmans endured. Still, the following discussion is not exhaustive.

Extrinsic, Intrinsic, Fundamentalist, and Quest Religious Orientations: Predictors of Prejudice?

In an attempt to better understand the nature of religious individuals and the interaction between religion and prejudice, Gordon Allport de-veloped the concepts of "extrinsic" and "intrinsic" religious orientation. Extrinsic religious orientation is associated with individuals who utilize religion for, or engage in religious activities because of, the social aspects of religion "such as security, comfort, status, or social support."[7] It has been asserted that many people who consider themselves "religious" fall into this group.[8] In contrast, an intrinsic religious orientation is associ-ated with individuals who value and follow the tenets of their faith for religious reasons and who model their behavior on their religious con-victions.[9] Allport and Ross wrote that an extrinsically motivated individ-ual "uses" his or her religion while an intrinsically motivated individual "lives" it.[10]

Over the years, many studies have shown that individuals with an extrinsic religious orientation are more likely than others to be preju-diced against outgroups and those with varying political views.[11] Most of these studies, however, involved issues of race rather than religious orientation. The studies also tended to show that individuals with an intrinsic orientation are less likely to demonstrate prejudiced and intoler-ant attitudes than those with extrinsic religious orientations.[12] Yet there are some individuals with intrinsic religious orientations who also dis-play a higher level of prejudice. Not surprisingly, there is some connection between these individuals and fundamentalist belief systems.[13] Recent research suggests that while intrinsically motivated individuals are less likely to demonstrate prejudiced attitudes toward racial minorities than extrinsically motivated people, they do demonstrate such attitudes toward homosexuals and others who are portrayed negatively by their faiths.[14] Given the demonizing of those who oppose the Christian Right message by leaders of the movement, it is quite possible that those who object to school prayer would fit easily into this category.

Furthermore, there appears to be a high degree of correlation between attitudes associated with both intrinsic and extrinsic religious orientation and the behaviors of those who have perpetrated discrimination against religious minorities and dissenters because of their response to issues such as school prayer. Further research is necessary to explore this connection more directly.[15] Intrinsically oriented individuals whose faith is consistent with Christian Right tenets and who may show less discriminatory attitudes in other contexts would be likely to discriminate against those whom their faith suggests are deserving of negative attention.[16] Thus, while their deep beliefs might lead to less discrimination against racial outgroups, if equality is central to that faith, that same faith might also suggest that religious outgroups and those who oppose issues such as school prayer are the enemies of God.

Similarly, those with extrinsic religious orientations would be more likely to be prejudiced toward religious minorities and particularly dissenters, because such bias tends to be based more on the fact that those groups differ from prevailing social norms and political beliefs than on any specific religious tenet, although the social norms and beliefs may themselves be supported by religious orientation. Thus, discrimination in this context is consistent with the social, personal, or political motivations generally associated with extrinsic religious orientation.[17] This does not provide a complete picture however. If both intrinsic and extrinsic orientations are consistent with discrimination against those who oppose school prayer, such discrimination ought to occur wherever there is a large number of religious people, but this is not always so. Since people of varied faiths can have intrinsic or extrinsic orientations, does faith or denomination matter to this analysis?

Significantly, as recent research has demonstrated, neither extrinsic nor intrinsic orientations can explain some of the inconsistencies in attitudes exhibited by both intrinsically and extrinsically oriented individuals of varying faiths and denominations. Thus, the distinction between those who hold fundamentalist and "quest" religious orientations becomes crucial in understanding tendencies toward prejudice among religious people. While most readers are familiar with the concept of fundamentalism, which is generally associated with a more rigid, biblically literalist, and authoritarian orientation,[18] the term "quest" in this context is less familiar. The term was coined by C. Daniel Batson and refers to a questioning approach to religious issues and a tendency to resist bright line, dogmatic, pat answers to questions.[19] In many ways, it is the opposite of a fundamentalist orientation.

A great deal of research has been done to demonstrate that fundamentalism is a strong predictor of intolerance and prejudice toward outgroups, while a "quest" orientation is associated with more tolerant attitudes.[20] In fact, fundamentalism can be an even stronger predictor of general prejudice than extrinsic religious orientation.[21] However, it is important to distinguish between orthodoxy and fundamentalism. The content of religious beliefs is not necessarily what causes the relationship between fundamentalism and prejudice, and it cannot be assumed that all orthodox believers or fundamentalists are indeed prejudiced. It is the tendency toward what some social psychologists call "right-wing authoritarianism" among fundamentalists that accounts for at least some of the fundamentalist-discrimination relationship.[22] Right-wing authoritarianism and fundamentalism have both been said to "encourage obedience to authority, conventionalism, self-righteousness, and feelings of superiority," and it has been suggested that it is the tendency to favor authoritarianism that is the driving force behind prejudiced attitudes exhibited by fundamentalists.[23] Still, religious beliefs can focus those prejudiced attitudes onto some targets more than others, such as homosexuals and those with opposing religious views.[24] This might account for the discriminatory attitudes exhibited by some intrinsically oriented fundamentalists, since such bias is consistent with their religious beliefs.

Given all of this, the advantage of viewing the issue through the fundamentalism/quest lens is that religious orientations can be placed on a continuum that considers more than the traditional extrinsic/intrinsic dichotomy alone can. Thus, a fundamentalist religious viewpoint can help explain why some intrinsically oriented individuals show higher levels of prejudice toward certain groups than extrinsically oriented individuals despite the general tendency for intrinsics to be less prejudiced.[25] It also implicates the role of authoritarianism and dogmatism in the facilitation of discriminatory attitudes.[26]

Moreover, these concepts can help researchers study and understand discriminatory tendencies across denominations and faiths. Studies that measure discriminatory attitudes across major denominations and faiths in the United States have consistently demonstrated that faiths associated with fundamentalist belief systems show the highest levels of prejudice toward a number of target groups.[27] Conversely, studies have shown that those with a "quest" orientation generally demonstrate less discriminatory attitudes than others.[28]

This is significant in the present context because much of the push for public school religious exercises has come from the predominately fundamentalist Christian Right.[29] These individuals have been engaged in a well-funded and well-organized campaign to influence and take over school boards.[30] Many of those associated with the Christian Right are poster children for an authoritarian and fundamentalist mind set. Thus, when such groups constitute the majority in a geographic area, or are otherwise able to influence school policy, they can have significant impact on school environments relating to religion and tolerance. This is evident in the fact that most of the cases of discrimination relating to public school religious exercises have arisen in areas dominated by fundamentalist and evangelical denominations or by denominations that have similar world views.[31]

If, as the research suggests, fundamentalism is a predictor of discriminatory attitudes, particularly against those who are negative objects of fundamentalist religious teachings and discourse, recent history suggests tensions will increase between Christian fundamentalists and others within our pluralistic society who oppose their agenda. Indeed, as Chapters One and Two show, the wave of fundamentalism that has been sweeping the country and the tension between religious pluralism and religious fundamentalism have created a fertile environment in which intolerance and hatred can grow when issues such as school prayer precipitate tension. Given the deeply felt beliefs on both sides of the school prayer issue and the religious orientation of many of those who most strongly support religious exercises in the public schools, it is no wonder that incidents like those described in Chapter One have been occurring with increased frequency over the last few years. However, the research cited above does not necessarily explain why discrimination can be facilitated by public school religious exercises in areas where fundamentalists are not the majority (although nonfundamentalist, extrinsically oriented individuals may be more likely than others to hold discriminatory attitudes) or whether discriminatory attitudes are as likely to be acted upon by children and adolescents as they are by adults.

In regard to the latter issue, peer pressure is quite significant. It is also important to note that some of the studies addressing extrinsic, intrinsic, fundamentalist, or quest orientations utilized high school students and college students (whose high school experience would be a recent influence). Others used adult subjects. Thus, while research on younger school children would be useful, the phenomena discussed in this section seem applicable across age groups, at least from adolescence on. Since the discrimination facilitated by public school religious exercises can be carried out by students, teachers, and other adults, the research is even more compelling in the present context. The next section demonstrates that other factors also support the connection between public school religious exercises and discrimination by school children.

Ingroup-Outgroup Dynamics, Peer Pressure, and the "Tagging" of Religious Minorities and Dissenters

Several studies have shown that school-age children can be among the most vicious toward those who are perceived as different, particularly when that difference is perceived negatively.[32] One remarkable study, documented in two books and the classic film *The Eye of the Storm*, demonstrated that when a teacher separated a class according to eye color and negatively portrayed one of the groups, the students in the positively portrayed group began to seriously discriminate against the outgroup.[33] This study is also supported by controlled experiments done by social scientists, and is consistent with much of the vast literature addressing ingroup-outgroup dynamics generally.[34] Moreover, these dynamics can occur regardless of the general religious orientation of the communities involved. The research suggests that it may be more pronounced in predominately fundamentalist communities, but as the studies mentioned above demonstrate such attitudes can be fostered almost anywhere there is an ingroup and a negatively perceived outgroup.

In school prayer situations, religious minorities and dissenters are often singled out as different, either directly by an authority figure[35] or indirectly by the situation and their reaction to it.[36] This is one of the properties of public school religious exercises in our pluralistic society. There is enough religious diversity in the country that any religious exercise has the potential to be offensive or inappropriate to at least a few students. Those students may be labeled as different simply because they do not participate in the exercise, because they participate differently, or because they or their parents object to the exercise. Thus, unless students conform to the offending practice and participate, they become "tagged" as "other." When a student or her parents object to the very religious exercises that have tagged the child, that tag is even more likely to become a scarlet letter, or worse, a target, although simply being tagged as different alone may have this effect.

In many of these cases, unlike the eye color experiment, the ingroup children have already learned negative messages about the religious outgroup at home or church, or from friends. This further facilitates the negative response. While those with fundamentalist or similar backgrounds may be more likely to have pre-existing negative beliefs about those who have different belief systems or lifestyles, anti-Semitism, anti-Catholicism, general xenophobia, and so forth are not simply the province of fundamentalists. Many people throughout society have these biases, and parents often pass these beliefs on to their children.[37] Additionally, as the eye color and similar experiments suggest, children do not necessarily need pre-existing bias to discriminate against those portrayed negatively by authority figures or peers. Simply being seen as different can be enough.

In some areas, religious differences may not be seen negatively, but in other areas they will. In these areas, children who do not participate in, or who protest against, public school religious exercises are potential targets for discrimination and harassment from their peers and others. How authority figures respond to this difference, as suggested by the eye color experiments, may be significant to how those tagged as other will be perceived. Thus, teachers and other school officials can be a mitigating or instigating force.[38] However, even when teachers and school officials attempt to mitigate discrimination, their attempts may be unsuccessful if the potential discriminators are influenced by negative messages at church or home or if the discriminators are influenced by adults outside the school. The fact that the tagging and the discrimination arise from a religious exercise sanctioned or condoned by the school may also send a message that the majority's view of things is the correct one and those who oppose it are outsiders.

Of course, even children who on their own might not treat their classmates harshly can become the perpetrators of discrimination and harassment when their peers are engaged in such activity. In the school setting, peer pressure is significant.[39] This remains true throughout childhood, although the level of pressure may fluctuate at different ages or in different settings.[40] Peer pressure can be especially problematic for those tagged as other. If even a few students seize on the differences pointed out through public school religious exercises and begin to discriminate, others may join in. In fairly homogeneous areas where some people have a fundamentalist outlook, even if fundamentalism is not the dominant religious view, students who do not share a fundamentalist religious orientation may nevertheless join in mistreatment of an outgroup that has been the focus of negative attention by their more zealous peers.[41]

The same peer pressure increases the discomfort and pain experienced by the victims of discrimination and intolerance in the school environment.[42] The influence and importance of peers for many school-age children make the process of being tagged as different, becoming the focus of negative attention, and standing up for oneself even more difficult and painful. In the school prayer context, the fact that a school-sponsored activity facilitated the process may cause students to feel they have nowhere to go for help. This was the case for Sally Walter and for the Herdahl and Herring children.[43] Common sense backs up the scientific data we have discussed. As children, most of us have witnessed, or suffered, the harsh treatment aimed at those who are labelled as "different" or "outsiders."

As noted above, all of this is significant in light of the emotional nature of the issue and the strong push for school prayer by Christian fundamentalists. As Chapter Two demonstrates, school board elections are being targeted by religious fundamentalists who have begun to view those contests as a new battleground. Unfortunately, these individuals have not generally shown a great deal of tolerance for those who do not share their religious or social views. Certainly, some individuals who hold these views can rise above the urge to be intolerant, but the views themselves do not promote a great deal of tolerance toward those with divergent beliefs.

For many school prayer advocates, the issue reflects a more general marriage between political agendas and religious belief. Thus, the issue is part of a broader world view that is supported by, or tied to, particular religious tenets.[44] Opposing this view can trigger a negative response from people with extrinsic or fundamentalist religious attitudes. Moreover, the belief system itself automatically divides people into ingroups and outgroups, even for those with intrinsic orientations—for instance, the "saved" and the "unsaved," the "righteous" and the "unrighteous."[45] Of course, Christian fundamentalism is not the only belief system that promotes ingroup-outgroup dynamics.[46]

Religious and political pluralism is likely seen by many vocal school prayer advocates as a challenge to the belief that "Christian" values, as defined by a particular group, are the nation's dominant values.[47] As a result, individuals who are armed with narrower views promoted by fundamentalism and the right-wing authoritarianism generally associated with it or who are interested in religion primarily for social gains are likely to see those with different religious and political beliefs as competing for valued social or political resources.[48] This can increase intolerance and prejudice toward those outgroups.[49]

It is important to be clear, however, that few social scientists have directly addressed the impact of public school religious exercises on religious minorities and dissenters. The few who have done so acknowledge the real danger of psychological harm inherent in public school religious practices and the likelihood that these practices will be used or abused to perpetuate discrimination.[50] The majority of the research discussed in this chapter points to the fact that regardless of the theoretical construct one uses to study the relationship between religion and prejudice, in many situations the dynamics of public school religious exercises make those exercises likely facilitators of discrimination. This research also demonstrates how "religious people" can commit the acts that were done to the Herdahls, Herrings, Bells, Bauchmans, and Walters. It also provides evidence that such conduct may be predictable when public school religious exercises occur, particularly in areas dominated or influenced by those with fundamentalist or authoritarian tendencies. The influence, power, and rhetoric of the Christian Right are likely to create situations in which the dynamics discussed in this chapter come to fruition. Ironically, those involved will likely paint the religious minorities or dissenters as the "bad guys" for not participating in, or for resisting, the practices in question.

Still, more research needs to be done. It is essential for social scientists to study the relationship between public school religious exercises and discrimination more directly. The research and literature on religious orientation, peer pressure, and ingroup-outgroup dynamics provide excellent starting points for new studies. The anecdotal and historical evidence is compelling, and the existing social science research points to a connection between public school religious exercises and discrimination, at least at some schools, but the dynamics of this connection and the effects of varying demographics within schools and school districts must be studied, along with the influence of Christian Right political activity. Such studies could be of great use in passing the type of legislation discussed in Chapter Eight and in formulating better policies to deal with religious issues in the public schools. Such studies may also help to create effective social mechanisms to protect children from discrimination without resort to the legal process. Greater awareness of the situations addressed in Chapter One, backed by clearly relevant social science data, may also persuade many of the 70 to 80 percent of the population who support school prayer to rethink that support.[51]

Given the incidents and history discussed in Chapter One, the political efforts and tactics of the Christian Right, and the long, tortured history of religious factions using government power to support their agendas, the likelihood of public school religious exercises giving rise to discrimination and even violence in the United States is increasing. The social science research discussed in this chapter demonstrates, at least in regard to those with fundamentalist-intrinsic religious tendencies, why the growth and rhetoric of the Christian Right and like-minded individuals can be a significant catalyst for the attitudes that give rise to situations like those described in Chapter One.

One final note: recently, efforts have begun to try to broker "peace" in controversial cases of religion in the public schools.[52] The idea is to find common ground for discussion between significantly divided parties.[53] The recent efforts by the First Amendment Center at Vanderbilt University to resolve disputes involving religion in the public schools are an excellent example.[54] Mediation techniques have been used to try to bridge the barriers that divide the opponents in these cases. Such efforts have been endorsed by people on both sides of the debate.[55] Some of the proposed solutions in these cases may themselves be unconstitutional, but the idea of trying to resolve these issues through emphasizing common interests and facilitating understanding between the parties would seem a good prescription in many situations. In other cases, however, the will of those involved or the power dynamics of the situation may lower the possibility of long-term success for mediated agreements.[56] Moreover, despite such efforts, discrimination facilitated by public school religious exercises is still occurring, and, as will be discussed later in this book, there is no effective legal remedy in many such cases. While a legal remedy in these situations is not likely to solve the social disputes underlying the problem, it remains to be seen whether the new efforts at brokering peace can help solve the problems. It would be wonderful if such efforts could do so in a manner consistent with constitutional mandates. For now, however, discrimination is a continuing threat.

Interestingly, Bruce Hunsburger, a social psychologist, has suggested that vigorously enforced laws may help to protect minorities from discrimination perpetrated by fundamentalists because their highly authoritarian dispositions make fundamentalists likely to obey laws with which they disagree.[57] Hunsburger has also suggested that other methods, such as causing fundamentalists to confront the "dark side" of their religious orientation and "its consequences," may help decrease prejudice in fundamentalists. However, as Hunsburger acknowledges, these suggestions are speculative.[58]

chapter five

Where Do We Go from Here?

BY THIS POINT, four things should be abundantly clear. First, when public school religious exercises occur, they sometimes facilitate discrimination against religious minorities and dissenters. Second, this discrimination is somewhat predictable when religious exercises occur at public schools in our pluralistic society, given the social dynamics these exercises create. Third, the frequency of religious exercises in the public schools is likely to increase as a result of the organized campaign currently being waged by the Christian Right and by the fact that most Americans are unaware of the discrimination facilitated by practices such as school prayer. Fourth, current constitutional doctrine in regard to public school religious exercises is being ignored in some school districts and is in a state of flux.

This naturally raises a question: what can be done about this? One's first response might be to look to the Constitution. After all, if the wall of separation between church and state is maintained, there will be no religious exercises in the public schools to facilitate such discrimination, right? Wrong. As demonstrated in Chapters One and Two, there are numerous school districts willing to knowingly violate the Constitution on issues like school prayer. Moreover, as Chapter Three demonstrates, even when school districts want to follow constitutional mandates, these mandates may be unclear and inconsistent. This leads to unpredictability when school boards and superintendents—faced with pressure to have, or not to have, religious exercises in the schools—must make decisions as to what is permissible, decisions that even the courts have difficulty making much of the time. Additionally, even currently constitutional activities such as moments of silence under appropriate state legislation can facilitate the kinds of discrimination addressed in this book.

Thus, while the Constitution remains the main tool in the struggle to determine what religious exercises are permissible or impermissible in the public schools, it is not the best tool for addressing the discrimination facilitated by such exercises when they do occur. As will be discussed in Chapters Six and Seven, this is also true because of the limited remedies available to victims of discrimination facilitated by public school religious exercises pursuant to the Constitution. This is not to say that the constitutional debate should be ignored. To the extent that it prevents many school districts from engaging in religious exercises, the Constitution is a significant prophylactic measure. Rather, the Constitution must be the major focus in any debate about what religious exercises should or should not be permissible in the public sphere. However, what "should" be permissible, or even what "is" impermissible, does not necessarily reflect what is actually going on in school districts throughout the country. The impermissible occurs every day, and the permissible is not static.

If not to the Constitution, where can we look to derive protection for victims of discrimination facilitated by public school religious exercises? The most logical place to look would be civil rights law and policy. There are some existing principles of antidiscrimination law that are uniquely equipped to deal with this problem. Ironically, as will be discussed in the next chapter, some of the shortcomings of antidiscrimination law and the use of law in general to resolve civil rights problems may prove to be beneficial in the present context. For example, one major shortcoming of antidiscrimination law that has been suggested by some of its proponents and opponents is that it may be too narrow in scope to effect any real social change and thus is simply a mechanism for redress in limited situations.

Of course, given the data discussed in Chapter Four and the long history of intolerance and discrimination facilitated by religious exercises in the public schools and by religious difference generally, a serious change in intolerant attitudes cannot be seen as a realistic goal of any civil rights legislation in this area. A more realistic goal of any such legislation would be simply to provide redress to victims of discrimination facilitated by public school religious exercises—a problem that is currently all but ignored, but which has serious ramifications. Additionally, any such legislation might serve a prophylactic purpose, because of the stigma and damages that can be associated with civil rights violations.

It would be wonderful if there were a means to legislate away religious intolerance and the zealous use of state resources sometimes used to give it force. However, as a civil rights scholar-attorney, I have significant reservations about any suggestion that law alone can transform such deeply embedded social phenomena, particularly in the short run. Law can serve as a normative factor to facilitate changes in behavior at certain levels, but it can also serve as a mechanism for justifying an entire system that perpetuates social inequities.[1]

In approaching the issues raised by this book, it is important to address them on several levels. First, and most basically, they must be pointed out and put in context so that they can be acknowledged and dealt with. Second, they must be analyzed within the context of the existing legal and social framework. Finally, a method must be developed to deal with these issues effectively at a time when the social climate makes it likely that the number of incidents will increase. One must be realistic about what may be achieved, particularly if the solution proposed is a legal one.

Realistically, the benefit of using civil rights principles in regard to the discrimination facilitated by public school religious exercises is the availability of more significant damages and the possibility that school districts could be liable for the discriminatory actions of third parties facilitated by school board policy or actions. Currently, school boards are not liable for such actions, as the *Bell* and *Bauchman* cases sadly demonstrate.[2] The higher damage awards might deter school boards from engaging in questionable activities and would also raise the ire of the taxpayers who elect school board members. Moreover, the stigma and bad publicity associated with committing a civil rights violation could also serve as a deterrent. Most importantly, the victims of the discrimination will receive more than simply an injunction and minimal damages for all their suffering. Thus, civil rights and antidiscrimination principles are well-tailored to provide redress and perhaps serve a deterrent function. Each of these points will be discussed in more detail in Chapters Six and Seven.

It is also significant that by addressing this discrimination as a civil rights violation we recontextualize it. We are no longer concerned only with the constitutionality of the school's actions or policies, but rather with the impact those policies and actions have on those likely to be the targets of negative attention. Certainly, constitutional claims may be brought, but their resolution would not be determinative of the discrimination issue. Schools engaging in activities that may be constitutional will have to do so in a sensitive fashion so that those activities do not facilitate discrimination. Thus, although it is currently constitutional to have voluntary student-initiated prayer at secondary school graduations in the Fifth Circuit, pursuant to *Jones II,* school districts that wish to allow this would have to be more sensitive to the potential discrimination this can cause. A school district that has a moment of silence pursuant to an appropriate state statute would need to be sure that policy is being effected in a manner that does not facilitate discrimination, such as that which occurred in the *Walter* case.[3]

Of course, pointing out that antidiscrimination law might be useful in this context is not the same as stating that there is existing law that does this, or that there is any way to have such a law that will not be so broad as to make school boards liable for behavior far beyond their control. The potential for using existing laws to achieve these goals is discussed in Chapter Ten. In Chapter Eight, however, I propose a statute that could more directly address this issue. The proposed statute demonstrates that it is possible to protect religious minorities from discrimination in the public schools without utilizing a vague or unnecessarily broad remedial scheme. As will be discussed in Chapter Eight, the key is to target only discrimination facilitated by religious exercises in the public schools, exercises over which the schools initially have control, whether they ultimately choose to delegate that control or not. Obviously, under this scheme the best way to avoid liability is either not to have such activities or to have internal policies in place that can effectively deal with incidents of discrimination when they occur. This will be discussed in more detail later in this book.

Even if the suggested remedial scheme set forth in Chapter Eight is not utilized, it is essential that discrimination facilitated by public school religious exercises be directly addressed as an issue of discrimination—that is, as a civil rights issue and not simply as a byproduct of a violation of civil liberties protected under the Constitution. Before getting to this point, which will be addressed in Chapters Six and Seven, it is important to discuss briefly two relevant issues that do not fit neatly into the discussion in later chapters.

The first of these is the potential for religious segregation occasioned by public school religious exercises in a pluralistic society. The other is the fact that the Christian Right has begun to usurp the discrimination issue through an organized campaign. It is ironic that while separationists have essentially ignored the discrimination issue as a separate legal entity, the Christian Right has demonstrated that it appreciates the power of claims of discrimination and victimization by endeavoring to paint religious Christians as victims of discrimination in the public schools and in society at large. Thus, if the victims of discrimination facilitated by public school religious exercises do not develop an organized voice, the Christian Right may in essence usurp the issue, despite having few verifiable instances of pernicious discrimination. Each of these issues will be discussed below.

The Potential for Religious Segregation

This section is necessarily brief because I am not aware of any research that has systematically studied the effect of public school religious exercises or environments (or perceptions of them) on geographic mobility. Such research would be invaluable, but for now I am limited to making observations that are necessarily speculative. However, because I believe they have merit, warrant further investigation by social scientists, economists, and educators, and point out yet another possible detrimental effect of public school religious exercises on religious minorities, a brief discussion is in order.

While poring over statements in newspapers and television transcripts by local townspeople who supported school prayer in relation to the *Herdahl* case I was struck by the statement of one woman in particular. She was asked by the reporter doing a television report for *60 Minutes* what she would do if her husband was fired or transferred and her family ended up having to move to a primarily Jewish town where there was Jewish prayer over the loudspeaker in the local public schools. The woman responded that she would never move there under any circumstances.[4] This single statement revealed a great deal about the provincial mind set of many of those who support the violation of constitutional mandates in regard to school prayer. More importantly, it raised the question of what Jewish, Muslim, or Buddhist families could do if faced with similar circumstances. After all, such families would virtually never be in the majority.

Perhaps Jewish families should live only in parts of Brooklyn or other cities where they might be in the majority; Muslims in certain suburbs of Detroit and Jersey City; Buddhists in Chinatowns in San Francisco and other major cities; Mormons in Utah; Catholics in parts of Boston, Philadelphia, Buffalo, and New Orleans; and so on. Of course, when written like this such an idea sounds ridiculous, but such religious segregation might be the result if the current trend toward public school religious exercises continues. Whether such segregation is de facto or de jure, to borrow terms from judicial analysis in cases involving racial segregation, would likely depend on the extent of state involvement in such religious exercises in a given geographic area and the nature of those exercises. Still, the potential for religious segregation is significant.

When one looks at the foundation of the Catholic schools in the United States, one can not ignore the role of organized Protestant prayer in the New York public schools and the discrimination it facilitated.[5] Bishop Hughes and other Catholic leaders wanted a Catholic school system, in part, to enable Catholic children to be educated in a less hostile environment.[6] In essence, they segregated themselves within a geographic area from the offensive practices in the public schools (though not all Catholics attended the newly founded Catholic schools). Fortunately, in New York and other cities there was a large enough Catholic population to support such schools.

What choices would Catholic families have had in areas with too small a Catholic population to support schools? What choice would a Jewish, Muslim, or Buddhist family have in most geographic regions today? If one cannot escape from such offending practices within a community, one is less likely to move there. Thus, one will remain where it is comfortable, perhaps missing opportunities in other areas. It is one thing if this is done voluntarily; it is quite another when one does so out of concern that the local schools and government will reinforce or inculcate alien religious beliefs in one's children. This effect on mobility could provide Congress with a basis to enact legislation like that proposed in Chapter Eight, since it impacts interstate commerce and the Commerce Clause has been a basis upon which Congress has claimed authority to pass other civil rights legislation.

If prayer is returned to the schools in the current political climate, whether student-initiated or not, constitutional or not, there is a significant likelihood that it will be sectarian in nature in many geographic regions. As discussed in Chapter Three, if it is student-initiated, sectarian prayer might be just as acceptable as nonsectarian prayer. The majority religion in any given area could dictate the nature of the prayer (particularly in areas where there is a willingness to disregard constitutional mandates in this regard). Given the situations discussed in Chapter One and the social dynamics explained in Chapter Four, this could make some areas particularly undesirable to certain faiths or denominations. In essence, many people would segregate themselves into areas where their faith, or like-minded faiths, are located. This would be especially so for families who could not afford private schools or who were considering moving to an area with no nonsectarian private schools.

Perhaps sectarian prayer in the public schools did promote religious segregation, and the increased religious pluralism in traditionally homogeneous areas over the last thirty years has been facilitated by the Supreme Court's ban on organized school prayer. While this is overly simplistic, an interesting study could be made of the factors behind the increased Jewish and Catholic migration to bible belt states such as Georgia, North Carolina, Texas, and regions such as central Florida since the 1960s, as well as of the increased geographic mobility and willingness to move to certain areas of members of other faiths. Of course, this is purely speculative and no doubt increased industry and the pluralistic nature of much of that industry is a major factor behind this increased mobility, but why didn't it happen sooner? There certainly have been recent incentives provided to industries to move to these areas, but many of those incentives, such as lower taxes, a ready workforce, and so forth, existed prior to the 1970s.

Put another way, if there were sectarian Southern Baptist or evangelical prayers in the public schools, would a business that was heavily Catholic, Episcopalian, Jewish, Methodist, or any combination of these or other religions/denominations with similar pre-existing geographic focii move to these areas? Consider Charlotte, Orlando, and Dallas. Each city has undergone incredible growth since the 1960s, and many religious minorities have moved to these areas (of course, there were certainly some members of these faiths already there). An environment like that in Ecru, Mississippi, and Pike County, Alabama, is not very welcoming to religious minorities.

While such anecdotal evidence certainly does not prove that this phenomenon would occur on a nationwide scale, one simply needs to think about what it would be like to send children to the Pike County or Pontotoc public schools. For those who agree with the majority faiths in those schools, try to imagine sending your children to a public school that reinforces a faith with which you disagree. No one could be sure of escaping the potential for discomfort at the least—harassment and violence at worst. Everyone is a religious minority somewhere.

A more in-depth discussion of the likelihood that segregation could be facilitated by public school religious exercises, and the effect school prayer and its limitation by the Supreme Court may have had on the geographic mobility of various faiths, is beyond the scope of this book. However, such work would be invaluable to understand the impact that public school religious exercises might have on the demographic makeup of entire regions in the United States. Perhaps it would prove to be a sporadic phenomenon, but it is quite possible that a direct correlation between public school religious exercises and religious segregation would be found. There is no question that many economic, social, technological, cultural, and non-school-related religious phenomena are key to these issues as well. However, the impact of public school religious exercises on geographic mobility should not be underestimated as was demonstrated by the statement of the woman interviewed in the *60 Minutes* report mentioned above.

Defining the "Victims" of Religious Discrimination

If you tune your television to *The 700 Club*, the Christian Broadcasting Network, *NET (National Empowerment Television)*, or any number of other "Christian" channels or programs, an interesting pattern emerges if you watch long enough. The viewer is told that "Christians" (I use the quotation marks here because in the context of these programs the term is generally used to refer only to certain evangelical Christians) are the victims of discrimination in our country and in our public schools. The First Amendment is being used to prevent "Christians" from freely expressing their religious beliefs through school prayer and other public displays. "Christian" children are prevented from reading their bibles or praying in school. They are the victims of discrimination, according to these programs.

Chapter Two provided several examples of this rhetoric of victimization that is frequently used by the Christian Right. Pat Robertson was quoted as saying:

> Just like what Nazi Germany did to the Jews, so liberal America is now doing to evangelical Christians. It's no different. It is the same thing. It is happening all over again. It is the Democratic Congress, the liberal-biased media and the homosexuals who want to destroy all Christians. Wholesale abuse and discrimination and the worst bigotry directed toward any group

in America today. More terrible than anything suffered by any minority in our history.[7]

Likewise, Robertson has written:

All over this country a frightening trend continues. The civil and religious liberties of American citizens—especially *Christian citizens*—are being trampled. . . . *It is time to stop the ACLU, secular humanists, and anti-family organizations that are destroying our freedoms* [emphasis in original].[8]

An article in the Christian Coalition's newspaper, *Christian America,* entitled "The Ghettoizing of the Gospel," demonstrates that members of the Christian Right can claim "victim" status while at the same time ignoring offenses to other faiths. That article included the following statement:

The unwarranted uproar that surrounded Gov. Kirk Fordice's simple statement of fact that "America is a Christian nation" serves as a chilling illustration of a contemporary cultural phenomenon: the "ghettoizing of the Gospel of Jesus Christ." In Nazi Germany, Joseph Goebbels' Ministry of Propoganda stigmatized the Jews until they were anathema in the eyes of the general public. Then, when public opinion was properly conditioned, the Jews were herded into ghettoes and later into concentration camps, where they were eventually destroyed. The same thing is happening to Christians in America today.[9]

Robert Simonds of CEE is a master of this rhetoric of victimization. For example, he has written:

We who are working hard to give our children "safe passage" through our schools must never be discouraged in our slow progress toward our goal. Trying to bring constructive school reform, to protect all American children from the chilling effect of anti-Christian teachers or administrators who are discriminating against our children of faith, many times openly persecuting them and their parents, is a very slow process, but it is happening.

Our victory over our children's detractors, as well as our children's public school education, and therefore their future, is worth a long struggle. God has carefully selected you and all of us at CEE for His victory. We must never accept anyone treating our children of faith as second class citizens, with discrimination and often persecution of Christian students.

Hiding behind false legalities and misinterpretations of the Constitution, God's true enemies would destroy religious freedom, and Christian students' right to pray or meet for reasons of faith in Christ.[10]

Other Christian Right leaders regularly make similar statements in speeches, sermons, and in writing. The rhetoric of victimization is a common feature in Christian Right literature and programming.

It is not a coincidence that concepts of victimization and discrimination are being used to evoke sympathy and support for the Christian Right's agenda. In fact, it is a brilliant media-savvy tactic, which is working. No doubt, there have been instances in which school officials have gone too far in enforcing the Establishment Clause, but these instances, which will be discussed further below, generally result from a misunderstanding of what the Constitution precludes and are rectified quickly, usually through informal mechanisms.[11]

The irony is, of course, that there are more serious and consistent victims of pernicious religious discrimination in the public schools, such as the Herdahls, Herrings, Bells, McCords, Bauchmans, and Walters discussed in Chapter One, and it is likely that this type of religious discrimination will increase. Yet, unlike the well-organized Christian Right, there is little organized effort to make people aware that this discrimination occurs, that it is tied to a long and tortured history of public school religious exercises, that there are psychological phenomena that make it predictable, and that virtually no one and no geographic area is immune from this discrimination.

Perhaps the ineffectiveness of many of those opposed to school prayer in getting this point across stems from the significant focus placed on the Constitution. Even in the *Herdahl* and *Herring* cases, which received national media attention, there was little mention of "religious discrimination." The focus was on the unconstitutional nature of the prayer and other religious exercises, not on the discrimination they facilitated.[12] Thus, instead of looking at the nexus between the government's actions and the discrimination as a discrete phenomenon, the problem was addressed more as a nasty byproduct of the government action and the nature of the local townsfolk. As can be seen throughout this book, however, there is a link between government action and the behavior of the townsfolk in case after case.

Regardless, the issue is being slowly usurped by those arguably most responsible for facilitating the recent discrimination discussed in this book, albeit unintentionally much of the time. The irony is that much of what they claim is discrimination consists of incidents in which the First Amendment was appropriately applied given current constitutional norms. Thus, when a public school does not allow organized public prayer sponsored by school officials, such as coaches at athletic events, this is seen as discrimination, although according to the courts the Constitution does not permit such prayer.[13] In a basic sense, it is discrimination. It is discrimination against illegal activity. However, it is not based in religious animosity against "Christians," but rather in a duty to uphold the Constitution.

Some of the "discrimination" alleged by the Christian Right results from the fact that public school curricula in general are pervasively secular and they foster a secular atmosphere at school. School officials, teachers, and administrators may make decisions in this environment that are insensitive to the needs or concerns of the orthodox, including born-again Christians. Some of these decisions may be mandated by the Constitution or academic concerns, but others may demonstrate poor judgment, incorrect assumptions, bad interpretations of what the Constitution permits or prohibits, or fear of bringing potentially divisive religious issues into school activities. To the extent that such instances constitute discrimination, they do not represent the kinds of vitriolic harassment and discrimination facilitated by public school religious exercises, and ironically, given the nature of these incidents, the First Amendment would likely provide a more appropriate remedy in these cases than in those described in Chapter One.

Still, there are some troubling incidents. These generally involve overzealous school officials who are trapped in a web between what is an unconstitutional establishment of religion and what is a constitutional free exercise of religion. Aware of this fact, Christian Right organizations are soliciting victims to use as "poster children" for their media efforts. For example, in the newsletters and magazines of some of these organizations there are requests for any incidents in which children have had their rights infringed in the public schools. Despite this effort, they have discovered few verifiable instances where "Christian" students' constitutional rights regarding freedom of religion were violated, at least instances that could not be peacefully rectified.[14]

The reality is that there have been some instances in which students were treated in an unfair or unconstitutional manner that denied them their rights. For example, a student was asked to remove his bible from class at a public school.[15] Other students have alleged they were prevented from praying privately. However, these instances are frequently reported inaccurately, are generally resolved informally, and are based more on a misunderstanding by school officials of the parameters of constitutional rights and duties than on any religious animosity fostered by school policies.[16] There is no question that students may bring a bible to school, pray privately, or engage in private religious conversations with their classmates.[17] Thus, while school officials may have made bad decisions in these instances, decisions with which those who value religious freedom should take issue, these incidents are a far cry from the pernicious discrimination described in Chapter One.

These incidents, and the way they are generally resolved, are different in nature from the experiences of the Herdahls, Herrings, Bells, and other families who have experienced the vitriolic hatred and discrimination facilitated by public school religious exercises. However, I do not mean to minimize the importance of resolving issues involving the denial of "Christian" students' constitutional rights. School prayer opponents and advocates alike understand the constitutional right of individual students to pray or bring their bibles to school. Those are rights that must be defended. This is possible primarily because they are clearly constitutionally protected rights, and once aware of this school officials usually comply with the Constitution. Of course, the same cannot be said for the school officials who promote unconstitutional religious exercises in the public schools.

Thus, the campaign by some in the Christian Right to portray themselves as the victims of discrimination often rests on the assumption that prohibiting an unconstitutional establishment of religion is discrimination, but it can also rest on real incidents in which students' rights are violated by overzealous school officials. What the Christian Right describes as "discrimination" is quite different, and often more easily resolved, than the discrimination addressed in this book. However, the most important thing pointed out by the campaign is the power evoked by the discourse of victimization and discrimination—a power the Christian Right understands very well. Combined with their campaign to influence school boards and local governments, this rhetoric can be a powerful tool to effect change and gain support for their agenda. Currently, they can define the debate because they are the only ones addressing it in a consistent and coherent fashion as a discrete issue. Despite numerous instances and a long history of public school religious exercises causing religious discrimination, it is those supporting such exercises, not those who oppose them, who seem to understand the power and importance of the discourse of discrimination and the utility of looking beyond traditional constitutional standards to define and refine the church-state debate.

Naturally, this returns us to the phenomena discussed in Chapters One through Four. If the pernicious discrimination facilitated by public school religious exercises were presented to the public in an effective fashion, serious public support might be rallied to deal with it. Ironically, those who favor the exercises that facilitate discrimination have taken over the role of "victim." Nevertheless, the victims of more serious religious discrimination are out there and will likely increase in number. They currently have no effective way to protect themselves directly from the discrimination facilitated by public school religious exercises. This is, of course, where civil rights principles and antidiscrimination law can be useful, both in addressing and calling attention to the issue.

The next few chapters will explore the nexus between public school religious exercises and civil rights principles. A statute that addresses the

AMERICAN RIVER COLLEGE

discrimination often facilitated by public school religious exercises will be proposed and analyzed, and the potential for using existing anti-discrimination laws to address the problem will be explored. Regardless of whether one agrees with the exact solutions proposed, the utility of applying civil rights and antidiscrimination concepts to this debate should become apparent. A great deal is at stake, and the current political climate makes it likely that the school prayer debate will continue and intensify. It is essential that the discrimination facilitated by public school religious exercises be directly addressed and policy be developed to deal with this discrimination.

chapter six
The Utility of Antidiscrimination Law

WHAT ARE CIVIL RIGHTS and antidiscrimination law, and what benefits does their application yield in the present context? For purposes of the present discussion, a somewhat limited conception of these terms will be presented. Civil rights are much broader than the area covered by civil rights law, and antidiscrimination laws deal with a broad array of discrimination against members of protected classes.[1] For purposes of this book, however, the focus will be on the ways in which civil rights principles and antidiscrimination laws address discrimination in education and employment, for these are the two areas that provide the best legal mechanisms for addressing the discrimination discussed herein. Specifically, the concepts of hostile environment harassment, as modified for educational settings, disparate treatment and disparate impact are useful in the present context.

Before addressing the utility of these legal concepts in regard to the issues raised in this book, it is essential to look at the way in which most antidiscrimination law functions in relation to the civil rights violations it is meant to remedy. Generally, antidiscrimination law is targeted to remedy specific instances of discrimination aimed at a member or members of a protected class or to end practices aimed at a protected class that have a negative impact on that class.[2] Some courts have focused a significant amount of attention on the individual nature of most antidiscrimination laws—i.e., holding that they are aimed at providing individual victims of class-based discrimination with a remedy rather than providing class-based remedies regardless of individual circumstance. While I disagree with this interpretation in some contexts, the debate that arises from such holdings is largely irrelevant for purposes of this book.[3]

Given the type of discrimination discussed herein, the key to any effective remedial scheme is its ability to enable individual victims or sets of victims (from the same schools) to obtain redress when public school religious exercises facilitate discrimination and to force school districts engaged in these activities to become sensitive and responsive to the negative impact on religious minorities and dissenters that religious exercises in the schools can foster. As demonstrated in Chapters One and Four, much of the discrimination facilitated by religious exercises will be based on religion and aimed at individual students who are members of faiths that are in the religious minority in a given school district. The remaining targets of the discrimination are likely to be dissenters who will be labelled as different simply because they dissent and perhaps will be perceived as being outside the majority faith whether they actually are or not.

Class-wide remedies are unnecessary in this context, because not all school districts will have these problems, and the question of who belongs to a religious minority will vary from school district to school district. The ability to reach the behavior of students, parents, and school employees, when that behavior is facilitated by school policies, is one of the key benefits of using antidiscrimination law to remedy the discrimination facilitated by public school religious exercises. As will be discussed in the next chapter, the remedies available under the Constitution are not designed to reach the type of discriminatory behavior discussed herein, especially when the discrimination is committed by third parties such as students or parents.

The key is that discrimination is a possible, even likely, byproduct of public school religious exercises in some areas, and a school that permits such exercises should be prepared to deal effectively with any discrimination that results. This is especially so once a student or parent complains about a discriminatory incident facilitated by a religious exercise. A good analogy arises in the context of hostile environment sexual harassment in employment and the schools. The law is aimed at the type of harassment facilitated by an employer's or school's policies and practices or by the inaction of an employer or school in the face of complaints of harassment.[4]

In general, civil rights principles are useful here. A government entity is engaging in, or facilitating, activity that has a proven potential to cause discrimination against students and their families, discrimination based on their religious preference or their position in regard to religion in the schools. The right to go to school free from constant discrimination and harassment should not be dependent upon one's religious views. At least in some contexts, religion has already been declared to be a protected class subject to civil rights protection.[5] Dissenters, who may not belong to a religious minority, are discriminated against because of their views in relation to religion and also may be regarded as a religious minority. Thus, in essence they too are being discriminated against based on religion. In fact, some federal antidiscrimination laws recognize that civil rights violations against those who are "regarded as" being a member of a protected class, even though not actually part of that class, should be remedied.[6]

When religious exercises occur in the public schools, discrimination may be facilitated in regard to a basic right—education—based on irrelevant characteristics. This is exactly the type of situation that civil rights concepts are best equipped to address. Looking at this issue through the lens of civil rights rather than the more traditional constitutional civil liberties lens opens up a new way of viewing the problem. By using antidiscrimination law, a favorite normative mechanism used to effectuate civil rights ideals, the discrimination itself can be addressed separately from the broader constitutional issues.

Of course, antidiscrimination laws can be criticized for not being terribly effective in achieving many of their stated goals and for making society believe that it has resolved problems that actually remain, problems that reach much deeper into society and the dominant social structure than laws can likely reach. When it comes to issues of race and gender, there is a great deal of merit to this criticism. For example, Critical Race Theorists have suggested that laws may reinforce the dominant racial hierarchies in society and that antidiscrimination laws, while useful in specific cases, serve more to assuage white guilt and support the myth of a "level playing field" than to actually undo the existing social structures that give rise to inequality.[7] When dealing with the intractable issues of race and gender, where research data and daily experience often demonstrate the deep reach of existing social hierarchies, this criticism makes sense. Antidiscrimination laws may help at some levels and may even effect deeper social change if left in place for long enough, but law alone is not capable of ending racism or gender bias.

In the current context, however, the goal is not to end religious discrimination on a societal scale. No one religious minority can be singled out for protection in regard to school-facilitated discrimination, because who belongs to a religious minority will vary from district to district. Thus, a complex web of socioreligious dynamics beyond the reach of antidiscrimination law would have to be untangled to undo the attitudes that underlie religious discrimination and intolerance. Religious hegemonics and discrimination are embedded in the theology of some religious denominations. Some would say that they are basic aspects of fundamentalism.[8] Moreover, some ways of practicing Christianity naturally promote the expression of religious differences by dividing people into a superior ingroup and unsaved outgroups (for instance, non-Christians cannot go to heaven unless they accept Jesus).[9] Religious proselytization or evangelism may exacerbate these differences.

Given that the majority of those expressing a religious preference in the United States are Christian and that the majority of those most active in promoting public school religious exercises tend to be evangelical, it would be unrealistic to try to create a law that would promote enough change in society to significantly lower the sentiments that promote religious discrimination without interfering with religious doctrine. Any law that would attempt to do so in the name of religious equality would surely run afoul of the First Amendment and rightly so. It is not government's place to alter religious doctrine in order to promote tolerance. However, government can pass laws aimed at limiting the impact of that intolerance on religious minorities, especially when the intolerance is facilitated by government institutions.

This is the focus of the antidiscrimination law discussed in this book. It is aimed at remedying or preventing discrimination in the limited context of public schools that choose to sponsor or allow organized religious exercises at school or during school-sponsored events. This may not be as grandiose a goal as the eradication of religious intolerance in society, but given the documented problems associated with public school religious exercises and the increasing religious pluralism and fundamentalism in the United States, even limited measures are essential. Perhaps, the use of antidiscrimination law will promote broader religious tolerance (simply calling attention to the problem may promote tolerance). That would be a wonderful byproduct. However, the immediate task is to provide redress for the increasing number of victims of religious discrimination facilitated by public school policies or practices, a task that antidiscrimination law is uniquely suited to perform.

Of course, stating that such discrimination is a civil rights violation, which should be afforded a remedy under antidiscrimination law, is only the first step. What law should be applied? Is there an existing cause of action that can be appropriately tailored to address this problem? The first question is not simple to answer because it is likely that no existing antidiscrimination law addresses this discrimination. Chapter Ten will discuss the application of existing laws. Chapters Eight and Nine will also set forth a proposed statute to address this problem. That statute is based on existing antidiscrimination laws and civil rights ideals, as tailored to the unique circumstances and constitutional limitations inherent in the public school context. No such law currently exists, at least at the federal level.

The second question is easier to address. There are three causes of action currently used pursuant to existing antidiscrimination legislation that could be tailored to the unique dynamics of this problem (others may be relevant in specific factual situations). However, they are not simplistic causes of action, and it is important to elucidate the issues arising from their application. These causes of action are "hostile environment" applied to cases of harassment, "disparate impact" applied to facially neutral policies that have a disproportionate negative impact on members of a protected class, and "disparate treatment" that would apply when teachers or school officials are the discriminators and a student is denied equal educational benefits.

The hostile environment cause of action is aimed at the type of discriminatory conduct to which public school religious exercises tend to give rise. The disparate impact cause of action is more applicable to allegedly neutral school policies or practices that give rise to discrimination. Disparate treatment would only be relevant when a teacher or other school official discriminates in regard to educational benefits as will be discussed briefly later in this chapter and Chapter Eight. For the reasons discussed below, all three may be useful in this area, but the hostile environment cause of action is of particular importance because of the similarities between harassment based on race or gender and the harassment based on religion as discussed in this book. Furthermore, in the workplace context, the hostile work environment cause of action is already applicable to religious harassment and can provide a direct analogy.[10]

Hostile Environment Harassment

Harassment that creates a hostile work environment based on membership in a protected class is actionable under Title VII of the Civil Rights Act of 1964 and several other civil rights statutes.[11] Likewise, according to the courts and the Department of Education Office of Civil Rights (OCR), an educational environment that is hostile to members of a protected class can be actionable in appropriate circumstances.[12] However, the nature and scope of liability for hostile educational environments have been questioned, and there is significant disagreement among courts about key issues.[13] The Supreme Court's recent decision in *Gebser v. Lago Vista Independent School District* clarified some of these issues, but not all.[14] Moreover, the federal statutes that have been used to support claims of hostile educational environments do not apply to religious discrimination.

Hostile educational environments will be addressed in more detail below. However, since the genesis of the cause of action was workplace harassment and courts and the OCR have frequently looked at hostile work environments as being at least partially analogous to hostile educational environments,[15] an understanding of hostile work environment harassment is quite useful for our purposes. Hostile work environment was initially recognized by the Fifth Circuit Court of Appeals in *Rogers v. EEOC,*[16] a 1971 case brought under Title VII, involving racial discrimination aimed at an Hispanic employee. Since then, the cause of action has been developed significantly by the courts and the Equal Employment Opportunity Commission.

As a general matter, workplace harassment that is sufficiently severe or pervasive violates Title VII's prohibition of discrimination in the terms and conditions of employment when it is aimed at an employee or group of employees based on membership in a protected class.[17] The Supreme Court addressed the hostile work environment issue for the first time in 1986 in *Meritor Savings Bank v. Vinson,*[18] a case involving sexual harassment. In *Meritor,* the Supreme Court set forth a general standard to be applied to hostile work environment claims.[19] The Court held that a sexually hostile work environment exists when an employee is subject, because of his or her sex, to unwelcome conduct that is sufficiently severe or pervasive to alter the conditions of employment and create an abusive working environment.[20] The Court also held that Title VII's protection is not limited to pecuniary interests.[21]

After *Meritor,* courts disagreed over the application of the general framework set forth by the Supreme Court.[22] Divergent views emerged regarding the appropriate objective reasonableness standard—i.e., the standard under which the severity or pervasiveness of the conduct should be evaluated;[23] views differed about whether the victim must demonstrate that the harassment seriously affected his or her psychological well-being or led the victim to suffer injury[24] or whether a harassment victim must demonstrate he or she subjectively perceived the work environment to be hostile.[25] The confusion over these issues meant that employers and employees might not know the full extent of their rights and duties and that particular conduct might be actionable in one circuit, but not in others.

In an attempt to clarify some of these issues, the Supreme Court revisited the issue of workplace harassment in *Harris v. Forklift Systems.*[26] The Court granted certiorari to determine whether injury to a victim's psychological well-being is necessary for a hostile work environment to be actionable.[27] The Court held that injury to psychological well-being was unnecessary for harassment to be actionable.[28] In addition, the court addressed the objective and subjective reasonableness questions,[29] holding that the severity or pervasiveness of harassing conduct should be evaluated under a reasonable person standard and that a victim of workplace harassment must also subjectively perceive the working environment to be abusive.[30] Significantly, in regard to the objective reasonableness standard, the Court may have created more questions than it answered.[31]

The Court held that conduct is sufficiently severe or pervasive when a reasonable person would find the working environment to be hostile or abusive.[32] However, the meaning of "reasonable person" under this standard is unclear. In this regard, the Court attempted to provide some guidance. It noted that its test for a hostile work environment cannot by its nature be mathematically precise.[33] Thus, the Court implicitly acknowledged that given the nature of hostile work environment claims, there must be some flexibility in the structure applied to those claims to account for the wide variety of situations with which courts will be presented. Such flexibility might include consideration of the perspective of a reasonable member of the victim's protected class. Moreover, "whether an environment is hostile or abusive can be determined only by looking at all the circumstances."[34] Such circumstances may include the severity and frequency of the alleged conduct, whether it involves physical threats or humiliation as opposed to a mere offensive utterance, and whether it "unreasonably interferes with" the victim's work performance.[35] The Court's mandate to consider the totality of the circumstances in a hostile work environment case reinforces the flexibility of the hostile work environment standard and lends support to the position that the perspective of the victim may indeed be an important factor among all of the circumstances.[36]

Significantly, the EEOC issued interpretive guidance regarding *Harris* and its effect on the EEOC guidelines applicable to sexual harassment.[37] That guidance takes the position that the reasonable person standard set forth in *Harris* does allow consideration of the perspectives of members of the victim's class and that this is consistent with the standard to be applied to other actionable harassment under federal antidiscrimination laws.[38] The EEOC's position in this regard remains consistent with the language of *Harris*.

Consideration of the victim's perspective could be important to any application of the hostile environment cause of action to the religious discrimination facilitated by public school religious exercises, because in some areas a strict "reasonable person" standard could lead to the perpetuation of the prevailing level of discriminatory attitudes and conduct in that community.[39] While the *Harris* opinion did set forth an objective reasonableness standard in the hostile work environment context, it did little to clarify the issue, because the application of that standard is subject to a variety of interpretations. It is quite likely that in the context of workplace harassment many courts will continue to apply a standard that acknowledges the victim's perspective,[40] although others may not.

Determining that a hostile work environment exists is not the end of the analysis. Employer liability is another significant issue. In the context of a hostile educational environment, there is at least a facial argument that school liability should be viewed as parallel to employer liability, but the Supreme Court rejected that argument in *Gebser*.[41] In many ways, school liability is an even more complex issue than employer liability, but since the issue of liability for hostile environment harassment was first elucidated in employment cases and several courts as well as the OCR have applied the general framework for employer liability to the school context, we will begin there. Because *Gebser* would not necessarily be binding in the religious discrimination context and because the proposed statute in Chapter Eight parallels the liability scheme in the OCR guidelines and Title VII to a great degree, rather than *Gebser*, concepts relevant to employer liability are important in this context.

The landscape of employer liability for hostile work environment harassment under Title VII recently gained some much needed clarity. In June of 1998, the Supreme Court decided two cases dealing with employer liability for workplace harassment perpetrated by supervisors. The two cases, *Faragher v. City of Boca Raton*[42] and *Burlington Industries, Inc. v. Ellerth*,[43] established the requirements for employer liability for harassment perpetrated by supervisors, but they will likely raise new questions.

The two cases utilized the same test for determining employer liability, but applied that test to different factual situations.[44] *Faragher* dealt with liability for severe and pervasive sexualized conduct that constituted a hostile work environment while *Ellerth* dealt with facts arguably relevant to both hostile work environment and quid pro quo harassment.[45] In *Ellerth,* the Court held that the distinction between hostile work environment and quid pro quo was not determinative of the employer liability issue.[46]

These cases were decided well into the editing process of this book, and thus the discussion of these cases, as well as *Gebser* (which was decided four days before *Faragher* and *Ellerth*), is necessarily brief. This is not a problem in the present context, however, for the reasons set forth in the discussion of *Gebser* below. The key to *Faragher* and *Ellerth* is the Court's use of agency principles to determine when an employer can be vicariously liable for the harassing behavior of its supervisors. The Court rejected the argument that the victim(s) of harassment perpetrated by supervisory employees must meet negligence standards in order to establish employer liability, or that the supervisor must be acting within the scope of employment when engaging in the harassing behavior.[47] Instead, the Court applied the "aided-by-the-agency-relation principle" set forth in §219(2)(d) of the RESTATEMENT (SECOND) OF AGENCY (1957), which can support liability in situations where the supervisor is acting outside the scope of employment.[48]

When a supervisor abuses supervisory authority by sexually harassing an employee, he is in a sense, automatically aided by his agency relationship with the employer, because his supervisory capacity gives him authority over the victim(s) and makes it less likely that the victim will respond in the same fashion she would if someone without power over her job duties were the harasser.[49] In *Meritor,* the Court had indicated that general agency principles should be applied in sexual harassment cases to determine employer liability for supervisory actions.[50] In *Faragher* and *Ellerth* the Court followed *Meritor* by looking to the law of agency to determine the standard for employer liability for the acts of supervisors.[51] However, the Court was cognizant of the holding in *Meritor* that employers should not be automatically liable for the acts of supervisory employees.

The Court was able to balance these concerns in the test it ultimately developed and applied in *Faragher* and *Ellerth*. That test is as follows:

> An employer is subject to vicarious liability to a victimized employee for an actionable hostile environment created by a supervisor with immediate (or successively higher) authority over the employee. When no tangible employment action is taken, a defending employer may raise an affirmative defense to liability or damages, subject to proof by a preponderance of the evidence, see Fed. Rule. Civ. Proc. 8(c). The defense comprises two necessary elements: (a) that the employer exercised reasonable care to prevent and correct promptly any sexually harassing behavior, and (b) that the plaintiff unreasonably failed to take advantage of any preventative or corrective opportunities provided by the employer or to avoid harm otherwise. . . . No affirmative defense is available, however, when the supervisor's harassment culminates in a tangible employment action, such as discharge, demotion, or undesirable reassignment.[52]

The Court clarified the operation of this test to some extent as follows:

> While proof that an employer had promulgated an anti-harassment policy with complaint procedure is not necessary in every instance as a matter of law, the need for a stated policy suitable to the employment circumstances may appropriately be addressed in any case when litigating the first element of the defense. And while proof that an employee failed to fulfill the corresponding obligation of reasonable care to avoid harm is not limited to showing an unreasonable failure to use any complaint procedure provided by the employer, a demonstration of such failure will normally suffice to satisfy the employer's burden under the second element of the defense.[53]

This test creates vicarious liability for supervisory harassment, but it does not create automatic liability, because the employer may assert the affirmative defense set forth in the test to avoid liability.[54] Given the dynamics underlying workplace harassment this test seems sensible. Since the supervisor is aided by his or her status in engaging in the harassment through the contact with, and control over, the victim provided by supervisory status, vicarious liability makes sense.[55] If the employer, however, reasonably acts to prevent harassment from occurring and promptly corrects the situation when it does occur, liability would seem incompatible with Title VII's purposes of promoting conciliation and deterrence.[56] Moreover, if the employer provided adequate preventative or corrective measures the victim(s) failed to take advantage of, such as a well-formulated harassment policy and complaint procedure of which the victim was aware, vicarious liability would seem inappropriate.[57] This second part of the affirmative defense meshes well with the first, because if the employer has inadequate preventative or corrective procedures in place, it would be hard to establish that the victim failed in his or her duty.

In *Faragher,* the Court also cited with approval a portion of the EEOC Guidelines on Sexual Harassment that recommends employers take "all steps necessary to prevent sexual harassment from occurring, such as . . . informing employees of their right to raise and how to raise the issue of harassment."[58] Therefore, the EEOC's recommendations regarding prevention and correction of hostile work environments, as well as court decisions addressing these issues in a manner consistent with *Faragher* and *Ellerth,* will likely be useful in interpreting when an employer has exercised reasonable care in preventing and correcting harassment and when a victim's failure to take advantage of such opportunities is unreasonable.

Neither the *Faragher* nor the *Ellerth* decision directly addressed the standard for harassment by co-workers or non-employees.[59] Employers are liable for the conduct of co-workers where the employer, its agents, or supervisory personnel knew, or should have known, of the conduct, and the employer failed to take immediate and appropriate corrective action.[60] Employers can also be liable for the acts of non-employees when the employer, its agents, or supervisory personnel, knew, or should have known, of the alleged conduct and failed to take immediate and appropriate corrective action, as feasible.[61]

The EEOC also provides guidance regarding measures an employer can take to avoid liability and eliminate harassment.[62] *Faragher* and *Ellerth* appear to support the EEOC guidance, or at the very least, not to vitiate it.[63] According to the EEOC, employers should take all steps necessary to prevent harassment, such as affirmatively raising the subject, expressing strong disapproval, providing sensitivity training, and implementing and disseminating appropriate harassment policies, sanctions, and complaint procedures.[64] Some courts have also addressed the adequacy of employer remedial action,[65] while other courts have addressed the adequacy of employer harassment policies.[66] *Faragher* and *Ellerth* clearly demonstrate that while it is not an absolute requirement, employers should have clear policies on harassment and mechanisms in place to help prevent and promptly correct harassing behavior.[67] The types of preventive measures mentioned above could prove significant in the context of religious harassment facilitated by public school religious exercises.

As noted above, analogies can be drawn between the types of employer liability (i.e., for supervisory employees, co-workers, and non-employees) and the roles of those involved in the harassment facilitated by public school religious exercises. For example, school employees might be treated like supervisory employees—i.e., as potential agents of the school—students as co-workers, and others involved in the harassment as non-employees. There is some support for this approach.[68] When these tests for employer liability are analogized in this manner, a coherent and reasonable model for school liability emerges. However, the courts that have considered the issue, most of which were dealing with sexual harassment under Title IX, have not all agreed that such an analogy is appropriate in the school context. *Gebser* completely rejected it.

In *Gebser*, the Supreme Court held that agency principles utilized under Title VII could not be used to impose vicarious liability for teacher-on-student harassment under Title IX.[69] Rather, the appropriate standard, according to the *Gebser* Court, is one of actual knowledge of the harassment by an "official who at a minimum has authority to address" the discrimination and "institute corrective measures on the [school's] behalf," combined with a response that amounts to "deliberate indifference to [the] discrimination."[70]

The Court rejected a more lenient standard, because unlike Title VII, the private right of action under Title IX is an implied right pursuant to the Court's decision in *Cannon v. University of Chicago.*[71] The Court further held that its earlier holding in *Franklin v. Gwinnett County Public Schools,*[72] that damages are available under the implied private right of action, must be interpreted consistently with the scope and nature of Title IX.[73] Since that statute expressly provides for an administrative means of enforcement and applies only to recipients of federal funding pursuant to Congress' spending power, the Court found that the remedies available under the implied right of action should not be disproportionate to the express remedial scheme set forth by Congress. That scheme requires that a violating school be informed of any violation and be given an opportunity to correct the violation prior to the revocation of federal funding.[74] The Court considered its actual notice requirement to be consistent with this express means of enforcement.[75] The Court also held that the contractual nature of Title IX—that it only applies when a school accepts federal funding and operates as a condition binding on a funding recipient—is quite different from Title VII which operates as a general prohibition against covered discrimination.[76]

The Court overlooked, or paid little attention to, several potentially important issues. The first is whether the Rehabilitation Act Amendments of 1986[77] and the Civil Rights Restoration Act of 1987,[78] each of which broadened the scope of Title IX, provide additional insight into Congress' view of Title IX.[79] A discussion of this would have been quite useful since the Court relied heavily on Congress' intent with regard to the remedial scheme under Title IX. Second, the Court glossed over the OCR guidelines, which directly addressed the issue of school liability and were drafted by an agency with special expertise in the area. While the Court was not bound to follow the guidelines, such guidelines by an agency with expertise in the area in question are usually entitled to some deference by courts.[80]

Finally, while the Court did analyze the school district's failure to promulgate an adequate antidiscrimination policy as required by Department of Education regulations, it dismissed the significance of that fact, finding that the failure did not create actual notice.[81] The Court did hold that the school district's failure in this regard could be sanctioned administratively. This holding places students who are sexually abused by their teachers in a double bind. If the student does not know who to complain to about the harassment due to the lack of a clearly disseminated policy, it is unlikely the school will have actual notice until the harassment/abuse has gone on long enough that a parent or other third party finds out. This is a particular concern when the student fears "telling" on his or her teacher, as Alida Gebser did,[82] or feels ashamed by the situation. In such cases, failure to have a policy in place will actually facilitate undetected harassment, thus thwarting Title IX's purpose of preventing sex discrimination in schools receiving federal funding, the very reason the Department of Education regulations require the grievance procedures in the first place. Additionally, in *Gebser,* the Court did not address the actionability of peer-on-peer harassment or the standards for school liability in such cases, nor did it address the standards for establishing a hostile educational environment generally. Given the approach and tenor of the decision, however, peer on peer harassment claims are not likely to fare well if the Court applies the rationale from *Gebser.*

Fortunately, despite these concerns about the *Gebser* decision, that decision is not necessarily relevant to the present discussion. Since *Gebser* was heavily based on the nature and structure of Title IX and since Title IX does not apply to religion, any measure created to address the discrimination that is the focus of this book need not be bound by the strictures of Title IX as interpreted by the Court in *Gebser.* In fact, school liability in the proposed statute set forth in Chapter Eight is modeled on Title VII, the OCR guidelines, and several pre-*Gebser* cases interpreting Title IX, all as modified for the unique factors underlying the discrimination facilitated by public school religious exercises. Interestingly, since the discrimination that is the subject of this book is facilitated by school policies or practices, *Gebser* may not apply on its own terms. In *Gebser,* the Court limited its analysis to "cases like this one [*Gebser*] that do not involve official policy of the recipient entity."[83] Thus, even under Title IX, if a school policy or practice facilitated the sexual harassment, school liability would likely be analyzed differently than in *Gebser.* For present purposes, then, the OCR guidelines, cases that apply them (or similar rules), and Title VII standards will be the primary focus.

Despite the Supreme Court's recent decision in *Gebser,* the current state of hostile educational environment claims is essentially a morass of conflicting decisions with only basic concepts commonly agreed upon. Issues such as school liability for student-on-student harassment have given rise to conflicting court decisions. As the above discussion implies, most of the cases that address hostile educational environments arise under Title IX and thus deal with sexual harassment. However, hostile educational environments based on race, color, and national origin have been found to violate Title VI of the Civil Rights Act of 1964.[84] Because the standards applicable to such claims under these statutes are generally the same, they will be addressed together here.

There is also potential liability for conduct giving rise to a hostile educational environment under 42 U.S.C. §1983, but that statute raises several unique issues and is more limited in regard to what and whose conduct can give rise to liability. These problems are even more pronounced in regard to liability for religious harassment. Because §1983 is one of the few existing laws that might support a claim for the conduct addressed in this book, even if in only a limited fashion, it will be addressed in greater detail in Chapter Ten. To the extent that a hostile educational environment might be actionable under that statute, the substantive cause of action would follow the general discussion in this chapter regarding hostile environment under Title VI and Title IX, although, as will be discussed in Chapter Ten, that would be neither the beginning nor the end of the inquiry under §1983.

Prior to the 1992 Supreme Court decision in *Franklin v. Gwinett County Public Schools,* which acknowledged but did not directly address the hostile educational environment cause of action in the context of teacher-on-student sexual harassment, it was not clear whether a cause of action for hostile educational environment actually existed under Title IX.[85] However, many courts had already recognized the cause of action. Still, the newness of the hostile educational environment concept gives rise to much confusion and disagreement over its parameters. Fortunately, and in a sense unfortunately, since religion is not covered under Title VI or Title IX, the problems with the cause of action under those statutes can be addressed in any proposed legislation to deal with the discrimination that is the focus of this book. Still, an understanding of the problems with hostile environment claims under Title VI and IX is important in the present context.

Significantly, much of the substantive analysis of hostile work environment claims is applicable to hostile educational environment claims.[86] Issues like the welcomeness, severity, and pervasiveness of the required conduct are treated in a manner similar to those in a hostile work environment claim. However, these issues are also considered in light of the age of the child being harassed and the nature of the educational environment.[87] Thus, conduct that creates a hostile environment for an eight-year-old might be different from that which does so for a high school student, and course content that might cause some students to feel harassed, such as that which might be involved in an AIDS prevention program, will not generally create a hostile environment and may be protected as a matter of academic freedom.[88] Moreover, the basis for hostile environment claims under Title VI and Title IX is discrimination in educational programs and/or interference with a student's enjoyment of an advantage or right enjoyed by other students on the basis of race or gender.[89] This is similar to the basis for a Title VII hostile work environment claim—interference with a term or condition of employment.[90]

Perhaps the biggest issue involved in hostile educational environment claims is the scope of the school's liability and what triggers that liability. This involves two distinct questions. First, in what situations and for whose conduct is the school liable for hostile educational environment harassment? Second, under what theory of liability is the school liable for conduct that creates a hostile environment? There are three potential groups of harassers that must be dealt with: (1) teachers and other school employees, (2) students, and (3) others (such as parents on school property, guest speakers, students from other schools at athletic events, and so forth). While the courts have agreed that there can be liability for harassment by the first group, prior to *Gebser*, they had not agreed on what situations give rise to that liability or on the theory of liability that should be applied.[91] Several courts have held that conduct by the second or third groups of individuals can give rise to school liability, but again holdings on the situations that can create liability and the appropriate theory of liability vary.[92] Other courts have refused to find student-on-student, or "peer harassment," actionable under Title IX.[93] Therefore, there is no one standard that governs these issues for every jurisdiction beyond the fact that a teacher sexually abusing or otherwise sexually or racially harassing a student in a sufficiently severe or pervasive manner could give rise to liability. Even then, whether, and under what theory, that liability can be attributed to the school remained a point of contention until *Gebser.*

As was suggested above, the best resources in regard to these issues for present purposes are the guidelines on harassment published by the Department of Education, Office for Civil Rights (OCR). There are separate guidelines for sexual harassment under Title IX and racial harassment under Title VI, although they are very similar in content.[94] Still, courts do not have to follow these guidelines, and there have been several decisions, including *Gebser,* that reject their approach to school liability.[95]

The guidelines apply Title VII concepts to the educational environment context. Thus, school liability for employees with supervisory responsibility and other employees with apparent authority are addressed under agency principles. Other harassers, such as students, employees who are not agents, and others are analyzed under the co-employee, "knew or should have known" test developed for Title VII.[96] As with Title VII, whether the school took immediate and appropriate corrective action is also central to a determination of school liability, and the duty to do so varies with the level of control the school can exercise over the situation and harasser(s).[97] Moreover, the age of the victims of the harassment should be considered in determining whether an employee had apparent authority or was otherwise acting as an agent of the school, as well as in determining what corrective action is appropriate.[98] While according to *Ellerth,* apparent authority is not generally applicable in the hostile work environment context,[99] it could be more relevant in the school context, where students might not know which school employees have actual authority or simply appear to have authority because they are adults.

Several courts have followed the OCR's approach or a similar one for teacher-on-student and student-on-student harassment.[100] However, even prior to *Gebser*, other courts had rejected this approach. One thing is clear: the OCR guidelines and the courts that have recognized student-on-student and third-party hostile educational environment claims hold that the school is not liable for the acts of harassment themselves, but rather for failing to provide adequate reporting procedures, harassment policies, or immediate and appropriate corrective action.[101] Thus, issues such as notice to the school of the harassment and the school's response become central to school liability. The basis for school liability is not the acts of the students or others who commit the harassment, but rather the failure to deal appropriately with that harassment or the fostering of an environment in which it is more likely to occur.[102] This is quite significant in the context of religious harassment, because when a school allows religious exercises that facilitate discrimination, but has no mechanism in place to address the discrimination that can result, an analogous situation exists. In the religious harassment context, the school's role is even greater in many situations because the school is likely to have an official policy allowing the exercises that give rise to the harassment.

Under the OCR's interpretation of Titles VI and IX, notice of the harassment can arise in any number of ways, most of which mirror notice to employers under Title VII. When a teacher or employee is the perpetrator of the harassment, notice may be presumed on agency principles. For harassment by employees who are not acting as agents of the school, for other students, and for third parties, the school must know or with exercise of reasonable care should know of the harassment in order to be on notice.[103] Thus, a school may be on notice when students or parents complain of the harassment, school officials or employees report it, outsiders report incidents they witness, or the situation is bad enough that the school should have known about the harassment had it been exercising reasonable care.[104] Moreover, if a school has no policy in place, or an inadequate one, the school can be found liable if the policies do not give the victims an adequate avenue for reporting incidents of harassment or reason to believe that anything would be done if it were reported.[105] In the religious harassment context, these methods of notice would closely fit the kinds of situations that arise.

Even if a school has notice, it can still avoid liability by taking immediate and appropriate corrective action. This is interpreted by the OCR in a fashion very similar to the way it is interpreted under Title VII, except that the age of the victim is also relevant to what remedial action is appropriate.[106] Thus, according to the OCR, and applying Title VII concepts, a school should investigate in a timely fashion any alleged incidents, and if the school determines that the incidents occurred, it should take action aimed at ending the harassment. What action is appropriate in this regard will vary according to the nature of the harassment involved, who the harasser is, and the context of the harassment. The school should also seek to prevent future incidents of harassment through appropriate policies and procedures, such as training for employees and age-appropriate classroom information for students to teach them what types of conduct cause harassment and how to respond to incidents of harassment when they occur.[107]

Numerous issues arise in regard to harassment in hostile work and educational environments. This book cannot, and need not, explore each of these in great detail. The hostile environment approach would seem a sensible and targeted way to address the harassment facilitated by public school religious exercises. However, there first needs to be some legal basis for applying the cause of action to religious harassment situations because neither Title VI nor Title IX applies to religion. There are some state statutes that arguably do so, but of course they only apply within states that have enacted them and must be interpreted to allow for hostile educational environment claims based on religious harassment facilitated by public school religious exercises—by no means a foregone conclusion.

Moreover, there must be a way to limit what types of religious speech or conduct can facilitate harassment, so that a line may be drawn between the type of conduct discussed in Chapter One and a student's simply trying to share his or her religious beliefs in an informal way. This is no simple matter and will be discussed in Chapter Nine in the context of the statute proposed in Chapter Eight. Whether or not such a statute is ever enacted, the utility of the hostile environment concept is clear in regard to the type of discrimination discussed in this book and exemplified in Chapter One. The hostile educational environment concept evinces the great benefits that can be derived from using civil rights principles and antidiscrimination law to address directly the discrimination facilitated by public school religious exercises, rather than relying strictly on the Constitution in the current political and legal climate. Of course, there are other concepts arising from antidiscrimination law that may be useful as well.

Disparate Impact and Disparate Treatment Discrimination

Disparate impact discrimination involves the application of facially neutral policies that have a disproportionate negative impact on a protected class. Implicit in the concept is a lack of provable intent to discriminate. For example, if an employer requires a high school diploma and a certain level of reading skill for mill worker positions that do not require reading skills, in an area where racial minorities have a lower rate of high school completion and literacy, these requirements would disproportionately exclude minorities from the mill positions on a basis unrelated to the job. This would create an actionable claim for disparate impact discrimination.[108]

In that situation, the employer probably intended to use the policy to exclude racial minorities, but perhaps not. However, the employer's intent is not determinative, since the effect of the policy had a disproportionate negative impact on minorities and was not job-related or justified by business necessity. This impact has been found to be actionable discrimination under Title VII.[109] Thus, since racial minorities are protected under Title VII, the implementation of these facially neutral policies in the manner described violates Title VII. It is interesting in the present context that this concept also applies to employment practices with a disparate impact based on religion under Title VII.[110] Of course, one cannot simply proclaim a "disparate impact." The impact needs to be supported by appropriate evidence, an issue subject to a great deal of scrutiny.

The disparate impact cause of action under Title VII has a complicated and conflicting history, some of which was clarified by the Civil Rights Act of 1991, which codified the cause of action after a series of court decisions that conflicted with the earlier understanding of disparate impact and how it is proven.[111] Those decisions dealt with issues such as who has the burden of proof and persuasion at different stages of disparate impact analysis.[112] However, issues such as what constitutes a "business necessity" and the parameters of "job relatedness" remain unclear even after the Civil Rights Act of 1991.[113] Also, even when business necessity and job relatedness are proven, issues remain regarding the effect of "less discriminatory alternatives" to the practice in question. Given so much confusion, this discussion is necessarily a very basic overview of disparate impact as it relates to employment—a legal concept involving far more complexity than needs to be addressed here.[114]

The focus is on employment because the analysis of disparate impact under Title VII provides the best definitional parameters for applying the concept to the issues that are the focus of this book. However, not all of the detailed issues raised by disparate impact in the employment context are relevant to the discrimination facilitated by public school religious exercises. The use of the theory in employment cases under Title VII demonstrates that to avoid liability an employer cannot simply argue that a policy is neutral and that the discriminatory results were not intended. Such an argument does not necessarily end the analysis. If this concept were to be applied to the religious discrimination discussed in this book, a school claiming that its policy on school prayer or some other religious exercise was nondenominational, and thus neutral and nondiscriminatory, could not escape liability if that policy facilitated a demonstrable discriminatory impact against a religious minority group or groups unless the school could show some sort of educational necessity for the policy—i.e., that the policy is necessary to the school's ability to perform its general functions.

Admittedly, this is stretching the concept beyond currently accepted boundaries, since the type of discrimination facilitated is actually intentional discrimination by others. However, the general idea still has merit. The supposedly neutral policy of allowing organized nondenominational religious exercises facilitates a disproportionately negative impact on a minority group. The nature of the policy and its impact are significantly different from the employment context, but the concept could be extrapolated to apply to the school prayer context.

Still, hostile environment seems to be the more useful concept, and through its focus on liability for inadequate policies and procedures it might protect against much of the same conduct disparate impact analysis would, although for very different reasons. In fact, if disparate impact were applied in the school prayer context, it would be more useful as a defense to claims of neutrality on the part of school boards, which have been able to avoid liability for hostile environment, than as a separate cause of action. Of course, the only way to analyze this issue properly is in the context of legislation that would permit such claims. Currently, there is no such legislation. However, the proposed statute set forth in Chapter Eight and analyzed further in Chapters Eight and Nine provides us with an opportunity to do this. The problems arising from the application of disparate impact theory to the public school religious exercise situation will be addressed further in Chapter Eight.

One final point should be made in regard to taking causes of action currently used in antidiscrimination law and applying them to the discrimination facilitated by public school religious exercises. Most of this discussion has focused on ways to combat or provide redress for the discrimination that manifests itself in the form of harassment. Both the hostile environment and disparate impact (as applied in this book) causes of action are tailored more toward discrimination and harassment that is facilitated by school policies or practices allowing organized religious exercises. However, there are cases in which school officials or teachers are alleged to have taken tangible academic actions against religious minorities or dissenters, such as disciplinary action or grade deflation, which affect the student's records or deny other educational benefits. Sometimes, this occurs because of the student's minority religious status and position vis-à-vis the religious environment created in the schools, but more frequently it is in retaliation for complaining about that environment or the policies that facilitate the religious exercises. The *Herring* and *Bell* cases included allegations of this type of discrimination.[115]

The heavy focus in this chapter on the hostile environment and disparate impact causes of action should not be taken to mean that other antidiscrimination law concepts such as disparate treatment (intentional discrimination) and retaliation would not be useful in cases involving appropriate allegations. In fact, a general focus of this chapter and book is that because discrimination is the issue here, civil rights principles, especially those developed in antidiscrimination law, provide a better way to deal with the problem than reliance on the Constitution alone. Thus, the statute proposed in Chapter Eight provides for disparate treatment and retaliation claims. These claims have been recognized in the educational discrimination arena in other contexts and will be elucidated further in relation to the proposed statute.[116]

In fact, to the extent that existing legal mechanisms such as §1983 are useful in cases of religious discrimination in the public schools, it is in the context of such tangible deprivations and discrimination that they are most likely to support successful claims.[117] However, as the information discussed in this book demonstrates, much of the discrimination that is likely to be facilitated by public school religious exercises will not be official action meant to harm the educational opportunities of the victims, but rather harassment by students, teachers, and others who may cause "tangible" physical or psychological harm but who may not have the power to effect discipline or grades. Of course, as is true under current antidiscrimination law, the types of conduct giving rise to the various causes of action available may intersect. Thus, the type of official behavior that could support a disparate treatment or retaliation claim may also support the pattern of conduct that gives rise to a hostile environment claim.

This chapter has discussed the potential usefulness of using civil rights principles and antidiscrimination law to directly combat the discrimination facilitated by public school religious exercises. Based on the discussion in Chapters Three and Seven, it should be clear that the constitutional approaches usually taken in this area are not terribly helpful in this regard. Next, I will compare the principles underlying antidiscrimination law and current church-state law. This comparison will further illuminate the possibility that antidiscrimination law is a much better way to address discrimination resulting from public school religious exercises than constitutional doctrines, since what is deemed constitutional is in a continuous state of flux. In fact, antidiscrimination law could be effective precisely because it can be applied when religious exercises in the public schools are deemed constitutional and because it has a remedial scheme more likely to affect those school districts that ignore constitutional mandates.

chapter seven

The Limitations of Using the Constitution

CHAPTER THREE SETS FORTH the basic parameters of constitutional law as it relates to public school religious exercises. Chapter Six provides a general overview of civil rights and antidiscrimination law concepts that might be used to address the discrimination that public school religious exercises can facilitate. This discussion raises the question of whether the constitutional norms reflected in Chapter Three are the appropriate focus when dealing with discrimination facilitated by public school religious exercises as opposed to the legality of those exercises themselves. This chapter will compare the traditional use of constitutional norms and discourse to address school prayer issues with the potential use of civil rights laws to directly address the discrimination that constitutional norms seem incapable of reaching in any meaningful way, apart from the ultimate disposition of the religious exercises themselves.

Earlier chapters pointed out a troubling legal problem with two facets: (1) the recent rise in the number of public schools willing to engage in unconstitutional religious exercises; and (2) the fact that what is constitutional in this regard has become blurry, causing some schools to allow religious exercises that may or may not be constitutional. Whether or not religious exercises are constitutional, the number of school districts that engage in them is likely to increase in the current political climate.

Naturally, when an exercise is deemed constitutional, such as voluntary student-initiated graduation prayer in the Fifth Circuit or moments of silence in some states, use of constitutional law principles is rather useless in addressing any discrimination that may arise from that exercise. As the *Walter* case demonstrates, however, even seemingly innocuous exercises such as moments of silence can give rise to religious discrimination and harassment in some areas. Since any religious exercise in a public school can call attention to difference in a negative way, particularly in school districts dominated by groups with less tolerant attitudes toward religious difference or political difference relating to separation of church and state, civil rights concepts are far more useful in addressing this discrimination.

Civil rights law can be targeted directly at the discrimination that results from the religious exercises rather than at the exercises themselves. Thus, the nature and constitutionality of the exercises become less relevant in dealing with the discrimination facilitated by them, and the educational environment and school policies in regard to discrimination become more of a focus. When school districts like those in the *Herring, Herdahl,* and *Bell* cases are involved, chances are greater that the level of discrimination will be higher. However, this is not necessarily going to be the case. It is possible that a school district may be in blatant violation of the Constitution, as were the school districts in those cases, and yet through extreme sensitivity to religious difference and strong policies against discrimination somehow manage to avoid incidences of discrimination. A school district like that would, and should, be challenged under the Constitution, but would not be liable under the civil rights principles addressed in this book. Likewise, a school district could go to great pains to stay within constitutional norms, having only a moment of silence or voluntary, student-initiated prayer (in jurisdictions where that is allowed) and yet foster an environment where religious tolerance is low, so that such exercises facilitate discrimination and lead to liability for civil rights violations. The school district would not be liable for allowing the prayer or moment of silence, but rather for not addressing the discrimination that results from the policy that allows those exercises.

In reality, the level and pervasiveness of religious activity is likely to be a good predictor of which school districts may be liable for civil rights violations. A school district or school willing to ignore the Constitution due to a prevailing religious zeal is more likely to be the locus for significant discrimination than a school district that simply has a moment of silence pursuant to state law. However, since the constitutionality of the religious exercises is not the key to addressing the discrimination under the civil rights/antidiscrimination law model, the focus of any inquiry would initially center on the level of discrimination, not on religiosity. Since that discrimination would have to be facilitated by public school religious exercises to be actionable under the scheme set forth in this book, the level of religiosity may be predictive of the level of discrimination in some circumstances, but not always. The key nexus is between the discrimination and the religious exercises/environment fostered or ignored by the school.

Of course, when one considers the grassroots campaign to influence or take over school boards, along with the legal activities of the ACLJ, the Rutherford Institute, and other Christian Right legal advocates, this is significant because new issues as to what is constitutional will continue to arise, and existing law in this area is in constant danger of being challenged. Thus, if we are truly to address the discrimination facilitated by public school religious exercises, we must target the discrimination directly and not simply the exercise. In fact, as demonstrated in Chapters One and Two, even when religious exercises are successfully challenged under the Constitution, they may continue in school districts that have the will to ignore or skirt constitutional mandates. This brings us to the next point, the relative strength of the remedies available under the Constitution and under civil rights/antidiscrimination law. A connected issue is the stigma attached to being a "discriminator" versus a violator of the Establishment Clause.

The remedies available under the Constitution and the conduct that may be reached are quite different from those under civil rights law. Certainly, injunctions and declaratory relief are available under both, but under the Constitution the conduct that may be enjoined or declared to violate the law does not include much of the discriminatory conduct facilitated by public school religious exercises and the environment they can foster. Moreover, the availability of damages for constitutional violations in the public schools is based on 42 U.S.C. §1983, which does not reach much of the discriminatory conduct in these cases.[1]

The remedies available for constitutional violations are naturally aimed at the conduct of the government actor and the constitutional rights that government action infringes. In the present context, that would generally not include the actions of students, nonpolicymaking employees (in most circumstances), or others (such as parents and townspeople). In the school prayer context, it is frequently the conduct of these types of actors that is discriminatory and not that of policymaking school officials, even if school policies fostered an environment where the discrimination was more likely to occur. More importantly, even if the school could somehow be charged with the discriminatory acts of these individuals, such acts are not the basis for the constitutional violation. The school district's policy or practice that violates the Establishment Clause is the constitutional violation and not the discrimination by others that it fosters. Two recent cases that deal with this issue are very instructive.

The *Bauchman* and *Bell* cases documented in Chapter One demonstrate the futility of trying to use constitutional norms to address incidents of discrimination and harassment facilitated by religious exercises in the public schools. The Tenth Circuit Court of Appeals' recent decision in *Bauchman* provides the best illustration of this point. The court spends a great deal of time explaining its reasoning as to why the alleged conduct of the choir teacher in that case, which included selection of a number of blatantly sectarian songs, regular performances at churches, and poor treatment of Rachel Bauchman, who did not share his religious views, was not unconstitutional.[2] The opinion also explained in depth why allegations of a twenty-year pattern of religious activity during school-sponsored events by that same teacher was not useful to demonstrate that he had a religious motive in engaging in the behavior about which the Bauchmans complained.[3] Not surprisingly, there was a vigorous dissent.[4]

Aspects of the majority decision are staggering in their departure from traditional understandings of Establishment Clause jurisprudence and evidentiary rules. However, for our purposes, this is not the most significant aspect of the decision, except to the extent that it demonstrates, as *Jones II* did, that even when existing precedent would appear to mandate a decision that the Establishment Clause has been violated by religious conduct in a public school, one cannot count on that result. This might be a result of judicial fiat, simply a difference in perspective on a somewhat muddy area of law, or a reflection that the judges involved wanted to allow or not sanction the religious exercises. The idea that judges sometimes use seemingly objective rules to justify decisions that may be motivated by their own values or personal interpretations of an issue is not new.[5] Given the age and makeup of much of the federal bench, and the fact that many Americans generally support school prayer,[6] it should not be surprising that some courts may lean toward allowing such religious exercises. However, this tendency alone does not appear to explain some of the leaps the majority took in *Bauchman*— leaps clearly not lost on the dissent or on any informed reader, regardless of political orientation. However, it is the treatment of the allegations of discrimination in *Bauchman* and *Bell,* which is quite consistent with existing precedent, that provides the best support for using civil rights law to address the discrimination facilitated by school prayer.

The discrimination involved in *Bauchman* included harassment by the choir teacher and other students, and ultimately an incident at a graduation ceremony where students, parents, and much of the choir violated a court order obtained by the Bauchmans and began singing blatantly religious songs, causing Rachel Bauchman and another Jewish student to run crying from the ceremony as parents and students jeered and spat on them.[7] As to the discrimination alleged in *Bauchman,* the court's response was clear and, under existing precedent and legal norms, quite accurate:

> [W]e must next address the relevance, if any, of her remaining allegations that she was subjected to public ridicule and harassment as a result of defendants' conduct. Certainly, Ms. Bauchman's allegations [that] she was criticized and retaliated against for opposing the religious content of the choir curriculum, taken as true, evidence a lack of sensitivity, crudeness

and poor judgement unbefitting of high school students, their parents, and especially, public school teachers and administrators. However, such claims do not rise to the level of a constitutional violation. Nor can they be used to breathe constitutional life into otherwise unactionable conduct. The fact that the defendants did not change their behavior in accordance with Ms. Bauchman's demands [that the religious exercises stop] and reacted negatively and/or offensively to those demands simply can not be viewed as support for her claim that the Choir's performance of religious music at religious venues furthered a religious purpose, advanced or favored religion or a particular religious belief, or otherwise entangled the public school with religion. We reject this "backdoor" attempt to substantiate an otherwise flawed constitutional claim and conclude the district court properly dismissed Ms. Bauchman's Establishment Clause claim.[8]

Essentially, the court is saying that the public ridicule and harassment that Rachel Bauchman endured was wrong, but not actionable under the Constitution. If it was based on gender or race, it might be actionable under Title VI or IX, but since religion is not protected under those statutes, and despite the fact that the conduct of a school teacher facilitated the discrimination at school, Rachel was out of luck. Unless there is some cause of action, independent of the Constitution, that directly addresses such discrimination, the number of Rachel Bauchmans without access to redress will continue to grow, and schools will be able to feel increasingly secure that they will not be liable for this kind of discrimination when it occurs. In fact, even in cases where the discrimination facilitated by school policy relating to religious exercises is far worse than in the *Bauchman* case, the result is the same.

In the *Bell* case, also discussed in Chapter One, the number and nature of incidents of harassment facilitated by a school policy on religious group meetings during school hours at school are too numerous to recount again here. One of the worst incidents was of course the fire bombing of the Bells' home.[9] While the panel of the Court of Appeals for the Tenth Circuit, which heard the case, acknowledged that 42 U.S.C. §1983 allowed for damages for the loss of the value of constitutional rights arising directly from the actions of the school and school officials that violated the Establishment Clause, the court did not allow relief for the discrimination, harassment, and tangible destruction inflicted by others that was facilitated by the school policies and the Bells' and McCords' objection to them.[10] The court held:

> A distinction must be made between the injuries caused by others and those inflicted by the actions of defendants that violated the Establishment Clause. For the reasons set out below, we believe that plaintiffs are entitled to recover compensatory damages for the loss of the inherent value of their rights under the Establishment Clause, even if they are unable to demonstrate consequential injury.[11]

This statement goes to the heart of the problem of attempting to use constitutional norms to remedy the discrimination that can be facilitated by public school religious exercises. The Constitution and §1983, which provides remedial measures for constitutional violations by municipal actors such as school boards,[12] do not generally reach the conduct of nongovernmental actors. A threshold issue for determining whether a particular actor's conduct is actionable for purposes of §1983 is whether that person was acting "under color of state law."[13] That term will be discussed in greater detail in Chapter Ten. Of course, when religious exercises or environments in the public schools facilitate discrimination and harassment, the worst incidents will frequently be perpetrated by nongovernment actors (who are not acting "under color of state law"). As in all of the cases in Chapter One, however, those actors may have been motivated or inspired by the attention called to the victims' religious differences or positions on religious exercises in the schools as the result of a school policy or practice allowing for religious exercises. But this alone is not enough to make the action government action for purposes of §1983 or to make it part of the Establishment Clause violation that will likely be the basis for any constitutional claim.[14]

This is a significant aspect of the "one-two punch" victims of religious discrimination facilitated by public school religious exercises face when attempting to obtain redress directly for the discrimination and harassment they have suffered. As *Bell* demonstrates, much of the conduct is not attributable to the government and thus not actionable under the Constitution, and, as *Bauchman* demonstrates, even if it were attributable to the government, the conduct that is the basis for the harassment and discrimination is generally not part of an actionable constitutional violation. In fact, neither court paid much attention to the incidents of discrimination and harassment, focusing instead on the Establishment Clause issues arising from the alleged government action.[15] This is also true of the court in *Herdahl*.[16]

This all makes perfect sense, given the current state of the law or at least the traditional approaches taken to these types of cases. While such incidents could conceivably help to demonstrate that the environment fostered by school policies violated the Establishment Clause and, if appropriate school personnel are involved, even support an Establishment Clause claim, the discrimination itself is generally not compensable or even relevant. These courts did not err in this aspect of their holdings and analysis—such a conclusion is compelled by the nature of constitutional claims and the reach of §1983. Add this to the fact that some school policies or practices regarding religious exercises/environments that give rise to discrimination might be constitutional in some jurisdictions, and the case for looking at the discrimination through the civil rights/antidiscrimination law lens is quite compelling.

Significantly, these are not the only limitations inherent in approaching the discrimination from a strictly constitutional perspective. The *Bell* case raises another significant issue in this regard, namely, the nature and level of damages that are appropriate for a constitutional violation as opposed to violations of civil rights/antidiscrimination laws. This is a significant issue because the scope, level, and methods for proving damages for constitutional violations vary significantly from those in civil rights/antidiscrimination law.

This issue has greater ramifications than simply how much money a party might receive, because the threat of significant damages may cause schools to think twice before facilitating or engaging in questionable behavior. It might also cause schools engaged in such behavior to be more sensitive to the discrimination issue. Since some schools may have their litigation costs covered by Christian Right–supported legal organi-

zations such as the ACLJ, the threat of an injunction and meager damages are not likely to induce the same reaction that the threat of significant damages for discrimination and the stigma attached to them would.
Thus, it is important to understand the differences in the damages available under constitutional claims and those based on violations of antidiscrimination law.

To understand the limitations on the damages available to redress a
constitutional violation under §1983, it is necessary to look at four Supreme Court cases: *Carey v. Piphus;*[17] *Memphis Community School District
v. Stachura;*[18] *Smith v. Wade;*[19] and *City of Newport v. Fact Concerts, Inc.*[20]
These cases have been the subject of a great deal of criticism and—at
least the first two—have also caused a good deal of confusion among
courts trying to apply the standards they set forth to new situations.[21]
Carey and *Stachura* deal with compensatory damages under §1983, while
Smith and *City of Newport* deal with punitive damages under that statute.

Carey was a case involving the denial of procedural due process by a
public high school under the Fourteenth Amendment to the Constitution. A student sued under §1983 to recover damages for the deprivation
of his due process rights. The Supreme Court held that the student could
recover compensatory damages only if he proved actual injury caused by
the denial of his due process (constitutional) rights.[22] The Court wrote:
"Rights, constitutional or otherwise, do not exist in a vacuum. Their
purpose is to protect persons from injuries to particular interests, and
their contours are shaped by the interests they protect."[23] The Court
rejected the notion that damages for an unspecified injury, which is inherent in the nature of a constitutional violation, may be presumed.[24]
Following the reasoning from *Carey,* if there is no provable injury
(which can include tangible benefits such as lost wages or other damages
such as loss of reputation, pain and suffering) resulting from a deprivation
of a constitutional right, compensatory damages are inappropriate because there is nothing to compensate for. In fact, the *Carey* Court
awarded nominal damages of one dollar because the student could not
prove he suffered any actual injury as a result of the due process violation.[25]

The *Carey* Court held that in order to determine compensatory damages arising from a constitutional violation we should look to analogous tort causes of action, because a significant focus of §1983 is to provide relief for injury resulting from constitutional deprivations, much as tort law is meant to provide relief for injury resulting from private wrongs.[26] This left open questions as to what rights are analogous to what tort causes of action, whether damages may be presumed for certain constitutional violations if they cannot be proven—as is true for a small number of torts—and whether there is any inherent compensatory value for the violation of a substantive constitutional right such as a First Amendment violation as opposed to a procedural due process violation. Some of these issues were clarified in *Stachura.*

In *Stachura,* the Supreme Court held that the "abstract value of a constitutional right may not form the basis for §1983 damages."[27] The Court also held that *Carey* did not "establish a two-tiered system of constitutional rights, with substantive rights afforded greater protection than 'mere' procedural safeguards."[28] The *Stachura* Court stated that the *Carey* Court "emphasized that, whatever the constitutional basis for §1983 liability, such damages must always be designed to 'compensate injuries caused by the [constitutional] deprivation.'"[29] Thus, it is inappropriate under *Carey/Stachura* to allow damages based on a trier of fact's perception of the abstract value or importance of constitutional rights. As a general matter, to be compensated pursuant to §1983 for an injury arising from a constitutional violation, one must prove that the violation caused actual injury, and one cannot be compensated simply for the abstract value of the deprivation of a constitutional right. This is still a somewhat muddy area because as the concurrence in *Stachura* points out, there are some constitutional violations that may cause "injury" simply by virtue of the violation.[30] However, even then the damage award must be proportional to the "actual loss sustained."[31]

In the context of cases arising from public school violations of the Establishment Clause through the sanctioning or sponsoring of religious exercises, the problem raised by this is clear. A student who suffers discrimination as the result of such a violation cannot obtain redress under the Constitution for the harm caused by nongovernment actors, which is likely to be the basis for the greatest actual injury suffered, and can only receive compensation if a court finds that the Establishment Clause violation itself (i.e., the constitutional deprivation) caused actual injury. Thus, the victims of discrimination facilitated by public school religious exercises cannot obtain redress for the discrimination, which would likely cause the bulk of actual injury, unless a government actor is directly involved. Such victims are essentially in a crap shoot as to whether they can receive any compensation for the Establishment Clause violation itself. Even if they can, that compensation is likely to be far less than it would be if the discrimination facilitated by the religious exercises were compensable. Unlike situations in which a direct injury is inflicted by unconstitutional government action, such as an illegal search and seizure or beating of prison inmates, an Establishment Clause violation is not as easy to link to a specific injury, and proving that the violation itself caused a particular injury may be harder to achieve.

This raises an odd possibility in cases such as *Bell, Herdahl, Bauchman,* and *Herring.* A court has to decide what injury is attributable to the state action depriving the victim of his or her constitutional rights and what is attributable to the actions of third parties. Thus, the existence of discrimination facilitated by the religious exercises, but carried out by students, parents, and others, could be used as the basis to find that the discrimination, and not the constitutional deprivation, was the cause of the bulk of injury. Ironically, in such circumstances the existence of severe and pervasive discrimination by third parties could increase the chance that little or no actual injury would be attributed to the government action giving rise to the constitutional deprivation. Of course, this is exactly what is implied by the reasoning in the *Bauchman* and *Bell* cases, which preclude redress for conduct perpetrated by third parties.[32]

Given this state of affairs, the damages available for a violation of the Establishment or Free Exercise Clauses are likely to be far lower than under traditional antidiscrimination damage schemes. This is so because it is precisely the harm caused by the discriminators (third parties and government entities) that is generally compensable under antidiscrimination law. That harm will likely be easier to substantiate in regard to the discrimination than the nexus between an Establishment Clause violation and any actual injury suffered as a result of that constitutional deprivation—although pain and suffering, etc. facilitated by such a constitutional violation would be compensable under §1983 to the extent that such an injury arises directly from the violation itself.

The *Smith* and *City of Newport* cases raise a different issue: the availability of punitive damages pursuant to §1983. As a general matter, the purpose of punitive or exemplary damages is to punish the wrongdoer(s) and not to compensate the victim (although the victim receives the award). Through the imposition of punitive damages, a trier of fact can say more than simply: "You did wrong and harmed the plaintiff." The trier of fact can express indignation at the nature of the wrong committed or the way in which the wrongdoer(s) committed the act(s) being sanctioned, assuming that the level of malice, recklessness, or intent necessary for punitive damages to be awarded can be met. In the civil rights context, this can be a powerful weapon if a judge or jury finds the acts constituting the civil rights violation to be intentional, malicious, or morally reprehensible. Moreover, punitive damage awards can sometimes exceed the amount of compensatory damages, and the fear of punitive damages might have a deterrent effect. Thus, the availability of punitive damages is a significant issue.

City of Newport dramatically limits the availability of this type of damages in §1983 cases. In that case, the Supreme Court held that punitive damages are not available against a municipal defendant (government entity) in a §1983 case.[33] Earlier Supreme Court decisions limited §1983 liability for governmental entities to municipalities (i.e., state and federal governmental entities cannot be properly sued under §1983).[34] However, in *Smith,* the Supreme Court held that individual defendants may be liable for punitive damages under §1983 if their conduct is "motivated by evil motive or intent, or when it involves reckless or callous indifference to the federally protected rights of others."[35] Therefore, while a school district cannot be held liable for punitive damages, individual board members, school officials, and teachers may be. Of course, it is the district that is more likely to have the money to pay a substantial punitive damage award. This is actually one of the reasons why the Supreme Court did not want municipal liability for punitive damages, since the taxpayers are the ones funding such a substantial award, and it is arguably wrong to punish them rather than the individuals who acted maliciously.[36]

More important in the present context is the point that since conduct must be motivated by evil intent, callousness, or reckless indifference to the federally protected rights of the victim(s) in order to get punitive damages under §1983, few defendants will be found liable for them in regard to religious exercises. The liability under §1983 flows from the Establishment Clause violation and not the discrimination by third parties that it may have facilitated. Since in most cases school boards and officials that allow school prayer and other religious exercises can argue that board policy or practice was not meant to facilitate a constitutional violation or the discrimination that resulted, and the board, officials, and teachers cannot be held liable for the acts of third parties under traditional constitutional doctrines, it would be hard to tie the "state action" or "state actors" to any evil intent in this regard. Moreover, reckless indifference would be hard to prove in many cases because unless the constitutional violations themselves are blatant as in the *Herring* and *Herdahl* cases, the unclear state of constitutional law regarding public school religious exercises could mitigate allegations of recklessness.

Significantly, since the focus of §1983 is necessarily the constitutional violation by the government actor(s), any punitive damages would be tied to that and not the discrimination by third parties it may have facilitated. Thus, much of the most evil and reckless conduct the victims of discrimination face could not be the subject of punitive damages under §1983 against individual government actors (unless those actors were involved in the discrimination as well as the violation), because it is beyond the reach of §1983. Yet that conduct could be the direct focus of antidiscrimination laws addressed to these issues. For example, if a school board resolution favoring organized public prayer at school events were passed and it caused discrimination that was known to the board members, school officials, and teachers, and if they did nothing to stop it, one could certainly argue that they were acting with reckless indifference, since they had created the policy facilitating known discrimination. The focus is not on the constitutional violation, but on the failure to rectify known discrimination facilitated by board action. Of course, another benefit of looking to antidiscrimination law would be that the punitive damage standards might be easier to meet, and Congress could draft legislation that would specifically allow punitive damages against school districts, which *City of Newport* would not preclude. This would be particularly appropriate in cases like *Herring* and *Herdahl,* in which it appears that most of the local taxpayers supported the district's policies and behavior.

Also, it is at least arguable that Title VI and Title IX, the civil rights statutes discussed in Chapter Six, allow punitive damages against state actors. In 1986, Congress passed the Civil Rights Remedies Equalization Act,[37] which abrogated the States' Eleventh Amendment immunity and specifically stated that the same remedies available against private defendants are available against the states in actions brought under Title VI, Title IX, and §504 of the Rehabilitation Act of 1973. Whether the Civil Rights Remedies Equalization Act was meant to roll back the presumption that government entities are immune from punitive damages remains an unanswered question. The few courts to address the issue have not agreed about it.[38] The language of the Act seems clear that all remedies available against private defendants are available against state defendants and there is no exclusion of punitive damages from this general statement, but at least one court has held that this is not dispositive in light of the historical backdrop against which the Act was passed and of the fact that the traditional presumption against government liability for punitive damages was not specifically abrogated.[39]

To the extent that punitive damages may be available directly against a state entity under Title VI and Title IX, it is at least arguable that state entities that intentionally or recklessly conduct or condone discrimination and harassment covered by those laws could be liable for such damages when that discrimination or harassment is actionable. It might also support any civil rights legislation passed to directly address the discrimination facilitated by public school religious exercises which specifically allows for punitive damages against school districts where appropriate, an option no longer available for constitutional violations redressed through §1983. This could affect the conduct of school boards and voters in school board elections and add a negative stigma to any holding that a district facilitated discrimination through its policies or practices, although the *City of Newport* Court found that the policies against such damages in the context of §1983 outweighed the benefits.[40] Of course, even in the absence of punitive damages against school boards, the other remedial benefits of using antidiscrimination law as opposed to traditional constitutional doctrines remain.

As will be discussed in Chapter Ten, the limitations on compensatory and other damages available pursuant to §1983 are not the only reasons traditional antidiscrimination law concepts would be more workable in this area. Over the last twenty years or so, the Supreme Court has decided a string of cases that dramatically increase the difficulty of establishing liability and demonstrating compensable injury under §1983. While the Constitution, as enforced through §1983, is certainly a potential tool for obtaining redress for some of the harms discussed in Chapter One, its reach is far more limited in regard to discrimination facilitated by public school religious exercises than that of antidiscrimination law. Of course, as will be discussed in the next few chapters, the one distinct advantage to §1983 is that it is currently the only game in town. Unless legislation or common law rules are developed to address the discrimination that is the focus of this book, people like the Herdahls, Herrings, Bells, McCords, Bauchmans, and Walters don't have very many options beyond §1983.

This is particularly troubling because, given the harsh reaction those who oppose religious practices in the public schools frequently face, many people may feel they have too much to risk and too little to gain if they object to such practices.[41] Moreover, school boards and school officials may feel they have very little to lose by engaging in activity that is unconstitutional or of questionable constitutional merit. In many places, a school board that stands up for school prayer is seen as heroic and the dissenters are seen as the bad guys.[42] There have been rallies in Pontotoc, Mississippi, to raise funds to pay the school district's liability for fees and costs that were awarded in the *Herdahl* case.[43] National and local speakers have spoken on behalf of the school board, and at the rallies the school district was portrayed as the victim and the Herdahls vilified.[44]

Those championing public school religious exercises are frequently portrayed as standing for traditional American values, and dissenters as opposed to those values.[45] However, if the paradigm were to shift and the basis for school board liability became religious discrimination and persecution, a stigma might attach to the actions of school boards or officials. The board would not be liable based on its unconstitutional behavior (although liability might attach for that), but for its facilitation of discrimination. Cast in such a light, the school board would no longer be the champion of traditional values, but the perpetrator of discrimination. This may not be dispositive of public reaction in every case, but it does recast the issue in a way that makes it far less politically comfortable for school boards, school officials, teachers, and others who support public school religious exercises.

As Chapter Five demonstrates, the Christian Right is acutely aware of the stigma that attaches to discrimination and has gone to great lengths to cast conservative Christians who agree with the traditional Christian Right agenda as the victims of discrimination and persecution. Given the severe discrimination that religious minorities and dissenters can face when public school religious exercises occur, looking at the legal issues through the antidiscrimination lens is legally desirable and may focus public attention on the discrimination issue, which is frequently subordinated to the constitutional issues that are the traditional focus in cases involving public school religious exercises. Thus, antidiscrimination law has several significant advantages over traditional constitutional claims when public school religious exercises occur. The former can reach conduct that is not unconstitutional, actors whose conduct cannot be the basis for constitutional liability, conduct that does not directly arise from a constitutional violation, and injuries that are based on the discrimination itself and not simply a constitutional deprivation. Additionally, proof and damage issues are more favorable for the victims of discrimination under antidiscrimination law, and the recasting of the issue as one of discrimination calls attention more directly to the discriminatory conduct facilitated by school policy or practice and may create a stigma that is politically uncomfortable for school boards, officials, and others who may support their actions.

chapter eight
A Model for Protecting Religious Minorities and Dissenters

A PROPOSED STATUTE aimed at the discrimination facilitated by public school religious exercises will be set forth and explained in this chapter. As noted in previous chapters, an antidiscrimination approach is better tailored to address this discrimination than traditional constitutional doctrines. Although the issues that arise from public school religious exercises have traditionally been addressed through constitutional doctrines, the proposed statute is not the first to advocate an alternative conceptualization of an issue regarding religion in the public schools.

In recent years, amidst an outcry that religious expression is being stamped out of the public schools and that religious people are being discriminated against on account of that expression, legislation has been passed in an attempt to protect those individuals from discrimination. First, the Equal Access Act[1] was passed in 1984, allowing religious and bible study clubs to meet in public schools during non-instructional time when other non-curriculum-related student groups are also permitted to meet. More recently, the Religious Freedom Restoration Act[2] was passed in 1993 in response to *Employment Division v. Smith,*[3] a decision that criminalized the ritual use of peyote by Native Americans in the Pacific Northwest. *Smith* was a highly questionable decision based on the Free Exercise Clause of the First Amendment, and RFRA had support from both sides of the church-state debate. However, while RFRA was certainly laudable in the context of the *Smith* decision, it quickly became a rallying point for those arguing that organized student-initiated religious activity should be protected, even when it occurs at school-sponsored events. As explained in Chapter Three, RFRA was recently found to be unconstitutional by the Supreme Court, although the Court left open the possibility that states could pass RFRAs of their own.

Given the information in Chapters One and Two, it seems ironic that the legislation passed in this area has frequently ended up benefiting the agendas of those who wish to return prayer and public religious exercises to the public schools, albeit more through its actual use than its stated purpose. Still, there are significant benefits of the Equal Access Act and RFRA, which this book does not question. While the EAA accomplished something the Christian Right had long sought through political and legal efforts—access for prayer groups to public schools[4]—it was drafted in a manner that provides equal access for any religious or political group if the other requirements of the Act are met. Thus, its purpose of nondiscrimination in access to school facilities by religious and political groups at schools that allow other noncurricular groups to use school facilities reaches beyond specific religious groups or doctrines. Although it is frequently used to allow Christian prayer groups to meet, this is perfectly consistent with the purpose of the Act, and "equal access" should certainly not be interpreted in a manner that singles out Christian groups and prevents them from meeting. Of course, in many areas religious minorities will not have sufficient numbers to form clubs and take advantage of the Act, but that does not vitiate its purpose or import.

It is interesting that a legislative solution was used to deal with the access problem, since that problem had traditionally been conceptualized in terms of the Constitution.[5] Given the state of constitutional law at the time the EAA was passed, it was by no means clear that the Supreme Court would allow religious groups access to primary and secondary public schools. In fact, some lower courts had denied access based on the Establishment Clause.[6] Congress chose to legislate access based on a careful balance between existing constitutional norms developed in the higher education context in the now famous *Widmar v. Vincent* case[7] and a departure from those norms contextualized for the unique setting of secondary public education.[8] The statute was challenged and found to be constitutional in *Board of Education v. Mergens*.[9]

Thus, a legislative solution to a problem traditionally conceptualized in constitutional terms under the First Amendment was successfully passed, and regardless of what one thinks of the results of the Act, it has generally served its purpose of giving religious and political groups equal access to schools that maintain a limited open forum for noncurricular student groups.[10] The proposed statute set forth herein looks to the Equal Access Act, along with federal civil rights statutes such as Titles VI, VII, and IX (discussed earlier) and state statutes that prohibit and penalize sectarian activity in the public schools,[11] as resources for developing a legislative scheme to protect religious minorities and dissenters from discrimination when religious exercises occur in the public schools.

If the interests of the religious majority can be protected from discrimination in the schools through mechanisms such as the EAA, it certainly makes sense to protect religious minorities and dissenters, especially when one considers the very real and classic forms of discrimination they often suffer when religion finds its way into public school activities. Moreover, since there are some school districts all over the country that have continued to disobey constitutional mandates due to community pressure or deeply felt beliefs, and since even when those districts ultimately comply they frequently do so very slowly and only under intense scrutiny, current legal mechanisms are not likely to protect the rights of minorities and dissenters.[12] This is especially true at a time when many school districts are being influenced by staunch school prayer advocates.[13] When people believe that God wants them to do something that goes against constitutional norms, Supreme Court precedent can be less than persuasive.[14]

In this environment, religious minorities need protection from, and remedies for, discrimination facilitated by public school religious exercises. Legislation that does so could also have the side benefit of indirectly forcing districts to comply with the Constitution for fear of discrimination suits. Moreover, as discussed in the last chapter, when an exercise is potentially constitutional as in *Jones II,* this type of legislation might cause districts to tailor religious activity in a manner that is more sensitive to the needs of religious minorities and dissenters.

So how would such a statute work? As is the case with most civil rights statutes, the statute would function to provide a remedy for those injured by discrimination, specifically discrimination resulting from religious exercises in the public schools. Like other civil rights statutes, it will also have a prophylactic purpose. Not surprisingly, the statute derives much of its language from existing civil rights legislation, ranging from the Americans with Disabilities Act to several Titles of the Civil Rights Act of 1964. However, as noted above, it also looks to the EAA and several state statutes that punish curriculum-related sectarian activity in the public schools.

Whether or not this proposed statute is ever adopted or used as a model for other legislation, it demonstrates that legislation addressing this problem is possible despite the complexities involved. Of course, as Chapter Six points out, legislation in this area can best be seen as a normative remedial solution that is not likely to solve the broader social conflicts underlying the discrimination.

Even if a legislative solution to this problem is never adopted, it is hoped that this book will call attention to the problem and to the possibility that by shifting the paradigm where appropriate, to call attention directly to the discrimination, some solution may be found. However, given the dynamics involved in the problem, a legislative solution would seem appropriate at least to provide some redress for the victims of discrimination. I hope that the proposed statute can serve as a model for any legislation or regulation created to deal with this issue. Even if it does not, any legislation in this area will ultimately have to deal with the issues raised in this chapter and Chapter Nine. Therefore, the discussion following the introduction of the proposed statute may be useful without reference to that statute.

Four major questions arise in regard to effectuating the proposed statute: (1) How will discrimination be defined given the nature of the harm and injuries resulting from public school religious exercises? (2) Who will be protected by the statute? (3) Who will be liable for the discrimination, and how can conduct like that involved in *Jones II* be implicated if only governmental entities can be liable?[15] (4) Will the proposed statute unconstitutionally impinge on free speech or the free exercise of religion? First, I will provide the proposed statute, and then I will answer the four questions above in light of its language. The first three questions will be addressed in this chapter and the fourth in Chapter Nine. The proposed statute reads as follows:[16]

I. *Rights of objectors and religious minorities in public schools protected:*
  a. Practices prohibited
    i. It shall be unlawful for any primary or secondary public school that receives federal financial assistance or any other entity to discriminate, or facilitate discrimination by others, in the school environment or at school events against any person on the basis of that person's religion or objection to public religious exercises in relation to such exercises that occur during school events or in the school environment.
    ii. It shall be unlawful for any primary or secondary public school that receives federal financial assistance or any other entity to retaliate against any person for objecting to religious exercises or practices in the public schools or for exercising rights under this Chapter.
    iii. No public school faculty, staff, or administrator, nor any person or persons invited, encouraged, or authorized by any faculty, staff, or administrator shall teach sectarian religious doctrine in a public school or engage in public sectarian or nonsectarian religious practices during school events or classes in the public schools, except as allowed elsewhere in this Chapter, by other federal law, or by the Constitution of the United States.
    iv. To the extent that religious practices are constitutional, they do not violate this Chapter unless they violate section I(a)(i) or (ii) of this Chapter; however, no student may be made to leave a room, event, or facility or be asked to wear any form of headgear, blindfold, or other device to avoid engaging in a religious practice. If such action is necessary to enable a student who objects to the practice to avoid participation, any resulting discrimination creates a per se violation of this Chapter.

v. Notwithstanding the exclusion of the Pledge of Allegiance and national anthem from the definition of religious practice and religious exercise in section II(i) of this Chapter, upon notice that discrimination is being facilitated against those who do not participate in or who object to such exercises on religious grounds, a school should take immediate and appropriate corrective action to address that discrimination as feasible.

b. Protection of private right to pray; Equal Access Act unaffected

    i. Nothing in this Chapter shall limit the right of individual students to engage in private prayer or other private religious exercises, to read the bible during free periods, or to engage in private dialogue of a religious nature with others who wish to discuss such topics during non-instructional time.

    ii. Nothing in this Chapter shall be construed to affect, interpret, or limit the Equal Access Act, 20 U.S.C. 4071 *et seq.*

II. Definitions as used in this Chapter:

a. The term "public school" includes any school owned or operated by the government and recognized as such by local, state, or federal law.

b. The term "entity" means any individual or organization, including school officials and employees acting in their individual or official capacities, and any local or state government.

c. The term "person" means any student or faculty member at any primary or secondary public school and any family member or associate of any student protected under this Chapter.

d. The term "discriminate" includes limiting, segregating, or classifying any person on the basis of his or her religion or objection to public religious exercise if such action is taken in relation to a public religious exercise; engaging in any religious practice, whether sectarian or non-sectarian, during any school-sponsored event, program, function, or during school hours that facilitates discrimination or creates an environment in which a religious minority or objector is deprived of equal educational opportunities or which is hostile to religious minorities or objectors and failing to take immediate and appropriate corrective action to remedy discrimination facilitated in this manner; and the utilization of any standards, criteria, or methods of administration that have the effect of discriminating on the basis of religion in relation to public religious exercises or objection to public religious exercises.

e. The term "facilitate discrimination" means to engage in a practice, condone or create an environment where religious discrimination or discrimination against objectors is more likely to occur than it would had the practice or environment not been created, whether that discrimination be perpetrated by employees, students, or others. Only discrimination facilitated by public school religious exercises is actionable under this Chapter.

f. The terms "public prayer" or "public religious exercise" mean any religious exercise that occurs during any school activity that is not considered "private" as defined in section II(g) of this Chapter.

g. The terms "private prayer" or "private religious exercise" mean religious activity or prayer engaged in by an individual privately that is not shared with any organized body of individuals or any religious activity or prayer engaged in by a group of people that does not create a disruption or occur during any school activity, event, class, or function.

h. The term "school environment" means land, buildings, or facilities owned or occupied by any public school; any public school class, activity, or function; and any off-campus activity conducted or sponsored by any public school.

i. The terms "religious practice" and "religious exercise" refer to any sectarian or nonsectarian religious practice, prayer, or exercise, but this term specifically does not refer to the Pledge of Allegiance, national anthem, or any affirmation of general social values or legal norms that contain no direct religious references or content except as provided in section I(a)(v) of this Chapter. Additionally, the terms "religion," "religious practice," and "religious exercise" as defined in this Chapter do not include any otherwise constitutional aspect of the secular curriculum of any public school including the sciences, history, English, or social studies.

j. The terms "objector" and "religious minority" include any individual or individuals, regardless of denomination or faith, who oppose public religious exercises or practices that are occurring in any public school or whose religion is in the minority in a particular school district that engages in, allows, or authorizes public school religious exercises. This term can refer to individuals whose religious faith is in the statistical minority or majority in the nation and those who subscribe to no faith at all.

III. Penalties for violation of this Chapter; judicial relief:

a. *Removal of federal financial assistance for intentional or reckless violations.* Any school or school district determined to be in violation of this Chapter, which was acting in contravention of established constitutional principles, will forfeit all federal financial assistance for two years immediately following the violation and every year thereafter until compliance is verified by a court of competent jurisdiction or by the attorney general of the United States. Such a district may also be subject to all other penalties or judgments allowed by this Chapter.

b. *Judicial relief.* Any person who suffers discrimination in violation of section I of this Chapter may assert that violation in a judicial proceeding against the offending entity(s) and obtain all relief described elsewhere in this chapter. The attorney general of the United States may also file suit in any court of competent jurisdiction upon receipt of complaint(s) of a violation of this Chapter after an investigation and obtain appropriate relief against the offending school district, school board, local government, and government officials. All damages and equitable relief authorized by Titles VI and VII of the Civil Rights Act of 1964, as amended by the Rehabilitation Act Amendments of 1986 and the Civil Rights Act of 1991, are available for violations of this Chapter where appropriate, except that there shall be no caps on damages as required by 42 U.S.C. §1981a.

c. *Discharge of offending employees.* Nothing in this or any other federal law shall be construed to limit the right of school districts or school boards to terminate or take other disciplinary action against any employee(s) responsible for violation of this Chapter.

d. *Multiple violations by school district.* If the attorney general of the United States shall determine after appropriate investigation that a school district has engaged in a pattern of offenses under this Chapter, that school district will lose federal financial assistance according to the terms and procedures set forth in section III(a) of this Chapter.

e. *Eleventh Amendment immunity waived.* The states shall not be immune

from suit under this Chapter. Eleventh Amendment immunity is
hereby abrogated for purposes of this Chapter.

f. *Establishment Clause and Free Exercise Clause unaffected.* Nothing in this
Chapter shall be construed to allow any government-sanctioned or
-sponsored expression of religion or interference with the free exercise
of religion that would violate the United States Constitution.

Defining "Discrimination" in the Proposed Statute

Perhaps the toughest issue relating to the proposed statute is the definition of actionable discrimination. This is also an important issue in regard to the use of existing statutes, as discussed in Chapter Ten. Certainly, the statute would be problematic if anyone could claim that any
school practice, no matter how innocuous, was actionable discrimination. Yet the statute must be broad enough to provide remedies for the
diverse harms that can result when religion mixes with public education
in an insensitive fashion. Additionally, two preliminary problems arise
from the beliefs of two very different religious groups.

First, religious sects like the Jehovah's Witnesses do not believe in
public affirmation of any political entity. Thus, saying the Pledge of Allegiance and singing the national anthem violate their religious tenets.
Similarly, atheists might find the references to God in these acts to be
offensive. The proposed statute is quite clear that these exercises are not
deemed "religious" for purposes of the statute. However, it would require that school districts engage in such activity in a way that does not
promote discrimination where possible—i.e., allowing students not to
participate and when it appears children are being harassed as a result of
nonparticipation, intervening to protect the children and sensitize those
harassing them.

Second, some people, including elements from within the Christian
Right, believe that school curricula collectively teach "secular humanism,"[17] which they believe functions like a religion.[18] Instruction that
promotes moral relativism and individualism or that teaches subjects
such as evolution, AIDS awareness, multiculturalism, and sex education

are examples of what these individuals believe to represent secular humanism.[19] Without engaging in a dialogue over whether, as defined by many within the Christian Right, "secular humanism" can be considered a religion, a dialogue best left to theologians and philosophers, the statute clearly precludes claims based on the secular curriculum generally.[20]

Courts have consistently held that government cannot establish secularism as a religion any more than it can establish any other faith. However, many of those who assert that current public school curricula teach "secular humanism" as a religious doctrine equate religious neutrality in the schools, which the Constitution mandates, with hostility toward religion. In other words, they claim that by teaching a secular curriculum that does not parallel their religious values the schools are essentially teaching a religion of secularism. To my knowledge, no court has upheld this position,[21] and it places the public schools in a no-win situation: by teaching a secular curriculum that responds to scientific discovery and current social issues the schools would be violating the Constitution by teaching "secular humanism"; by not doing so to meet the requirements of the Christian Right's doctrine the schools would have to destroy much of the current curriculum and might potentially be in violation of the Establishment Clause by weakening the secular curriculum to respond to the religious needs of one or two factions. The statute essentially avoids this debate by placing it outside the parameters of the statute. The secular curriculum is not considered "religious" for purposes of the statute; it cannot lead to actionable discrimination under the statute.[22]

While this might seem an arbitrary line to draw, it is in keeping with the logic behind the statute and the types of situations that create the need for this kind of legislation. Since its purpose is to protect those who object to, or are victimized as the result of, religious exercises in the public schools, the statute would be rendered meaningless if the definition of "religious exercise" included aspects of the school curriculum that are not generally associated with religion. If it did, any school district might be sued based on its regular curriculum. Of course, if a student subscribing to the values expressed by the Christian Right or others who oppose "secular humanism" was subjected to discrimination facilitated by an organized religious exercise in the school as defined in the proposed statute, that student would be protected as would students of any faith or no faith at all. For example, if there were a "celebration of atheism" in the form of an organized, public religious exercise that facilitated discrimination against fundamentalists or other religious persons, the statute would apply. However, it would have to be akin to a religious exercise or practice and not simply the inculcation of secular subjects or ideas.

Explaining that these two concerns cannot lead to actionable discrimination does not answer the question of exactly what is actionable discrimination under the proposed statute. Clearly, the purpose of the statute is to remedy and prevent discrimination that is directly caused by religious exercises in the public schools or is facilitated by such religious exercises. The definition of discrimination contained in section II(b) of the statute includes practices that would cause a child to be held out as different or that would deprive a child of the same educational opportunities afforded other students. This would include situations where religious exercises facilitate harassment or discrimination of students as occurred in the *Bell, Herring, Walter, Bauchman,* and *Herdahl* cases.[23] The statute recognizes that the threat of discrimination raised by religious exercises in the public schools comes not only from the meshing of church and state, but from the peer pressure and harassment of students deemed "different." Realistically, children are not known for their kindness to those who do not fit the norm, and the dynamics of religious intolerance and the creation of a religious ingroup and outgroups can greatly exacerbate the situation.[24]

The statute states that religious practices, whether sectarian or nonsectarian, that occur during any school-sponsored event, program, or function, or during school hours can support a violation of the statute if they facilitate discrimination (discussed further below), create an environment that would deprive an objector or religious minority of equal educational opportunities, or if they create an environment hostile to such individuals. This provision recognizes that there are some practices that are currently considered constitutional, or may be considered constitutional in the future, that may still facilitate discrimination if carried out in an insensitive fashion. Additionally, this provision recognizes that many school districts engage in activities that are unconstitutional and have effects that go beyond any violation of constitutional rights.[25] This is where some of the traditional causes of action available under other anti-discrimination laws come into play.

Hostile environment harassment is actionable under the proposed statute. This is significant because once the school is legally on notice of the harassment (see Chapter Six) it must take immediate and appropriate corrective action to remedy the situation. If it does not, the school can be liable for any harassment facilitated by the allowance or sponsorship of religious exercises in the school. Therefore, a school can be liable for a hostile environment created by students, relatives of students, and other people as well as school employees and officials. The trigger for potential liability is a school's policy or practice of allowing or sponsoring religious exercises at school or during school activities or functions. The school's response and policies relating to any harassment facilitated by those religious exercises will determine whether the school district itself is liable. Regardless, as will be discussed below, the individual harassers can be liable for their actions whether they be school employees/officials or not. Additionally, as is the case in a hostile work environment, a single comment—even one resulting from a school practice—is not likely to be sufficient to create a violation of the statute.[26] The cause of action would function in the manner discussed in Chapter Six and, where feasible, the OCR guidelines discussed therein.

Moreover, as mentioned in Chapter Six, school districts can be liable for disparate impact and disparate treatment discrimination as well as for retaliation under sections I(a)(i) and (ii) of the proposed statute. Whether or not a school is liable under the disparate impact theory will depend on whether the school has any facially neutral policies regarding public school religious exercises or activities that have a negative disparate impact on religious minorities or dissenters. Frequently, that negative impact will be the harassment that could be independently actionable. Hostile environment harassment may still be an available cause of action in such a circumstance, but the availability of the disparate impact claim may serve as a backup due to some of the defenses available in hostile environment situations.

Additionally, the disparate impact theory could be useful in situations like those alleged in the *Herring* case. As you may recall, in that case a school policy precluded the Herring children from wearing their Stars of David because they were said to be gang symbols (in rural Alabama) while Christian students were permitted to wear crosses, and the school allowed the Gideons to hand bibles out during instructional time. It could be argued these policies had a profound and negative differential impact on religious minorities. In such a situation, the totality of the various incidents might support a hostile environment claim (and definitely would in a case like *Herring*), but under disparate impact theory each of these policies could be actionable without regard to other incidents and policies. This could preclude schools from carefully enacting policies or engaging in practices that seem facially neutral, such as the gang symbol policy in *Herring* or an equal access policy that does not actually provide "equal access" to groups not favored by the religious majority, policies that have a disparate impact that by itself would not be actionable under a hostile environment theory. However, to be actionable under the proposed statute, there would have to be some connection between the disparate impact and the religious exercise(s) that triggered the statute.

Disparate treatment would come into play if a school, school official, or employee took action against a student in the religious minority, or one who opposes religious exercises in the school, on the basis of the minority or dissenter status of that student. Examples would include teachers' lowering the grades of such students and other grade inequities tied to the students' status; disciplining of minority or dissenter students; differentials in workloads; forcing students to wear headgear; unreasonably segregating students to avoid hearing an offending prayer or religious exercise; unequal access to facilities, school-related activities, or learning tools; or any other intentional actions or inactions that prevent such students from obtaining educational opportunities on an equal basis with other students. While the hostile educational environment cause of action can be based on the school's role in, and response to, harassment by students and others who may also be liable, the disparate impact cause of action would be available only against the school district and board, and the disparate treatment cause of action would be available against the school district, school board, school officials, and school employees with the power to affect a complaining student's educational opportunities. (As to individual defendants, only those who did affect such opportunities could be liable.)

The statute is also violated if school employees or officials retaliate against a student for filing a claim under the statute or for objecting to religious activity in the public schools. Claims of retaliation would be governed by the standard for retaliation claims under Title VII as modified for the school context. For example, in the school context, retaliation might involve grade deflation, unwarranted discipline, verbal abuse, or requiring work not required of other students.

The final aspect of the definition of discrimination is the use of standards, criteria, or methods of administration that have the effect of discriminating on the basis of objection to public religious exercises. This is similar to language contained in the Americans with Disabilities Act[27] and refers to any methods of administration, policies, or rules that relate to religious practices in a public school that cause or facilitate any result that is deemed discrimination elsewhere in the statute. For example, this provision can be relevant to hostile educational environment claims in which school administrative policies either foster the hostile environment or are inadequate to remedy it. It could also be relevant to a disparate impact claim based on a method of administration, policy, or rule that has a discriminatory impact on religious minorities or dissenters.

The phrase "facilitate discrimination" is defined separately in section II(e) of the statute and refers to any religious practice that creates an environment in which religious discrimination is more likely to occur than had the practice not been effectuated. In this context, it does not matter whether the discrimination facilitated by the practice is perpetrated by students, school district employees, or others. What is required is that the discrimination be facilitated by a school practice that sponsors, authorizes, or allows religious exercises at any public school event, program, or function.

A natural issue that arises from this term is what constitutes a religious exercise or practice for purposes of facilitating discrimination. If an activity is not a religious exercise or practice, it cannot facilitate discrimination under the proposed statute, even if it is religious in nature. Perhaps the best way to address this given the rather broad definitions of "religious exercise" and "religious practice" contained in the proposed statute is to begin by stating what they are not. The statute makes clear that it does not limit the rights available under the Equal Access Act and that it cannot be used to justify an unconstitutional interference with the free exercise of religion. Thus, as a general matter, religious club meetings pursuant to the Equal Access Act would not constitute "religious exercises" or "religious practices." Nor would individual students saying prayers, reading from the bible, or even proselytizing, so long as such activities are not organized, constitute public religious exercises. Additionally, if a school were to rent school property to a religious organization in the evenings or on weekends pursuant to an access policy also applicable to non-religious organizations, such meetings would not constitute a religious exercise or practice under the proposed statute.[28] However, if a school promotes a religious environment, as in the *Herring* and *Herdahl* cases, such activities, and any discrimination or harassment they facilitate, could be considered as part of the overall environment promoted by the school.

The types of religious exercises or practices that are really the focus of the proposed statute, and most likely to facilitate discrimination as defined therein, are organized public prayer (including student-initiated prayer) at school events or during instructional time, bible reading, religious meetings that do not comply with the Equal Access Act, moments of silence conducted in a religious manner, distribution of bibles, religious assemblies, and other activities like those alleged in the *Herring, Herdahl, Bauchman,* and *Bell* cases. Of course, to be actionable under the statute, such activities must directly cause or facilitate discrimination. The primary difference between direct causation and facilitation for purposes of the statute is that an activity or practice directly causes discrimination when the activity itself directly results in provable discrimination, while an activity or practice facilitates discrimination when, as noted above, it makes it more likely to occur by serving as the catalyst for harassment or other discriminatory conduct.

The definition of "facilitate discrimination" may seem broad to some and perhaps too narrow to others. However, it does recognize that the danger from public school religious exercises leading to discrimination against religious minorities and those who object to such exercises is not just the harm inflicted on objectors' constitutional rights, but also invidious discrimination such as harassment, being segregated from the main group, and other similar conduct. It recognizes that the risk of harm comes not only directly from the school's practices, but also from the environment that those practices foster, as was demonstrated in the *Herdahl* and *Walter* cases.[29]

Significantly, the statute does not make actionable every annoyance, slight, or discriminatory comment of a religious nature that occurs in a public school. It does acknowledge that when discriminatory conduct results from a religious exercise at a public school event or class, the exercise has facilitated real harm, which can be actionable. It is the link to the religious exercise at an event or at a time or place sponsored by the public school that brings the discriminatory conduct within the statute's aegis. Religious discrimination that occurs for other reasons might be actionable under other causes of action if severe enough, but would not be a violation of this statute.

Additionally, if a school engages in a pattern of religious activity and individual activities within that pattern give rise to separate incidents of discrimination, the cumulative effect of such incidents can be a violation of the statute, even if the incidents would not be violations if considered individually. The fact that the incidents result from separate activities does not dissociate them from the pattern engaged in by a school. Conversely, if the school engages in practices that do not clearly violate the Constitution or the statute, and it endeavors to remedy promptly and appropriately any resulting discriminatory conduct, the district might be shielded from liability under the statute, even if those practices are questionable.[30]

Despite the parameters provided in this chapter, there really is no precise definition for the terms "discrimination" and "discriminate" as

they are used in the proposed statute, because there are no precise limitations to the different types of harm caused by religious exercises in the
public schools. However, the discussion in this section should demonstrate that the definition is limited enough to protect districts who are
not engaging in inappropriate behavior or who engage in behavior that
might be close to the lines drawn by the statute, but act in a sensitive
manner. School districts can avoid any violation of the statute simply by
not engaging in or permitting religious exercises at school events.
Should districts choose to engage in such activity, they should be prepared to do so in a fashion that is sensitive to the needs of objectors and
religious minorities.

In all likelihood, the greatest impact of the statute would be on districts that intentionally violate constitutional norms, who intentionally
engage in practices that are close to the line, or who implement such
practices in an insensitive fashion. It should be remembered that while
discrimination as defined in this proposed statute is relatively broad, the
statute is only implicated when a school engages in or allows religious
practices at school events or during school hours.[31]

Who Is Protected by the Proposed Statute?

The answer to this question is both simple and complex. The primary
focus of the statute is on protecting religious minorities and dissenters.
This is a simple enough concept until one has to consider exactly how
"religious minority" and "dissenter" are to be defined for purposes of
the statute. Moreover, while an obvious focus of the statute is the protection of students who are subject to discrimination facilitated by public
school religious exercises, what happens when that discrimination filters
up to family members as in the Bell and Herdahl cases? Additionally, what
if a teacher objects to religious exercises or a religious atmosphere and
is subject to discrimination as a result of that objection or of the atmosphere itself? The first of these issues is the most significant, and it must
be answered with consideration of the overall purpose of the statute, the
situations that give rise to the need for such a law, and the fact that fear

of the significant discrimination and ostracism that can arise when one objects to religious exercises in the public schools keeps many from objecting under the current legal framework.[32]

First the term "religious minority" must be defined. Section II(j) of the proposed statute demonstrates that whether one belongs to a religious minority for purposes of the statute is dependent upon whether one's faith is in the minority in the municipality or school district where the discriminatory practices are occurring. Whether one is in the religious minority nationally, or even one's state, is not the relevant inquiry. Thus, any denomination or faith can be a religious minority somewhere. Members of some faiths, such as Jews, Muslims, Buddhists, Hindus, Wiccans, and Daoists, are likely to be in the religious minority virtually everywhere in the country. Others, such as Catholics, Seventh Day Adventists, Eastern Orthodox, and Mormons, are likely to be in the religious minority in many areas, but may not be in certain geographic areas. The same would be true for atheists or agnostics. However, as the *Herdahl* case demonstrates, Lutherans, Pentecostals, and others who may not usually be thought of as "religious minorities" can be in the distinct minority in some school districts.

Protecting all such individuals is in keeping with the purpose of the statute—to protect the victims of discrimination facilitated by public school religious exercises. If schools engage in religious activities and discrimination against religious minorities occurs, the victims are going to be the minority in the specific school district involved. To use an overly limited definition of "religious minority" would not serve the purpose of the statute or adequately cover the problem the statute is meant to redress. The vast majority of Americans who identify with a religious faith are of some Christian denomination, and many other Americans are atheists or agnostics. To preclude Christians, atheists, or agnostics from protection under the statute makes no sense, since one Christian denomination may be a minority in an area dominated by others, and in a school that has religious exercises an atheist or agnostic is a likely target should discrimination arise. In fact, it is quite possible that a denomination that constitutes the majority in a school district where religious persecution is occurring may itself suffer discrimination elsewhere. The *Bauchman* case provides a likely example of this: most of the discriminators in that case were Mormon, but in other areas Mormons may be the victims of discrimination by others.

It is true that many of the school districts involved in this kind of discrimination will be in areas dominated by fundamentalist or evangelical faiths, or faiths with similar world views.[33] This is due both to the overt nature of such faiths and the fact that many who subscribe to these faiths are great supporters of school prayer, as are many of their political and religious leaders. The cases contained in Chapter One and the information in Chapter Two point this out quite clearly. However, given the ongoing campaign to bring organized religious exercises back into the public schools, those exercises can occur anywhere, as recent incidents in California, New Jersey, and Florida demonstrate.[34] While it might be poetic justice were individuals such as the discriminators in *Herdahl, Bell,* and *Herring* subject to discrimination in some other area as the result of the campaign to support public school religious exercises, principles of nondiscrimination must protect all children. Someone who is a potential perpetrator in one area can be the victim in another. Of course, the odds are that the same groups will be in the majority in many of the school districts that facilitate such incidents. For example, Southern Baptists were the majority faith in the school districts in both *Herdahl* and *Herring,* although a Southern Baptist child would be protected if subject to discrimination in a town dominated by members of another faith or denomination.

What the foregoing discussion should make clear is that the term "religious minority" cannot be narrowly defined based on preconceptions and stereotypes about who is and who is not in the religious minority nationally or even regionally. The fact that religious exercises that facilitate discrimination are more likely to occur in areas dominated by faiths with fundamentalist world views only suggests where the statute is most likely to be used, not where and for whom it may be used generally.

A related issue is who can be considered a "dissenter" under the proposed statute. This term is also defined in section II(j) of the proposed statute. Significantly, while dissenters are protected under the statute to the same extent as members of religious minorities, their status is unrelated to their religious faith or denomination. It is possible that they could be of the majority faith in a given area. Their status is instead dependent upon their position vis-à-vis the religious exercises that facilitate the discrimination. A "dissenter" is anyone who objects to the religious exercises or atmosphere in a public school, or who objects to the discrimination or discriminatory environment facilitated by such exercises or atmosphere.

It is particularly important to protect dissenters because many people are afraid to come forward with complaints because of the often overwhelming, even violent response they may face.[35] Given the reception those who complain of public school religious exercises often receive, whether they be in the religious minority or majority, the protection and provision of redress for those who suffer discrimination when they complain about religious exercises should be a central purpose of any mechanism created to address this problem. While many dissenters will also be in the religious minority, the proposed statute recognizes that others will not be, and through its remedial scheme it attempts to provide relief for those with the courage to come forward even when they are likely to suffer discrimination as a result. Perhaps this will encourage more individuals to do so. The number of reported challenges to public school religious exercises only represents those very few incidents in which individuals have come forward and the case has worked its way through the system far enough to be reported.[36]

In an article that discusses the role of ceremonial deism in society, Steven Epstein succinctly summarizes this point:

> Simply stated, the ostracism that befalls plaintiffs who challenge cherished governmental endorsements of religion is so extreme that most who are offended by these practices bite their tongues and go about their lives. Moreover, in view of the dicta in Supreme Court and lower court cases suggesting that ceremonial deism passes constitutional muster, those who might be inclined to file suit must consider not only the hatred and violence that their litigation will engender, but also the dismal prospect that suffering through such harassment will be worth their while.[37]

Of course, the types of religious exercises discussed in this book frequently go beyond ceremonial deism, and Epstein's point resonates even stronger in these contexts. Significantly, the ostracism, hatred, and violence that Epstein refers to is the very type of conduct this book addresses, although it may be based on the attention called to minority status by religious exercises in addition to dissent. Given the current state of constitutional law and the inadequacy of other laws to address discrimination and harassment head on, there is no great incentive for many people to endure the pain that dissent will likely inflict.[38] Although it provides better remedies for the behavior that inflicts pain on dissenters, the proposed statute will not be a panacea that causes all those who might complain to come forward. Still, it could provide an incentive for more people to do so. Likewise, for those who "cherish" governmental endorsement of religion and see those who oppose it as deserving of ostracism, hatred, or violence, the statute may create a disincentive to act on those beliefs. As Chapters One, Two, and Four point out, when religious exercises do occur in the public schools, many school officials, employees, students, and members of the public who strongly support those exercises will react harshly, even when blatantly unconstitutional exercises are challenged.

The next issue relating to who is protected under the statute arises from cases such as *Bell* and *Herdahl,* in which parents and other relatives of the children become the targets for discrimination and harassment, either because of their minority status, their relationship to the children, or their objection to the religious exercises. Frequently, the parents are vilified because of their role in complaining of the religious practices or discrimination and because, when a lawsuit begins, they must generally file suit on behalf of their children. Thus, the parents may be seen as the ones really behind any objection to the religious exercises.

In the *Bell* case, this likely led to the burning down of the Bells' house and in the *Herdahl* case it led to death threats and other conduct aimed at Lisa Herdahl. The harm to the parents and other family members caused by the hatred and discrimination in these cases is real, and as the *Bell* case poignantly demonstrates, sometimes tangible. Yet schools whose policies or practices facilitate the controversies that give rise to such behavior are insulated from liability for this kind of harassment and destruction under traditional constitutional doctrines.[39] Making the schools liable for such conduct is problematic, even under the proposed statute, because it does not generally occur at school or school-sponsored events. Thus, inadequate school policies or failures to remedy the discrimination are not relevant considerations because the school is not likely to have any authority over the discriminators or the environment where the discrimination occurs. Of course, if the discrimination occurs at school events or activities, or is somehow directly condoned by school officials, a different situation arises.

Under the proposed statute, a school could be liable for discrimination inflicted on the parents or other relatives of a student if it was facilitated by religious activity at the school, if the discrimination occurred at school events or activities, and if it met the other requirements for a cause of action under the statute. If a hostile environment claim is involved, the objective reasonableness standard would be based on someone of the parents' age, and the school would be liable only to the extent that it could have taken immediate and appropriate corrective action or appropriate preventative measures such as proper policies and procedures for reporting and investigating instances of harassment. If it can be proven that school officials are directly involved in the conduct or that school officials intentionally condoned or recklessly influenced those engaged in the conduct, the school can be liable, regardless of where or when the discriminatory incidents occur. Under these circumstances the school more clearly causes or facilitates the discrimination.

In situations like the firebombing in *Bell,* it would be hard to find the school district or school officials liable for such an incident without making a blanket statement that schools are vicariously liable for any conduct that could be tied to public school religious exercises they support, condone, or allow—regardless of how unpredictable or unusual. While I am sympathetic to the benefits of that type of blanket statement, it would likely prove unworkable because of the wide range of religious exercises, environments, discriminatory actors, and incidents that the statute must take into account.

To create automatic vicarious liability would also put schools allowing religious activities that are arguably constitutional in an untenable position: they would be liable for any discrimination that flowed from those activities, whether or not the school district had the ability to stop or affect that discrimination. One need only think of a school district in a state that has a statute allowing or mandating a moment of silence. If the school complies with that law in an insensitive fashion by infusing a religious tone to the exercise (which could make it unconstitutional as well), is aware of discrimination against students resulting from it, and does not take appropriate corrective action, that district could be liable because it had the power to address the situation and did not. However, that same district should not be held liable if an individual in the town decides to blow up the vehicle of a family that opposes the practice unless the district had knowingly or recklessly incited that kind of behavior. As a practical matter, to propose otherwise would significantly decrease the chances that any legislation like the proposed statute could be passed.

However, this does not leave families like the Bells without redress under the proposed statute. As will be discussed further in the next section, the statute allows suits against the individuals or organizations that directly support or engage in such conduct aimed at the families of complaining students. Thus, the statute allows suits not only against school districts, boards, officials, and teachers, but also against others involved in discrimination that is caused or facilitated by public school religious exercises. Moreover, the statute does not preclude any other cause of action available under other law. Whether the proposed statute is a viable basis for a claim will depend on whether the conduct giving rise to the claim is in response to attention called to the victims' religious status by a public school religious exercise or to the victims' objections to such exercises.

Another related point must be addressed. While it is obvious that the proposed statute protects students from actionable discrimination that occurs on school grounds, if a student is harassed in other places by other students as part of a pattern of conduct facilitated by public school religious exercises and the school is either directly aware of this harassment or is otherwise liable for incidents occurring at school, the off-campus conduct can be considered along with any on-campus incidents in determining the school's liability and appropriate remedies. This is because the school has the power to address the overall pattern of conduct through its disciplinary control of students at school and because the school's policy or practice in regard to religious exercises is the catalyst for the incidents. It also reflects the fact that the school has the power to address the sensitivity with which those policies or practices are carried out or whether they are carried out at all.

The final issue concerning who is protected under the proposed statute relates to teachers and other school employees who are subject to discrimination as the result of their objection to religious exercises or the attention those exercises call to their status as religious minorities. Title VII and some state laws address religious discrimination in employment, and it is not the purpose of the proposed statute to usurp the role of these other statutes in this regard. In fact, the primary focus of the statute is on protecting students who do not have the protection of a statute like Title VII in regard to religion. However, when discrimination is aimed at a teacher or other school employee because of that employee's objection or response to public school religious exercises or because those exercises call attention to the employee's religious status, the employee could seek redress under the proposed statute.

Significantly, because employment is involved, the statute would utilize Title VII standards where appropriate, since there are some differences between the employment context and that of the students and others protected under the statute. The primary benefit of using this statute is that teachers who face discrimination because they object to religious practices in the public schools are covered even though they are not protected under Title VII on that basis (unless the discrimination can also be shown to be based on religion). Additionally, section III(b) of the statute would allow greater damages than are currently available under Title VII. The availability of these damages is in response to the fact that the harm is not caused by ordinary religious discrimination, but rather by discrimination facilitated by religious exercises sponsored or allowed by the school.

Determining Who Can Be Liable under the Proposed Statute

As mentioned above, the proposed statute allows governmental entities, government officials (such as school board members and principals), employees (such as teachers), and other discriminators (such as parents who engage in the harassment and organizations that directly instigate it) to be liable for violations. Of course, each of these categories of potentially liable entities raises questions about when and why those within that category can be liable. The scope and nature of liability should vary between the categories, and this can have a significant impact, depending on the facts of a given case.

First, any school district, school board, school, and state or local government can be liable for violations of the statute. Liability would be determined based on an entity's role in any statutory violation. Given the numerous ways in which school districts, individual schools, and local governments interact in the various states and cities across the United States, this makes sense, but it still begs the question of what "roles" or conduct can trigger liability. The answer depends on the facts of a particular case and on what claims are filed based on those facts. However, there are several general rules derived from Title VI and Title IX that greatly clarify this issue. Perhaps the most important one is that government entities such as school boards are not always liable for the conduct of others under a theory of vicarious or *respondeat superior* liability.

In the hostile environment context, the school may be directly liable for its own conduct or the conduct of its agents, but when school officials or agents are not the ones engaging in the conduct giving rise to the hostile environment, and in all other situations, liability is based on the governmental entities' policies and practices, whether they are policies of action or inaction.[40] Thus, in a case involving a hostile educational environment, a government entity might be liable based on the harassing conduct of its agents, because it did not have adequate policies in place to deal with harassment or because it knew or should have known of the harassment and failed to take immediate and appropriate corrective action. The governmental liability in the latter two situations is not based on vicarious liability for the acts of the harassers, who may be students or even parents, but rather for the school's failure to address the situation adequately.[41]

In the disparate impact context, the government entity that created or is responsible for the policy or practice with discriminatory impact is directly liable based on that policy. In such cases, it is the actor. In the disparate treatment context, the cause of action is based on the denial or loss of enjoyment of some educational opportunity caused by someone with the power to deny or affect that opportunity. Thus, agency liability is essentially presumed because the discriminator is given the power, either actually or apparently, by the school or school board.[42] Additionally, according to OCR guidelines a school can be vicariously liable under Title VI for disparate treatment discrimination committed by other employees acting within the scope of their employment.[43] The same would be true for claims of retaliation.

It is essential to remember that in order for a statutory violation to occur the discrimination must be facilitated by a public school religious exercise. Therefore, the governmental entity involved must allow, condone, or sponsor some religious practice during the school day or at school-sponsored events or activities. However, there need not be any malicious intent or recklessness for this provision to be triggered. Even in a case where a school believes it is acting in accord with the Constitution in sponsoring or allowing a religious exercise, such as in the *Jones* case, the school can still be liable if its policies or the exercises it allows facilitate discrimination.

The purpose of this book and its focus on this issue from the discrimination perspective is that there is frequently a connection between public school religious exercises and discrimination. Schools need to be put on notice that if they allow or sponsor such exercises, they must do so in a sensitive fashion with an appropriate means of discovering, investigating, and redressing any complaints of discrimination that arise. While governmental entities' policies and practices relating to discrimination are the focus of government liability, the statute must be triggered by a religious exercise condoned, sponsored, or allowed by a school or other governmental entity relating to the schools. It is important that the activity that triggers the proposed statute not be confused with that which creates governmental liability, although the former may certainly be relevant to the latter. This is particularly true in cases like *Herring, Herdahl,* and *Bell.* Of course, as is clear from the language of the statute, it does not apply to any nonpublic school.

Another issue in regard to the liability of governmental entities is state liability. Generally, state governments are not involved in the conduct that creates liability under the statute and thus are irrelevant to the issue. However, some state governments, such as Alabama and Mississippi, have repeatedly attempted to pass legislation to facilitate public school religious exercises. Other states have successfully passed moment of silence legislation. As with local governmental entities, states that pass such legislation essentially facilitate any discrimination related to the religious exercises the legislation allows or mandates, and in some states the rhetoric and focus of the executive or legislative branches of government may add to this problem.[44]

In the absence of legislation, state policies, or executive orders that allow religious exercises or moments of silence, the issue of state liability disappears. However, when state government acts in regard to religious exercises in the public schools, the state cannot insulate itself from liability under the proposed statute by asserting Eleventh Amendment immunity. Thus, the proposed statute is consistent with Title VI and Title IX, which through the Civil Rights Remedies Equalization Act,[45] waive states' immunity. In the present context, this makes perfect sense. If a state government authorizes local entities to engage in or allow activity that may facilitate discrimination, the state should not be insulated from liability. In fact, in such a situation, it would behoove the state attorney general or the appropriate state agency to draft guidelines to help local school districts carry out the law in a sensitive fashion and effectively deal with any discrimination facilitated by the religious exercises mandated or permitted by state law.

In such cases, the local and state entities should be jointly liable for discriminatory conduct relating to activities the state law allows, but the school district should be solely liable for discrimination facilitated by its own policies or practices that go beyond or do not carry out the state law in the manner prescribed by the state. Exactly which entity is liable, and for what, when this type of case arises is a matter for the state and local government to work out. A complainant need only demonstrate that state and local laws, policies, or practices allowed for religious exercises in a public school and that those exercises caused or facilitated discrimination against the complainant that was not appropriately addressed by the state or local governmental entity in a timely fashion.

Additionally, individual school, school board, and local government officials acting in their official and individual capacities can also be liable for conduct that violates the statute. Whether an official is acting in an official or in an individual capacity can be determined using principles developed under §1983.[46] Allowing individual or official liability serves both a prophylactic and a remedial purpose. By allowing individual school officials to be named as defendants in a discrimination suit and by allowing them to be liable individually for conduct that they engage in outside of their official capacities, additional pressure is placed upon school officials to be sensitive to the discrimination issue in both their official and personal capacities. The fear of being personally liable for damages or being named as a defendant in a discrimination suit in their official capacity may motivate school officials to think carefully about the discrimination that is the focus of the proposed statute and this book. This would be particularly important with school officials like those in the *Bell, Herring,* and *Herdahl* cases discussed in Chapter One. Additionally, plaintiffs who prevail under the statute will be able to obtain redress for conduct that is attributable to the behavior of officials, even when the governmental entity itself may not have directly acted. An example of this is, when a school principal allows a religious exercise that facilitates discrimination on his or her authority, or directly causes discrimination, or when a school board member, acting individually or through official action, harasses a student or family.

Moreover, any offending official or employee may be disciplined by a school district or local government as it deems appropriate. This right is specifically preserved in section III(c) of the statute so that local governments and school districts can take immediate and appropriate corrective action as they see fit. By adopting the standards from §1983 in regard to official versus private conduct, the proposed statute does not allow individual liability for official actions, even though in circumstances such as the *Herdahl, Herring,* and *Bell* cases that might be desirable.

Additionally, teachers and other school employees may be liable for their discriminatory conduct. Schools can be liable for the conduct of teachers and other employees as set forth above. However, teachers and other employees can be liable in their individual capacities for discriminatory conduct when the teacher or employee is acting outside the scope of his or her employment and is not otherwise acting as an agent of the school. In such a case, the teacher or employee would be liable under the category of "other discriminator." In other words, the employee would be liable for the same conduct for which any third party would be liable when that conduct is engaged in outside of the scope of employment and is not performed in any other agency capacity. In that case, the teacher or employee would essentially be acting as a private third party who also happens to be a school employee.

This feature of the statute is not necessarily in line with the other federal antidiscrimination laws discussed in this book. However, by imposing individual liability on employees and third parties acting independently of the school, although facilitated by religious exercises in the schools, the statute is better able to reach those responsible for the conduct itself in addition to the school and school officials who facilitated and failed to remedy the conduct appropriately. Moreover, to the extent that these individual defendants can pay, they will also be responsible for damages. This may have a deterrent effect, and more importantly through joint and several liability the school district will not be solely responsible for damages caused by the actions of third parties that were facilitated by school action/inaction in regard to religious exercises.

This still leaves the question of when nongovernmental actors can be liable under the proposed statute. This is a very tough question to answer when one considers the variety of actors who may engage in conduct that constitutes discrimination under the proposed statute. The discrimination for which these actors may be liable is limited to harassment through the hostile educational environment theory. Inherent in this is the idea that the harassment must be tied to the educational environment or to a pattern of conduct relating to that environment. Thus, the proposed statute cannot be used as a civil "hate crime" statute or as a means to avoid the strictures of intentional infliction of emotional distress or other tort claims for conduct unrelated to the school environment. Moreover, as with any hostile environment claim, for liability to attach the conduct of the nongovernmental actors must be severe or pervasive enough to create a hostile environment as discussed in Chapter Six. When a third party's conduct is not sufficiently severe or pervasive, that third party is not liable under the proposed statute, but the conduct can still be considered in regard to school liability for the harassment facilitated by a school's religious exercises. This is especially so when the "third party" is a school employee acting in his or her individual capacity.

Significantly, the conduct need not take place at school for it to be related to the school environment. In cases like *Bell* and *Herdahl* where a pattern of conduct that begins at school as the result of issues facilitated by school policy on religious exercises also involves off-campus harassment, that harassment can be actionable under the statute. However, the complainant would have to establish the nexus between the educational environment and the off-campus incidents. Conduct unrelated to the school environment would not be actionable under the statute. This reflects the need to balance the importance of addressing head on the type of discrimination the statute is aimed at and avoiding rampant liability for all acts of religious discrimination alleged to relate to public school religious exercises. As explained above, third parties and nongovernment entities are likely to be liable for such off-campus discrimination (at least by adults).

This also raises the question of who can be liable as a third party under the statute. Here I draw an admittedly arbitrary line. Only legal adults who are not students at the school involved can be liable as third parties under the statute. Thus, parents, faculty, and coaches of other schools (acting outside of the scope of employment), townspeople, and school employees (acting outside of the scope of their employment) are personally liable for otherwise actionable conduct. This does arbitrarily preclude students from being personally liable (beyond any discipline imposed by the school) and parents from being vicariously liable for their children's conduct. However, sound policy supports this exclusion.

Holding students liable either directly or through their parents for harassment facilitated by public school religious exercises would be unwieldy, given the peer pressure and social dynamics involved with child and adolescent behavior. Also, the school has more influence over the conduct of children both in and out of school than others in this regard, since the school can choose how best to implement in a sensitive fashion any policy or practice relating to religious exercises. Moreover, the school can create policies to facilitate reporting, investigation, and redress for student-on-student harassment. Much of this conduct will occur in the school environment, and to the extent that it occurs outside, the school still retains more influence over students than outsiders. Thus, school liability is the best way to address student-on-student discrimination. This is particularly compelling when one considers that behavior is only actionable under the proposed statute if it is caused or facilitated by religious exercises in a public school. Also, as a practical matter, any legislation that would hold children and adolescents liable (directly or through their parents) for the type of conduct the proposed statute addresses is not likely to pass.

The final issue relates to outside organizations and their leaders that specifically promote harassing or discriminatory conduct toward religious minorities or dissenters vis-à-vis their relationship to public school religious exercises. Such individuals and organizations can be liable to the extent that they cause, directly contribute to, or directly promote harassment of religious minorities and dissenters in relation to public school religious exercises. The call to harass or discriminate must be clear and specifically suggest that harm be done to dissenters or religious minorities—i.e., a statement that dissenters are evil or bad and deserve no better is not enough. To the extent that such individuals or organizations (through acts by members performed on behalf of the organization) are directly involved in the conduct, they would be liable to the same extent as other third parties.

Organizations and their leaders have a right to advocate public school religious exercises. They even have a right to malign those who oppose such exercises or who are in the religious minority. The proposed statute would not reach such conduct. Many of the organizations mentioned in Chapter Two engage in this type of conduct and rhetoric. These organizations and their leaders would not be liable under the proposed statute unless they went a step further and directly advocated that organization members or others cause harm to dissenters and religious minorities. Even then, the causal connection between the organization's activities and any harm caused would have to be proven. The same would be true for the activities of any organizational leader who was personally responsible for a call to violence or harassment. Organization leaders are, of course, liable for their own personal conduct when it would be actionable if another third party engaged in that same conduct.

chapter nine

The Proposed Statute and the Free Speech and Free Exercise Clauses

IN IMPLEMENTING THE PROPOSED STATUTE, the Free Speech and Free Exercise Clauses of the First Amendment must be considered,[1] for if challenges are raised to the proposed statute or to the use of existing statutes as discussed in Chapter Ten such challenges are likely to come from alleged violations of the Free Speech or Free Exercise Clauses. Fortunately, the proposed statute and the causes of action envisioned under it pose few problems in this regard. The primary questions that are likely to be raised would go something like this: (1) Does the proposed statute violate the free speech rights of students and employees in regard to religious speech? (2) Does the proposed statute violate the free speech rights of harassers through the hostile environment cause of action? (3) Does the proposed statute in any manner violate the Free Exercise Clause of the First Amendment? Significantly, these questions would likely be raised in response to any legislation applied to the problems that are the focus of this book.

As will be seen in greater detail below, the statute essentially stays clear of potential free speech and free exercise concerns by regulating discrimination and not speech or religion. In other words, because the proposed statute is not aimed at the religious exercises themselves, but rather at the discrimination they may facilitate, it does not place unconstitutional restrictions on speech or the exercise of religion.

In regard to the potential interaction or conflict between the proposed statute and constitutional norms, I am reminded of Ira C. Lupu's interesting article *Statutes Revolving in Constitutional Law Orbits*,[2] in which Lupu discusses some of the benefits and risks attendant upon statutory drafting in traditional constitutional spheres. In response to the current tendency of many judges to defer to other branches of government in constitutional interpretation, relaxed enforcement of constitutional protections, and the weakening of what many consider fundamental rights, he points out:[3]

> [A] number of scholars have called for a new public law. Indeed, it has become a commonplace refrain among political progressives that law reform must arrive through legislative, administrative, and executive action rather than through constitutional litigation. The burgeoning field of "legisprudence" is in no small measure an attempt to develop intellectual underpinnings for a movement that will strive, as much as possible, to achieve results through nonconstitutional means of legal change [footnotes omitted].[4]

This has led to the drafting of legislation that operates in close constitutional orbits. As examples of this, he looks at the Equal Access Act and the Religious Freedom Restoration Act, which are discussed in this book, as well as at the proposed Freedom of Choice Act.[5]

Despite the fact that the Equal Access Act is one of the better attempts to draft such legislation,[6] the statute proposed in Chapter Eight carefully avoids such a close constitutional orbit. In fact, the underlying presumption of the proposed statute is that traditional constitutional norms are inadequate to address the problem the statute is aimed at, and thus looking to antidiscrimination law provides a better solution. The Equal Access Act applied a modified test reminiscent of, but not identical to, existing constitutional standards, but used the test in a new context.[7] The proposed statute applies a conceptualization of the harms that can arise from public school religious exercises different from that under the Constitution and therefore takes the situation out of the constitutional sphere. It is a statute cognizant of the limitations inherent in constitutional norms, which may also apply to the conduct it is aimed at. Therefore, it may be seen as yet another attempt to "achieve results through nonconstitutional means of legal change,"[8] although one whose orbit lies much farther outside the constitutional sphere.

The proposed statute does not attempt to alter, extend, or roll back existing constitutional doctrine in regard to public school religious exercises. As noted above, it goes in a different direction, a direction not shaped by the traditional constitutional analysis of these claims. To the extent that it applies to conduct that also violates the Establishment Clause, it does so for different reasons. At worst, it is redundant in such situations; at best, it provides a broader remedy for injury facilitated by public school religious exercises.

In taking this approach, however, the proposed statute must be carefully crafted to avoid trying to solve constitutional concerns raised by threats to current Establishment Clause doctrine through concepts such as student-initiated prayer. It also must be cognizant of free speech and free exercise rights, so as to steer clear of them to the greatest extent possible. As Lupu points out, statutes that lie in close constitutional orbits run the risk of being found unconstitutional or being affected by the ebb and flow of the constitutional doctrines that they orbit.[9] Thus, attempts to closely tie the proposed statute to constitutional doctrine would be risky indeed and not well suited to the task at hand.

Free Speech Issues and the Proposed Statute

The potential free speech issues implicated by the proposed statute involve a broad, complicated, and some would say incoherent body of law.[10] These concerns are (1) whether the proposed statute violates the free speech rights of students and employees in regard to religious speech, and (2) whether the proposed statute violates the free speech rights of harassers through the hostile environment cause of action. To determine whether or not free speech rights are impinged under legislation such as the proposed statute, it is essential to look at what that legislation does and does not do in regard to speech and at whose speech, if anyone's, is regulated.

Arguably, this is where the analysis should end in regard to the Free Speech Clause because, simply put, the proposed statute does not regulate speech. It provides relief for discrimination. It does not attempt to make "religious speech" illegal. Nor does it attempt to punish anyone directly for speech. In fact, as discussed earlier in this book, students cannot be held liable directly or through their parents under the proposed statute.[11] To the extent that others can be liable under the proposed statute, that liability is based on the discriminatory conduct in which they engage and not because they have engaged in speech. Although discriminatory expression can constitute the actionable conduct, the idea that legislation can appropriately support liability for a discriminatory pattern of conduct that involves speech or other expression is at the heart of the hostile environment concept.[12] Both public and private employers have been found liable for such conduct in the employment context, and in the educational context several courts and the OCR have found schools liable.[13]

It would be wonderful if I could end this discussion here, because even a basic discussion of the Supreme Court's free speech doctrines in the public school context, for someone like myself who does not generally study those doctrines for more than limited purposes, is akin to running an intellectual marathon on an obstacle course with one leg tied behind the back. I ask readers who have spent years studying these doctrines to excuse me if I occasionally trip, for I must briefly analyze the free speech doctrine as developed by the Supreme Court in regard to the public schools. I do so because some might attack this kind of legislation as a prior restraint on speech, since it might cause schools to develop policies limiting harassment of protected students. Schools also might challenge the statute arguing that the Free Speech Clause prohibits them from regulating the conduct that can give rise to a hostile environment under the proposed legislation, and the application of the statute to private individuals might be challenged under the Free Speech Clause.

Perhaps the two most important cases in this regard are *Hazelwood School District v. Kuhlmeier*[14] and *Tinker v. Des Moines Independent Commu-*

nity School District.[15] *Bethel School District No. 403 v. Fraser* is also germane
to these issues.[16] *Tinker* involved a school district ban on the wearing of
arm bands by students to protest the Vietnam War and the subsequent
disciplining of students who wore arm bands in violation of that policy.[17]
The Court held that the policy violated the students' First Amendment
rights and that students and teachers do not "shed their constitutional
rights to freedom of speech or expression at the schoolhouse gate."[18]
The fact that the school policy regulated personal political, or "pure
speech," as opposed to disruptive or school-sponsored speech was highly
relevant to the Court.[19] For present purposes, the most important holding in *Tinker* was that schools do have the right to regulate speech that
would "materially and substantially interfere with requirements of appropriate discipline in the operation of the school" or infringe the rights
of other students to "be secure and to be let alone."[20] This will be discussed further below.

 Hazelwood involved the censoring of two articles and the material surrounding them in a school-sponsored student newspaper at a public high
school.[21] The Court reiterated the holding from *Tinker* set forth above,
but differentiated the newspaper situation because it involved school-
sponsored speech pursuant to the school's journalism curriculum and
rules regarding the student newspaper.[22] The Court gave great deference
to the judgment of school officials that regulate school-sponsored speech
"so long as their actions are reasonably related to legitimate pedagogical
concerns."[23] The way the Court viewed this has been much criticized.[24]
For present purposes, however, the decision, not the criticism, is the
issue to consider in regard to the proposed statute.

 Perhaps the most significant aspect of the decision is its holding that
"[a] school need not tolerate student speech that is inconsistent with its
basic educational mission, even though the government could not censor similar speech outside the school,"[25] and the related holding that the
public schools are not public forums unless school officials "'have by
policy or practice' opened those facilities 'for indiscriminate use by the
general public,' or some segment of the public."[26] The Court went on
to hold that if school facilities have been "reserved for other intended
purposes, even communicative purposes, school officials can impose rea-

sonable restrictions on "the speech of students, teachers and other members of the school community" because no public forum is created.[27] Moreover, the Court stated that "[t]he government does not create a public forum by inaction or by permitting limited discourse, but only by intentionally opening a nontraditional forum for public discourse."[28] This is unlikely to occur in most educational settings. Thus, according to *Hazelwood,* when school-sponsored activities are involved and the school has not created a public forum, speech can be regulated so long as the regulation has a "valid educational purpose."[29]

The *Hazelwood* Court specifically distinguished *Tinker:*

> The question whether the First Amendment requires a school to tolerate particular student speech—the question that we addressed in *Tinker*—is different from the question whether the First Amendment requires a school affirmatively to promote particular student speech. The former question addresses educators' ability to silence a student's personal expression that happens to occur on school premises. The latter question concerns educators' authority over school-sponsored publications, theatrical productions, and other expressive activities that students, parents, and members of the public might reasonably perceive to bear the imprimatur of the school. These activities may fairly be characterized as part of the school curriculum, whether or not they occur in the traditional classroom setting, so long as they are supervised by faculty members and designed to impart particular knowledge or skills to student participants and audiences [footnote omitted].[30]

Thus, depending on the nature of the speech and when or where it occurs, there are potentially two different tests that could apply to it: those set forth in *Hazelwood* and *Tinker.*

Before applying those tests to the concerns raised by the proposed statute, it is worthwhile briefly to address the *Fraser* case, which involved a nomination speech for a student government candidate (delivered by another student), which was filled with sexual innuendo. The student who delivered the nomination speech was suspended and removed from a list of potential graduation speakers.[31] The Court upheld the discipline, holding that schools need not tolerate speech that is inconsistent with their "basic educational mission," that schools may "disassociate" themselves from vulgar speech so as to show others that such speech is "inconsistent with the 'fundamental values' of public school education," and that a "determination of what manner of speech in the classroom or in school assembly is inappropriate properly rests with the school board."[32] Although decided before *Hazelwood, Fraser* serves to reinforce its holding and demonstrates that schools have a great deal of discretion in determining what speech may be properly limited at school-sponsored events and activities.[33]

There are essentially two types of speech, opponents might argue, that are hindered by legislation such as the proposed statute. The first type is religious exercises, which trigger the proposed statute, and the second the conduct that can give rise to hostile environment liability. As discussed above, the proposed statute does not directly address either of these expressive activities, but rather focuses on the discrimination, which the one facilitates and the other contributes to. Still, challenges to the proposed statute based on free speech might be made. Thus, it is worthwhile to look at the proposed statute through the lens of the free speech cases discussed above. Significantly, even if the *Hazelwood* or *Tinker* test is applied, the proposed statute should emerge unscathed by the taint of actionable free speech violations. It is likely that the *Hazelwood* test would apply to most of the religious exercises that trigger the proposed statute and to discriminatory expression and conduct that occur during school-sponsored events, while the test set forth in *Tinker* would apply to other discriminatory expression or conduct that occurs in the school environment.[34]

Hazelwood is the easier of the two to apply in the present context because avoiding discrimination and harassment could certainly serve "legitimate pedagogical" concerns and be reasonable in the school environment.[35] Thus, any school policies or regulations that develop in response to the proposed statute and seek to limit discriminatory conduct in the school environment would likely fare well under *Hazelwood* and the significant discretion it leaves school officials, discretion that makes it harder to implicate the proposed statute in an actionable free speech

violation. Moreover, *Fraser* might support the limitation of discriminatory speech just as it did vulgar speech.[36]

The more stringent *Tinker* standard is also less problematic in the context of the proposed statute. A key aspect of the *Tinker* standard is that
a school may regulate speech that infringes the "rights of other students
to be secure and to be let alone."[37] These are exactly the rights the
proposed statute is aimed at—the right of students in the religious minority and dissenters to be let alone and not subjected to a pattern of
vitriolic discriminatory conduct facilitated by public school religious exercises. A school policy that appropriately responds to allegations of discrimination, in order to comply with the statute, would also serve this
purpose. If a school were to enforce an overly broad policy, however,
which limited speech rights not implicated by the discriminatory conduct addressed by the proposed statute, the school might be guilty of a
free speech violation. Even then, the proposed statute is not the cause
of the violation, but rather the overzealous attempt at enforcement.
Therefore, regardless of which standard applies, the proposed statute
would not appear to violate the Free Speech Clause, either directly (because it does not prohibit speech) or when boot-strapped to a claim
based on school policies or practices enforcing the proposed statute.

The Supreme Court's "forum" doctrine, which considers whether the
school or a particular event is a closed forum, a limited public forum, or
a traditional public forum (also discussed in *Hazelwood*), is worthy of
separate discussion at this point because it may have additional relevance
when (unlike in the cases discussed above) a public forum is involved or
alleged.[38] This is particularly important to third parties who might claim
that the proposed statute, or its enforcement, impinges their free speech
rights. Under the forum doctrine, the limitations that may be placed on
free speech rights vary according to the type of forum that is involved.
As an initial matter, it is important to remember that we are only discussing public schools here. The government may not violate the First
Amendment, and it is bound to uphold it; however, private institutions
are not so limited.[39]

The forum doctrine as developed by the Supreme Court provides
three types of forums, with varying levels of protection for speech atten-

dant to each.[40] Traditional public forums, such as public parks, are the most open and free speech rights are broadest there.[41] They are public forums because they for "time out of mind, have been used for purposes of assembly, communicating thought between citizens, and discussing public questions."[42] Limited public forums must be created by a policy or practice of the government entity that controls such a forum. The government entity must open the forum "for indiscriminate use by the general public" or a portion of the public.[43] Once designated as a "limited public forum," however, any speech regulation in that forum is subject to the same strictures as in traditional public forums as long as the forum remains open.[44] Thus, any content-based speech regulation in such a forum can be justified only if narrowly tailored to serve a compelling governmental interest, but reasonable "time place and manner" restrictions are allowed if content-neutral and "narrowly tailored to serve a significant governmental interest."[45] Closed forums provide the least protection for free speech rights, and government may place reasonable restrictions on speech in such forums so long as those restrictions are not meant to suppress speech due to opposition on the part of public officials.[46] The forum doctrine, and particularly "limited public" forums, are discussed in some detail in Chapter Three in the context of public "student-initiated" prayer. Thus, for present purposes, I will address only those issues not discussed in Chapter Three.

In *Hazelwood,* the Supreme Court held that public schools are not generally public forums as defined for First Amendment free speech purposes.[47] Moreover, the Court has specifically recognized that schools have the right to limit speech appropriately at school-sponsored events, activities, and classes.[48] Thus, unless a school truly opens its facilities or events to "indiscriminate use by the general public" or "some segment of the public," schools can regulate speech at school-sponsored events consistent with *Hazelwood.*[49] Therefore, if students, teachers, or third parties alleged that the proposed statute or its enforcement by a school violated free speech rights, they would be best served by establishing that a public forum existed, which as discussed above, will be quite hard to do in the public school setting.

Moreover, courts have held that religious speech in particular can be limited in the public school context, pursuant to *Hazelwood*.[50] A line might be drawn, however, between personal/private speech and school-sponsored speech.[51] Cases like *Jones II* and *Adler,* discussed in Chapter Three, muddy this analysis in the context of allegedly private student-initiated religious speech that occurs at school-sponsored events such as graduations. An easy answer to this problem is provided by the *Black Horse Pike* case, which held that school graduation ceremonies have not generally been considered public forums.[52] Thus, as discussed above, the school has far greater flexibility to regulate such speech. *Adler,* however, held a high school graduation ceremony to be a limited public forum, and the implication of *Jones II* is that the graduation there was a public forum as well.[53]

While it is hard to believe that schools would actually open graduation ceremonies to "indiscriminate speech," due to the disorder that could create, these holdings are troubling, because if schools can simply declare a ceremony, function, or event to be a public forum, whether it really functions as one or not, and obtain judicial recognition of this, student-initiated prayer could pose serious free speech problems, and those enforcing the proposed statute would have to be careful not to overstep the constitutional limits created by this situation. As noted above and in Chapter Three, however, it is somewhat ridiculous to assume that the schools involved in these cases would really maintain these events as public forums, even if only for students, thus allowing a gay or lesbian student, a socialist, or a satanist to share equal time with students delivering a prayer at a graduation or other event.

If a public school event were considered a public forum, which *Hazelwood* and logic would seem to preclude ordinarily, it still might be appropriate to limit the religious content of speech if the event itself were school-sponsored.[54] As explained above, however, if those events were public forums, the most stringent test available under the Constitution, the strict scrutiny test, would have to be met in order to justify censorship.[55] The strict scrutiny test requires that the questioned governmental action, in this situation the limitation of religious speech at a school-sponsored event or activity, be narrowly tailored to serve a compelling governmental interest.[56]

Both preventing discrimination and avoiding violations of the Establishment Clause could be compelling governmental interests.[57] Thus, whether the proposed statute is narrowly tailored to serve either of these compelling interests would become the likely focus of the inquiry, although since the purpose of the statute is aimed at discrimination and not at the Establishment Clause per se, the compelling interest of preventing an Establishment Clause violation may be less relevant. The proposed statute is arguably narrowly tailored to prevent discrimination because it does not preclude practices that are otherwise constitutional, but rather requires that religious practices be conducted in a fashion that does not cause discrimination against objectors and religious minorities. It also mandates greater sanctions when unconstitutional religious activity facilitates discrimination. The proposed statute is meant to remedy and prevent discrimination on the basis of religion or objection to public religious exercises in the public schools. It is not aimed at religious speech itself. Thus, it could be persuasively argued that the statute is narrowly tailored to prevent discrimination because it does precisely what it is meant to do and does so in the most narrow way possible, by targeting only discrimination that is caused or facilitated by public school religious exercises.

To the extent that an activity at a school-sponsored event that has been declared a public forum both gives rise to liability under the proposed statute and violates the Establishment Clause, it may be limited or prohibited to prevent a violation of the Constitution.[58] The Establishment Clause itself imposes the compelling governmental interest, and if the only way to avoid such a violation is to preclude the religious exercise, such a limitation would be narrowly tailored. A violation of the Establishment Clause cannot be justified in the name of free speech.[59] The proposed statute, however, is aimed at the discrimination caused by the exercise and not at the exercise itself. Thus, the proposed statute would be irrelevant when a violation of the Establishment Clause serves as the basis for limiting religious speech at a public school exercise, although any limitation pursuant to the Establishment Clause would lower the chances of triggering the proposed statute.

Another concern would be presented by a situation in which a speaker unexpectedly delivered a religious message at a public school event, for example, if a student or speaker without warning engaged in a religious exercise during a public school event. As explained above, at school-sponsored events *Hazelwood* might allow for appropriate censorship of religious speech, although the proposed statute would not require this. The problem with spontaneous religious speech is how this might be regulated when the speech is unexpected (even prior review of comments, which could pose other concerns, would not prevent a speaker from ad libbing content). Perhaps the best solution in such a case would be to make known beforehand that a religious exercise is inappropriate in that situation and not invite or allow a speaker who engages in such an exercise to speak at any school-sponsored event again. Since the statute mandates that the school take immediate and appropriate action to remedy the discrimination, the school should do its best to prevent spontaneous religious exercises from facilitating discrimination (to the extent this is feasible given the unexpected nature of such exercises) as well as to appropriately remedy any discrimination that does occur.

The final point regarding free speech for present purposes relates to the hostile environment cause of action. As noted above, some might try to use the Free Speech Clause as a defense to a hostile environment claim under the proposed statute. The above discussion deals with this in the context of the broader free speech concerns raised by the proposed statute. I would be remiss, however, if I did not also point out that the free speech defense has not precluded public employers from being found liable in the context of hostile work environment claims. While the interaction between hostile work environment claims and free speech rights remains a complex issue from a theoretical perspective, courts frequently ignore it.[60] It also has not precluded the hostile educational environment claim from being applied to harassment committed by teachers and students.[61]

The *OCR Guidelines on Sexual Harassment* under Title IX provide an excellent example of this, although those guidelines also apply to university settings and thus raise free speech rights and issues beyond those discussed in this chapter:

> Title IX is intended to protect students from sex discrimination, not to regulate the content of speech. OCR recognizes that the offensiveness of

particular expression as perceived by some students, standing alone, is not a legally sufficient basis to establish a sexually hostile environment under Title IX. In order to establish a violation of Title IX, the harassment must be sufficiently severe, persistent, or pervasive to limit a student's ability to participate in or benefit from the education program or to create a hostile or abusive educational environment.

Moreover, in regulating the conduct of its students and its faculty to prevent or redress discrimination prohibited by Title IX (e.g., in responding to harassment that is sufficiently severe, persistent or pervasive as to create a hostile environment), a school must formulate, interpret, and apply its rules so as to protect academic freedom and free speech rights. For instance, while the First Amendment may prohibit a school from restricting the right of students to express opinions about one sex that may be considered derogatory, the school can take steps to denounce those opinions and ensure that competing views are heard. The age of the students involved and the location or forum may affect how the school can respond consistent with the First Amendment [footnotes omitted].[62]

The guidelines then provide some examples of this policy in practice. One of those examples is quite relevant to the kind of discrimination the proposed statute is aimed at and the way that statute is intended to function. The example as set forth in the OCR guidelines reads as follows:

Example 2: A group of male students repeatedly targets a female student for harassment during the bus ride home from school, including making explicit sexual comments about her body, passing around drawings that depict her engaging in sexual conduct, and, on several occasions, attempting to follow her home off the bus. The female student and her parents complain to the principal that the male students' conduct has created a hostile environment for girls on the bus and that they fear for their daughter's safety. What must the school do in response? *Answer:* Threatening and intimidating actions targeted at a particular student or group of students, even though they contain elements of speech, are not protected by the First Amendment. The school must take reasonable and appropriate actions against the students, including disciplinary action if necessary, to remedy the hostile environment and prevent future harassment.[63]

While the sexual nature of the conduct in this example is quite different from the present context, the overall pattern described is reminiscent of the harassment in the *Herring* and *Herdahl* cases.[64] The key point is that according to the OCR guidelines, "[t]hreatening and intimidating actions targeted at a . . . [student] . . . even though they contain elements of speech, are not protected by the First Amendment."[65]

The cause of action described in the OCR guidelines is quite similar to the cause of action as applied pursuant to the proposed statute.[66] First, as discussed in Chapter Eight, governmental liability for hostile educational environments under the proposed statute is not based on vicarious liability for the speech of students but rather on the school's failure to remedy the harassment.[67] Second, to the extent that others, such as teachers and parents, are liable based on their speech, it is not the speech itself that creates the liability, but the discrimination it causes. This is also similar to the hostile work environment situation for public employers, including schools. If a teacher successfully sued a school for sexual harassment based on a pattern of harassing comments made by faculty or school officials, the school's liability would not be based on the speech itself, but on the environment the speech created.[68] Of course, this arguably begs the question of whether the two are really separable despite the implication by the courts and the OCR that they are.

Free Exercise and the Proposed Statute

A troubling dynamic is posed by the Free Exercise Clause. It is not troubling because the statute is likely to violate the Free Exercise Clause, but because public school prayer advocates have increasingly focused their attention and arguments on that clause (as well as on the Free Speech Clause).[69] Significantly, the proposed statute specifically states in section I(b)(i), that nothing in it shall "limit the right of individual students to engage in private prayer or other private religious exercise."

That clause was included to prevent the statute from being construed as a means to limit the rights of individual students to engage in private religious exercise. Moreover, section III(f) states that the statute cannot be used as a basis to violate the Establishment or Free Exercise Clauses, i.e., the statute itself would be violated if implemented in a fashion that violated the Free Exercise Clause.

The only exercises of religion implicated by the proposed statute are those that take place publicly during the school day, at school events, functions, or other school activities. Even then, the statute focuses only on activities that cause or facilitate discrimination against religious minorities or objectors. Thus, the only free exercise argument that could be made in opposition to the statute is that there is a right to unhindered public free exercise of religion at public school events or during public school activities, a right that precludes redressing the discrimination inflicted on religious minorities or dissenters as a result of those exercises.

Such an argument might be made based on the type of reasoning in *Jones II,* but would not likely be implicated in situations such as those under the proposed statute where the practice itself is not being challenged as unconstitutional, but rather the discriminatory results of such practice. In fact, in section I(a)(iv), the proposed statute specifically states that practices that are constitutional do not violate the statute unless they violate the sections relating to discrimination or the facilitation of discrimination. This is significant, because constitutional religious exercises do not violate the statute unless they inflict actionable discrimination on religious minorities or dissenters. Even then, the purpose of the statute is to remedy the discrimination, not to stop an otherwise constitutional religious exercise. This might be done through conducting the exercise in a more sensitive fashion or by severely disciplining anyone who engages in discriminatory conduct. It is essential not to forget that it is the discrimination that is actionable, not the religious exercise itself. The religious exercise is simply the catalyst that brings the resulting discrimination within the realm of the proposed statute and the problems it was designed to address.

Simply put, the statute does not preclude the free exercise of religion or free speech. It precludes discrimination. To the extent that it supports remedies directly based on any religious practice per se, such practices would be unconstitutional anyway.[70] Thus, neither the Free Exercise nor Free Speech Clauses of the First Amendment would be violated by the proposed statute set forth in Chapter Eight.

chapter ten

Can Existing Law Help?

THE STATUTE PROPOSED in Chapter Eight is just that, a proposed statute. It is not existing law, and although the material discussed in this book suggests there is a need for such legislation, there is no guarantee that it will be enacted. This does not mean that individuals who suffer discrimination such as that discussed in Chapter One have nowhere to turn for redress. There are existing legal mechanisms that could be used to afford some of the protections available under the proposed statute; however, the use of existing laws to remedy and prevent discrimination against religious minorities and dissenters resulting from religious exercises in the public schools is limited by the nature of those laws and jurisdictional considerations. Therefore, while some of the conduct addressed in this book might be remedied through existing legal mechanisms, most of it will not be, and the remedies available are generally far more limited than those available under antidiscrimination laws.

In the federal realm, §1983 is applicable, but as will be discussed below there are significant limitations on the use of that statute. Also, as discussed in Chapter Seven, the remedies available under that statute are quite limited in this context. Titles II and IV of the Civil Rights Act of 1964 might be twisted to address this problem, but as will be discussed below, they have not been used in this manner in the past, and it would be a significant stretch to say that they properly apply to the situations that are the focus of this book. The only other option comes from state law. Examples of this are, state antidiscrimination laws that protect against religious discrimination and apply to education, state laws that prohibit sectarian religious teachings and practices by public school employees and officials at school activities, claims based on state constitutions, and common law claims.[1] As will be seen, there are few state laws that provide any real benefit in the present context, and to the extent that there are state laws useful in this area, they are limited to the jurisdictions that enacted or recognize them (which are frequently the states that least need them).

42 U.S.C. §1983

In Chapter Seven, I explained that while §1983 is the primary vehicle for obtaining redress for constitutional violations committed by local governments, including school boards, as currently interpreted by the courts it is of limited usefulness in regard to discrimination facilitated by public school religious exercises, because it requires a constitutional violation, does not generally reach the conduct of nongovernment actors, and is limited to the conduct that gives rise to the constitutional violation, in these cases usually an Establishment Clause violation.[2] Therefore, it generally cannot reach the discrimination facilitated by public school religious exercises, except to the extent that discrimination is carried out by a state actor and is part of a constitutional violation.

It does not reach the conduct of those most frequently involved in this type of discrimination: other students, parents, outsiders, and school employees acting individually (although when school employees are involved there is at least a possibility their conduct could be covered, but that would not matter unless the discrimination was also tied to the constitutional violation). As a general matter, §1983 allows individuals to bring suit based on constitutional violations perpetrated "under color of law" by covered government officials and municipal entities.[3] Conversely, the purpose of the statute proposed herein, and of a cause of action for discrimination facilitated by religious exercises in the public schools generally, would be to provide redress that is not available under the Constitution for discrimination resulting from actions that may or may not be constitutional.

I need not rehash the issues discussed in Chapter Seven. Instead, I want to use those limitations as a starting point. This chapter will only look at the conduct and injury for which §1983 may be able to provide redress—i.e., conduct relating to a constitutional violation inflicted under color of law and injury that flows from that violation. As will be seen, there are numerous hardships involved in sustaining a §1983 claim, even when these threshold requirements are met. It is extremely hard to succeed on a claim under §1983 because of procedural and substantive barriers erected by the Supreme Court over the last twenty years.[4]

Section 1983 litigation is a complex web of constitutional law, rules, and tests gleaned by the Supreme Court in interpreting §1983 and of tort standards, which are sometimes analogized with the constitutional tort framework created by §1983.[5] Section 1983 doctrine is neither simplistic nor concise, and I do not pretend to address it here in a comprehensive fashion. Rather, I address those concepts that are relevant to the issues in this book, while staying mindful of the statute's limited utility in situations where the discrimination is not part of a constitutional violation or where no unconstitutional conduct has occurred at all. With this caveat in mind, §1983 may be useful for redressing some discrimination facilitated by public school religious exercises when appropriate facts are alleged.

As noted above, §1983 is applicable to actions taken "under color of state law" that violate constitutional or certain other federally protected rights.[6] Local governments, local government officials acting in their individual and official capacities, and state officials acting in their individual capacities may be liable under §1983.[7] However, state governments are immune from suit under §1983, as are state officials acting in their official capacities.[8] Others acting "under color of law" may also be liable, but they must generally be acting as an agent of the state toward the state's ends.[9] There are a variety of standards analogous to tort law regarding general factors of liability that may apply to the actions of officials, depending on the constitutional violation alleged.[10] Moreover, for municipal liability to exist the constitutional deprivation must be tied to a policy, pattern, or custom of conduct to support a §1983 claim.[11] Relatedly, municipal entities can act only through their officers and employees, but a municipal entity cannot be held vicariously liable under the doctrine of *respondeat superior* for the actions of its employees and officials.[12] Additionally, issues of qualified or absolute immunity for government officials are frequently relevant to §1983 claims.[13]

Needless to say, these issues combine to create a voluminous body of law, and the concerns they raise have produced a similarly voluminous body of scholarship addressing §1983. While my personal interests in this area lie more with the scholarship, as is the case with much of the legal discussion in this book, I am generally only concerned with the doctrinal legal norms that currently exist or are likely to develop in the near future. The reason for this is simple. I am discussing these issues to explain what courses of action are, and are not, available to the victims of discrimination facilitated by public school religious exercises under current legal mechanisms. While this is practical, given the broader purpose of this book and the need to remain focused on that purpose, it is unfortunate because there is a richness in much of the scholarship addressing §1983 as well as the First Amendment issues discussed earlier in this book, which I cannot even hope to capture with the very basic analysis that is most appropriate to the task at hand.

Significantly, that analysis demonstrates that the best way to bring the discrimination that is the focus of this book within the realm of §1983 is to tie that discrimination to a constitutional violation (a must) and to focus on those acts carried out by school officials and employees. One other option, discussed further below, is to try to show that the actions of third parties and students were taken "under color of law" because they were facilitated by school conduct or occurred at school events. As will be seen, this latter argument, while sometimes useful given the right facts, is generally quite weak.

The constitutional violation most likely to be involved in cases of discrimination facilitated by public school religious exercises would be an Establishment Clause violation. Other possible violations that could be involved would be free exercise and free speech violations where implicated by the facts in a given situation. One might also try to utilize the Equal Protection Clause of the Fourteenth Amendment, but even assuming state action, any school policies or practices supporting an equal protection claim based on religion would be subject only to rational basis scrutiny, which strongly favors the government actor.[14] Although in cases of overt discrimination carried out by school officials, this approach might have some merit as well.

I will focus on the Establishment Clause here, but the following discussion can be easily extrapolated to address any constitutional violation that §1983 is used to enforce. First, as I have repeatedly pointed out, absent a constitutional violation §1983 is essentially useless as a tool to combat discrimination facilitated by public school religious exercises. Moreover, there must be a nexus between any discrimination suffered and the constitutional violation—religious discrimination by private actors unconnected to a constitutional violation renders §1983 equally unavailing in the present context. Finally, an entity subject to §1983 liability must be involved, and the proper test for liability given the entity and type of violation alleged must be met. Thus, a school board, other municipal entity, municipal officials acting "under color of law," and state officials in appropriate circumstances (acting in their individual capacities) may be liable, but only for harm arising from a constitutional violation, as discussed in Chapter Seven.

Thus, if a teacher, school administrator, or school board member was directly involved in the discrimination, several questions would need to be answered in order to establish liability: (1) Is the discrimination part of a constitutional violation, or does it amount to one by itself? (2) Is the employee or official acting in his or her official or individual capacity? (3) For municipal liability, is there an actionable policy, pattern, or practice involved? (4) Do any immunities attach to the actions of the official or employee involved in the violation? (5) Is the injury alleged tied to the constitutional violation or some other factor? If someone other than a government official or employee is the discriminator, some of these questions may also be relevant, but the key question would be: Was the discriminator acting "under color of law?"

As the *Bell* and *Bauchman* cases demonstrate, courts that have considered §1983 liability for discrimination facilitated by public school religious exercises have generally denied relief for the most egregious discrimination, either because it is not considered part of the constitutional violation or those engaging in the discriminatory conduct are not governmental actors. In the present context it can be presumed that those courts believed the discriminators were not acting "under color of law" in regard to the discrimination and/or that the discrimination was not part of any constitutional violation.[15] The irony, of course, is that *Bauchman* involved allegations of discriminatory and harassing conduct on the part of Rachel Bauchman's teacher, and the court dismissed that conduct as being in poor taste or insensitive, but not a constitutional violation.[16] Let's assume for a moment that the court was not so quick to dismiss this conduct. Are there any grounds under which the conduct might be actionable pursuant to §1983?

We arguably have someone acting "under color of law." A school teacher has authority over students given by the state. In regard to the choir and music classes at West High School, the teacher involved in *Bauchman* had such power. The court found no Establishment Clause violation, but let's presume for a moment it did (as the dissent suggested the facts in the amended complaint would have warranted). The violation would, of course, be based on the infusion of religion into the curriculum by the teacher and not the discrimination.

Would there be a nexus between the constitutional violation and the discrimination by the teacher if a constitutional violation were found? The court implied not.[17] However, I am not so sure of this. It certainly might be argued that the unconstitutional conduct facilitated the choir teacher's discrimination against Rachel Bauchman because without that conduct little attention would have been called to her minority status and the discriminatory conduct arose in the context of her status vis-à-vis the religious exercise. I believe under these circumstances injury arising as a result of the teacher's discrimination arguably flows from the constitutional violation and may be cognizable under §1983. The fact that the *Bauchman* court found otherwise demonstrates that even when seemingly compelling facts are available to support a §1983 claim for redress for discrimination facilitated by allegedly unconstitutional public school religious exercises, one cannot count on a court to find a constitutional violation or actionable discrimination.

What if others, such as students, parents, or outsiders began to discriminate because of the situation? According to *Bell,* the actions of such people, even if facilitated by the religious exercise are not cognizable under §1983.[18] This seems consistent with the current state of law under §1983. If these people are not government-empowered actors acting "under color of law," §1983 would appear inapposite. One might argue that the nongovernment actors are acting under color of law since their conduct is spurred or facilitated by the school's religious activities. Nongovernment actors can be liable under §1983 when acting under color of law or in conspiracy with government.[19] However, it is not easy to establish that a private citizen was acting under color of law.[20] Given the types of situations discussed in this book, such relationships for private discriminators are likely to be exceedingly rare. In these rare cases, §1983 might apply, but only to the discrimination directly flowing from the constitutional violation itself.

Another excellent example is provided by the *Herring* case, in which there were numerous allegations of harassment by students, which was facilitated by public school religious exercises, but there were also allegations amounting to a pattern of conduct by school officials and employees, which might support liability for injury caused by that conduct,[21] for example in-class "Happy Birthday, Jesus" parties, blatantly sectarian assemblies, bible distribution, the prohibition on wearing Star of David jewelry, and the request that one of the Herring children write an essay about "Why Jesus Loves Me."[22] There can be little doubt that, if proven, these allegations would support an Establishment Clause violation and thus trigger §1983. Some of the other allegations discussed in Chapter One may also establish a Free Exercise Clause violation.

In regard to injury caused by the discrimination directly attributable to the school officials, immunity would not seem to be an issue because much of the conduct alleged violates clearly established law developed under the Establishment Clause.[23] In fact, such conduct thumbs its nose at that law. A pattern, policy, or practice could be established to show municipal liability since much of the conduct was engaged in with the knowledge, and sometimes direct involvement, of high-ranking school officials acting in their capacities as school officials. Moreover, the unconstitutional conduct was regular and not sporadic. Section 1983 would be quite useful here. Or would it?

Much of the worst discrimination was carried out by students and others who did everything from spitting and jeering at the Herring children to verbally and physically attacking them and vandalizing their personal property. The incidents were worse after blatantly religious activity, but most of this conduct was carried out by private individuals without government authority. As *Bell* and *Bauchman* vividly demonstrate, this conduct is likely to escape liability under §1983.[24] Unfortunately, as Chapter One demonstrates, in many, if not most, cases of discrimination facilitated by public school religious exercises, this type of conduct will be the primary form of discrimination. Even when brazen school officials and employees, such as those in the *Herring* and *Herdahl* cases are involved, liability under §1983 arises from their constitutional violations and not simply because they engage in other activity that a court considers in bad taste or unbecoming a school employee.[25] In many cases involving discrimination facilitated by public school policies or employees, recovery under §1983 will be at best a crap shoot and at worst a no-win situation—at least in regard to the harm caused by the discrimination as opposed to the constitutional violation.

The Civil Rights Act of 1964

It is possible that some of the conduct that would violate the proposed statute might be actionable under Title IV of the Civil Rights Act of 1964, which deals with public education, but this is most definitely a reach, given the nature and purpose of that law.[26] It is also possible to try to make Title II of the Civil Rights Act of 1964, which deals with public accommodations, applicable to some of this discrimination.[27] If application of Title IV is a reach, however, application of Title II is a full leap, given its purpose and the situations to which it is generally applied. At the outset, I want to be honest that to my knowledge these statutes have never been applied to situations involving religious exercises in the public schools, but they could be amended to do so. I will address Title IV first.

The public accommodation provisions of the Civil Rights Act of 1964 are generally applied in cases involving privately-owned establishments that affect interstate commerce or are supported by state action.[28] The public accommodation provisions do protect on the basis of religion,[29] however, and discrimination is supported by state action for purposes of the public accommodation provisions when it is carried out under power of any law, statute, ordinance, or regulation; is carried out under color of any customer usage required or enforced by state or local officials; or is required by any state or local government.[30]

It is significant that courts have applied the public accommodation provisions to state-owned and state-run facilities.[31] Moreover, the provisions have been applied to private schools that are nonsectarian and directly receive no public funds,[32] so at least in the broad sense they are applicable to schools. Still, the public accommodation provisions of the Civil Rights Act of 1964 were primarily meant to apply to privately-owned public facilities such as restaurants, recreational facilities, and movie theaters.[33] Thus, the biggest problem with any attempt to apply the public accommodation provisions to religious exercises in the public schools would be whether that chapter even applies to public schools, since public schools are not generally open to members of the public.[34]

The fact that there is also a public education chapter in the Civil Rights Act of 1964 suggests that the public accommodation provisions were not meant to apply to public schools. Of course, the public education provisions also have a limited scope, and perhaps where Title IV does not apply, Title II might apply to the public schools. The reality is that no one has tried to make the argument that the public accommodation chapter could apply to religious discrimination in the public schools, and therefore it is a novel argument, which is not directly supported by the purpose and history of the statute.

At first glance, the public education provisions of the Civil Rights Act of 1964[35] would seem to apply more directly to discrimination based on religion in the public schools. However, those provisions are meant to apply primarily to issues of desegregation.[36] Thus, they have not been applied to discrimination resulting from religious exercises in the public schools. In fact, the provision that empowers the attorney general to bring suit on behalf of citizens specifically refers to desegregation or the belief that the legal action "will materially further the early achievement of desegregation in public education."[37] Significantly, however, the provision regarding personal suits arising from discrimination in public education simply states that "nothing in this subchapter shall affect adversely the right of any person to sue for or obtain relief in any court against discrimination in public education."[38]

Therefore, it is possible that although the primary purpose of the chapter regarding public education was aiding desegregation, its language could support other claims when appropriate. Interestingly, it could be argued that there is a form of segregation involved in many religious exercises in the public schools, since objecting students or religious minorities are often asked or forced by circumstance to leave the room or otherwise set themselves apart during such exercises. Admittedly, this is stretching the definition of segregation beyond its usual meaning, but arguably it could be considered an "assignment of students within a public school" based on their religion.[39]

While to my knowledge no aspect of the Civil Rights Act of 1964 has been used in an effort to protect students in the religious minority from discrimination based on religious exercises in the public schools, several provisions of that Act are broad enough to potentially encompass such claims. Unfortunately, there is no precedent for this use of the Civil Rights Act of 1964 and thus no guarantee that such claims would even be considered actionable thereunder. I pity the lawyer forced to engage in the legal contortions that would likely be necessary to get a court to accept the applicability of these laws to the context of discrimination facilitated by public school religious exercises, but there are some interesting possibilities. Perhaps through amendment, these provisions, or Titles VI or IX (Title IX of the Education Amendment of 1972), which do not currently apply to religion,[40] might be made to serve a purpose similar to that served by the proposed statute outlined in Chapter Eight.

For now, however, the Civil Rights Act of 1964 does not have great utility in combating the discrimination facilitated by public school religious exercises, except as a model, as discussed in Chapters Six and Eight.

State Law

The types of state laws that might apply to discriminatory conduct facilitated by public school religious exercises can generally be broken down into four categories: (1) state laws that prohibit and sanction sectarian religious exercises in the public schools, (2) state antidiscrimination laws that apply to religion and to education, (3) state tort claims, and (4) claims based on state constitutions. Each has varying utility and may exist in a differing number of jurisdictions. Thus, I will explore each as a separate entity. (As explained below, however, state constitutions are beyond the scope of this discussion.)

Perhaps the most interesting protection comes from state laws that prohibit sectarian practices in the public schools. Excellent examples of such laws are provided by statutes in Nevada,[41] New Mexico,[42] and Alaska.[43] Essentially, these statutes prohibit school officials or employees from engaging in sectarian practices or teaching sectarian doctrine in regard to public school functions. Thus, their function is more prophylactic than remedial—i.e., they do not provide redress for discrimination but rather provide incentive for school officials and employees to avoid engaging in some of the types of conduct that might facilitate discrimination. However, few states have such laws; they are rarely enforced; and depending on the breadth with which they are drafted and the ebb and flow of constitutional doctrines, the laws themselves might be unconstitutional under the Free Exercise Clause. Given the very limited number of jurisdictions that have passed such laws, the likelihood that they will rarely be enforced, and the fact that they do not directly address the discrimination that is the focus of this book, these laws are more an interesting novelty than a comprehensive remedy for the problems this book raises, although a novelty worth mentioning as a possible preventative measure.

State and local antidiscrimination laws might provide a more direct basis for addressing the discrimination issue,[44] so too might state and local government rules, including school board antidiscrimination policies.[45] Unfortunately, it is highly unlikely that the school districts, cities, and states where the most egregious discrimination based on religious activity in the public schools takes place would voluntarily enact such policies. Additionally, in the local government context it is unlikely very many local governments will make such rules applicable to this type of conduct or consistently enforce them. Similarly, the information contained in Chapters One and Two suggests that while a state may have a statute or policy on the books, a local school district may not comply with that statute if it is already engaging in unconstitutional religious exercises unless severe sanctions were available. Despite these concerns, state and local antidiscrimination statutes are perhaps the best potential means currently available to protect the rights of religious minorities and objectors in public schools that engage in religious activities. Unfortunately, comprehensive laws are most likely to exist in the states and school districts that least need them.[46] Moreover, I am unaware of any situation in which a state antidiscrimination law has been used to provide redress for discrimination facilitated by public school religious exercises, so even where they do exist they would have to be found to cover such discrimination or expanded to do so.

The next type of state law that could be germane to at least some of the discrimination facilitated by public school religious exercises is state tort law. Specifically, I suggest, common law claims for intentional or negligent infliction of emotional distress (hereinafter IIED and NIED), assault, or battery might be relevant.[47] Of course, there are variations between the states in regard to what causes of action are recognized, how they function, and whether or not local governments are subject to such claims, and if so, to what extent. IIED and NIED are most relevant and might be applied to a variety of discriminatory conduct facilitated by public school religious exercises.

Unfortunately, not all states recognize IIED, and few states recognize

NIED as a separate tort. To the extent that IIED is recognized, it is very hard to prove and generally requires extreme and outrageous conduct that goes "beyond all possible bounds of decency" and is "regarded as atrocious, and utterly intolerable in a civilized community."[48] Also, the distress caused must be so severe "that no reasonable man could be expected to endure it," and the conduct must be intentional or reckless.[49] It is very hard to prove IIED claims, and the standard for such claims makes the cause of action an ineffective tool for general use in combating the types of discrimination addressed in this book, even in the jurisdictions that allow such claims. While the standard for NIED is easier to meet given appropriate facts, it is not recognized as a separate tort in very many jurisdictions, at least not in a form useful in the present context.

Assault or battery might be useful in situations where conduct supporting those claims can be proven. However, those found liable for any of these torts will not necessarily be able to pay any judgment, and school districts cannot generally be held liable for these types of intentional torts in most states. Thus, tort claims might be useful if the jurisdiction where the discrimination occurs recognizes them, the victim can prove appropriate facts and meet the appropriate burden of proof, but such claims, given the chance of success, will likely do little to stop schools from engaging in the practices that facilitate discrimination. Moreover, few victims will be able to make the requisite showing for the most relevant torts unless they can prove they were subject to violent, extreme, or outrageous conduct.[50]

State constitutions may also provide a basis for claims relating to discrimination facilitated by public school religious exercises. As with state antidiscrimination laws, however, I am not aware of any state constitution being utilized in this manner, although many state constitutions may serve as preventative measures, along with the U.S. Constitution, through state religion clauses. Moreover, what substantive rights are available in regard to religion under state constitutions, whether those rights are enforceable, and if so, how, varies greatly from state to state. Since few, if any, state constitutions are likely to provide a remedy for the types of discrimination addressed in this book, and because a discussion of state constitutional provisions that apply to religion or discrimination generally would raise a number of issues not relevant to the present discussion, state constitutional claims will not be analyzed further here.

Ultimately, while there may be protections available at the federal or state level under existing law, the clarity and breadth of those protections are questionable. Given the issues pointed out earlier in this book, there is a need for legislation applicable in all the states that will directly protect the rights of objectors and religious minorities in school districts that engage in religious exercises that facilitate discrimination. That legislation must not infringe the rights of students to engage in constitutionally protected religious expression, such as private prayer, discourse, or access to school facilities. Unfortunately, current legal mechanisms are not well equipped—at least as currently applied—to do this.

chapter eleven
Somebody Make It Stop

CONSIDERING EVERYTHING I have learned while researching and writing this book, I fear for children like those involved in the cases described in Chapter One. I fear for the victims because of the pain they will endure at the hands of their tormentors. I fear for the tormentors because instead of being educated to respect the views of those who are different, many seem to be acculturated to respond negatively to difference and to think in provincial, factional terms. Given the experiences of the Herring, Herdahl, Bell, Bauchman, and Walter children, and of the victims of similar discrimination whose cases will never be heard for fear of backlash, I can see in my mind's eye a school child in turmoil.

I picture that child as being Jewish and in elementary school, perhaps because of my own background. However, the child could be Catholic, Protestant, Muslim, Buddhist, atheist, and could be in primary or secondary school. The salient vision is what I picture this child saying— not to me—but to his or her tormentors, classmates, neighbors, teachers, parents, and society at large. The child is saying: "Please, somebody make it stop." When I began the research for this book I would have assumed this fictional child was the victim of an exceedingly rare phenomenon. Now, I realize the fictional child is a reflection of the reality many children in this country face, a reflection of the way the children whose stories are described in Chapter One must have felt.

When public schools and public officials attempt to engage in religious activities, there are bound to be innocent victims. Those victims will often be members of the religious minority or those who object to religious practices in the public sphere. While there is currently a significant push for legislation that focuses on the rights of the majority and those who wish to practice religion in the public sphere, little is being done to protect the rights of religious minorities and objectors who are injured by such practices and the behavior they facilitate. In fact, the discrimination issue is rarely addressed separately from the constitutional issues to which it is so often tied.

At first glance, when one considers the notion of public school religious exercises and thinks of one's own town, school district, and neighbors, the plight of students and families like those discussed in Chapter One may seem remote. When people hear of situations like those faced by the Bells, Herrings, Herdahls, and Bauchmans, they may think or convince themselves that perhaps these are just isolated incidents not tied to any broader social, historical, or political phenomenon. Some might even think, "That's what they get for trying to stop school prayer and force their will on the majority."

Ultimately, two questions must be addressed when we discuss the discrimination facilitated by public school religious exercises. Is it really a problem? Is it a problem that warrants legal intervention? This book has endeavored to address these two questions and the broader dynamics that give rise to them. The problem is that the traditional legal and political discourse applied to "school prayer" situations overlooks the legitimacy of the discrimination issue as an entity separate from the constitutional and political issues.

However, as was shown earlier in this book, the discrimination caused or facilitated by these religious exercises is widespread, predictable given the social dynamics involved, and likely to get worse unless the discrimination itself is considered. Cases like *Herdahl, Herring, Bell, Bauchman,* and *Walter* are simply recent examples. Given the number of documented and published cases that involve discrimination of this sort, it is quite troubling that none of these cases was able to address or redress the discrimination directly, relying instead on traditional constitutional principles that are not equipped to deal with this type of discrimination effectively. It is even more troubling that, as Nadine Strossen has written, the cases actually filed "represent only the tip of the iceberg,"[1] an iceberg that is likely to grow bigger given the inevitable clash between increased religious and social pluralism and the resurgent and politically active evangelical awakening currently taking place in the United States.

To fault the Christian Right for exercising their political rights and freedoms is neither desirable nor useful in this context, nor is simply ignoring the issue in the hope that it will go away, thinking perhaps that these events are the work of a few radical or uncultured people. The reality is that the Christian Right, which shares the same rights as other Americans to engage in political discourse and try to influence policy, is a well-organized political force bent on influencing school policy at the grassroots level, and many of those educators and school board members who support it are anything but uncultured radicals. Moreover, Americans generally support efforts to return prayer and other religious exercises to the public schools, so on these issues the Christian Right has much support.[2] This is particularly troubling because so few people are aware of the discrimination that frequently accompanies these exercises. Most people do not consider the possibility that given the increasing religious pluralism in America, they may one day belong to a religious minority or be the one objecting to the religious indoctrination of their children in a public school.

The Christian Right might be one of the major social and legal forces working in this area, but to address the issue we must look to the problem itself and not simply blame those whose politics may facilitate the exercises that give rise to the problem. Unfortunately, we do not generally do this. Of course, there are articles that mention some of the horribles addressed in Chapter One.[3] In the end, however, the focus always seems to be on the traditional constitutional discourse and how these situations represent a threat to religious freedom or demonstrate the reasons why many are afraid to stand up for that freedom.[4] There is nothing wrong with this, because the constitutional issues go to the heart of religious freedom in America, and the debate over those issues has ramifications far greater than the discrimination that is the focus of this book.

Yet, should the magnitude of the constitutional debate and the important implications of that debate warrant a tunnel-visioned approach to these discrimination issues, one that cannot see beyond that debate to a solution that may lie elsewhere in the legal or social sphere? Surely, these significant instances of discrimination and the many more they represent are not simply a byproduct of unconstitutional behavior unworthy of separate attention. In fact, some instances of discrimination are facilitated by conduct that is constitutional. In order to be properly addressed, this discrimination must be considered in its context, which may necessarily implicate behavior that has constitutional significance, but it must also be looked at for what it is—discrimination and harassment of an outgroup based on differences that are called to people's attention and exacerbated by practices in the public schools. Given the nature of religious tension, peer pressure, social stigma, ingroup-outgroup dynamics, and the clash between pluralism and those fighting to hold onto what they see as the core values of society, this dynamic should not be surprising.

In this book, I have attempted to demonstrate the factors underlying discrimination caused or facilitated by public school religious exercises and through the anecdotal and historical evidence presented in Chapter One to show that this is a problem that is neither new nor old. Rather it is a manifestation of the age-old problem of factions, with the more dominant faction in certain locales using its power to enforce its will and cast negative attention on those who are different or who object to the majority's attempts to use the public schools to reinforce its message or beliefs.

An additional concern results from the dearth of social science research into this problem. Given the fact that much of the activity giving rise to this dynamic is both unconstitutional and taking place behind school doors, as well as the fact that the phenomenon itself is rarely acknowledged, it is hard to blame social scientists for this. Still, the research on religious discrimination, ingroup-outgroup dynamics, and peer pressure among children and adolescents provides a great deal of useful information for anyone wishing to delve into this issue. Moreover, the increased brazenness with which school districts are willing to engage in the types of activities that facilitate discrimination could help researchers to identify potential subjects and environments within which to study the phenomenon.

As a legal scholar looking at the dynamics of this issue, the benefits to social science research in this area are clearly apparent to me. Before one can walk, one must crawl, and in any fight to gain proper attention for this problem broader social data would be an invaluable tool. I hope that this book has achieved its goals of identifying the problem, demonstrating that in the current sociopolitical climate it is likely to get worse, contextualizing it as a separate concern from the traditional constitutional issues generally focused upon in "school prayer" cases, and showing that antidiscrimination law could be useful to provide a legal remedy for the injury caused by this kind of discrimination.

There are many cases in which a practice meant to inject religious values into public education ends up separating out religious minorities and objectors for discrimination, harassment, or other harm. Unfortunately, those who are most involved in the fight to bring prayer and other religious exercises back into the public schools do not appear particularly sensitive to the needs of religious minorities and objectors. They are fighting for a holy cause, one that leaves little room for redressing the needs of those most opposed to, or negatively affected by, their policies and politics.

Since constitutional law involving the separation of church and state is in a constant state of flux, and there are organizations and school districts pushing the envelope between constitutional private religious expression and unconstitutional public religious expression in the public schools, there is no way to gauge for sure what will be precluded by constitutional mandate. Even when practices are deemed unconstitutional, many school districts choose not to follow constitutional mandates despite Supreme Court decisions requiring compliance.[5]

Only by directly addressing the discrimination issue and recognizing the nexus between it and the religious exercises and environments that facilitate it can we begin to see change or at least appropriate legal mechanisms in regard to this problem. Providing remedies for those who suffer discrimination as a result of religious activity in the public schools based on the discrimination itself will help religious minorities and dissenters gain protection and attention to their plight. Fortunately, the same statutory provisions that could provide such protection could potentially serve as prophylactic measures, causing schools and local governments to implement policies in a more sensitive and nondiscriminatory fashion.

Regardless of the majority's support for religious exercises in the public schools, injury is frequently inflicted on religious minorities and objectors when such activity occurs. In the words of the Reverend James Forbes, "I believe that no government should ever inflict suffering upon the religious minority."[6] Hopefully, there will come a time when no government does. Unfortunately, given the current state of affairs, that time seems a long way off.

I am reminded of an exchange between the primary characters in Jerome Lawrence and Robert E. Lee's play, *Inherit the Wind,* which was loosely based on the famous "Scopes Monkey Trial" of 1925.[7] In that exchange, the fundamentalist lawyer, Matthew Harrison Brady, whose character is based on William Jennings Bryant is being cross-examined as a witness by Henry Drummond, whose character is based on Clarence Darrow. The exchange develops as follows:

Brady: We must not abandon faith! Faith is the important thing!

Drummond: Then why did God plague us with the power to think? Mr. Brady, why do you deny the one faculty which lifts man above all other creatures on the earth: the power of his brain to reason? What other merit have we? The elephant is larger, the horse is stronger and swifter, the butterfly more beautiful, the mosquito more prolific, even the simple sponge is more durable! Or does a sponge think?

Brady: I don't know. I'm a man, not a sponge.

Drummond: Do you think a sponge thinks?

Brady: If the Lord wishes a sponge to think, it thinks.

Drummond: Does a man have the same privileges that a sponge does?

Brady: Of course.

Drummond: This man wishes to be accorded the same privilege as a sponge! He wishes to think!

Brady: But your client is wrong! He is deluded! He has lost his way!

> *Drummond:* It's sad that we aren't all gifted with your positive knowledge
> of right and wrong, Mr. Brady [emphasis and stage directions omitted].[8]

Long before the 1990s, we won the same rights as the sponge in this clever exchange of dialogue. However, in some schools students in the religious minority or those who object to the institutionalization of the majority's religious practices are persecuted for exercising their rights or simply for being different. This persecution is not ordinarily caused by a specific law as in the Scopes trial, but by those with whom the students must interact on a regular basis: their classmates, neighbors, and teachers. I continue to hear that child's voice as he is tormented by those around him: "Please, somebody make it stop." Before we can, we have to focus on "it."

Notes

Chapter 1

1. 330 U.S. 1 (1947)(despite utilizing this phrase, the Court held that tax dollars could be used to subsidize bus fares for parochial school students as part of a program that did the same for students attending public and nonparochial private schools).
2. The *Everson* court, which brought the term "separation of church and state" into common parlance, in turn cited the earlier case of Reynolds v. United States, 98 U.S. 145, 164 (1879), which borrowed the phrase from the writings of Thomas Jefferson. Specifically, Jefferson used it in a letter he wrote to the Danbury Baptist Association, in which he stated: ". . . I contemplate with sovereign reverance that act of the whole American People which declared that their legislature should 'make no law respecting the establishment of religion, or prohibiting the free exercise thereof,' thus building a wall of separation between church and state." Edwin S. Gaustad, SWORN ON THE ALTAR OF GOD: A RELIGIOUS BIOGRAPHY OF THOMAS JEFFERSON (Eerdmans 1996) at 98–99. In this letter, Jefferson offered his understanding of what the religion clauses of the First Amendment meant. *Id.* More recently, the Court has questioned the accuracy of this metaphor in describing the "practical aspects of the relationship that in fact exists between church and state," while acknowledging it is "a useful figure of speech." Lynch v. Donnelly, 465 U.S. 668, 672 (1984).
3. 374 U.S. 203 (1963).
4. 370 U.S. 421 (1962).
5. For the sake of consistency and ease of reading, I use the phrase "public schools" throughout this book, since it is commonly used today. However,

in the early period of public education, these schools were sometimes called "common schools," since the Common School Movement was a driving force in support of public education at that time. That movement did support a nonsectarian Protestant religious foundation for state-sponsored schools, but the movement arose at a time when virtually everyone who would attend was Protestant. Lloyd P. Jorgenson, THE STATE AND THE NON-PUBLIC SCHOOL, 1825–1925 (Univ. of Missouri Press 1987). As Catholic immigration increased, the Protestant orientation of the movement and the schools heightened tensions between Protestants and Catholics. *Id.* In writing about the historical incidents described in the first part of this chapter, I use the phrase "public schools" to refer to the "common schools" as well.

6. Jorgenson, THE STATE AND THE NON-PUBLIC SCHOOL at 76–83; Vincent J. Lannie and Bernard C. Deithorn, *For the Honor and Glory of God: The Philadelphia Bible Riots of [1844]*, 8 HIST. OF EDUC. QUART. 45 (1968)(the date was originally misprinted as "1840" and was corrected in a later issue).

7. *See* James Hennesey, AMERICAN CATHOLICS: A HISTORY OF THE ROMAN CATHOLIC COMMUNITY IN THE UNITED STATES (Oxford Univ. Press 1981) at 117–118 (hereinafter AMERICAN CATHOLICS); Jorgenson, THE STATE AND THE NON-PUBLIC SCHOOL.

8. Hennesey, AMERICAN CATHOLICS at 117–118.

9. Jorgenson, THE STATE AND THE NON-PUBLIC SCHOOL at 23–30, 69–110.

10. *Id.* at 23–28.

11. *See generally* Michael Feldberg, THE PHILADELPHIA RIOTS OF 1844: A STUDY IN ETHNIC CONFLICT (Greenwood Press 1975)(hereinafter PHILADELPHIA RIOTS)(Feldberg acknowledges the role of the bible dispute in sparking the May riots, but also places those riots within the broader ethnic and socio-economic clashes between "natives" and "immigrants").

12. Jorgenson, THE STATE AND THE NON-PUBLIC SCHOOL at 28–30; *see also* Leo Pfeffer, GOD, CAESAR AND THE CONSTITUTION (Beacon Press 1975) at 174–175.

13. Jorgenson, THE STATE AND THE NON-PUBLIC SCHOOL at 72–83; Hennessey, AMERICAN CATHOLICS at 122–124; Pfeffer, GOD, CAESAR AND THE CONSTITUTION at 174–176.

14. Pfeffer, GOD, CAESAR AND THE CONSTITUTION at 174–178. Of course, as is the case today, there were some communities that rose above such behavior.

15. James Madison, "Federalist No. 10," in THE FEDERALIST PAPERS (Clinton Rossiter ed., Penguin Books 1961); *see also infra* note 52.

16. Jorgenson, THE STATE AND THE NON-PUBLIC SCHOOL at 83–85.

17. Pfeffer, GOD, CAESAR AND THE CONSTITUTION at 176–179.

18. Hennesey, AMERICAN CATHOLICS at 125. Father John Bapst, the priest

involved in the incident, later became the first president of Boston College. However, the incident continued to haunt him, eventually causing him to be placed in an asylum. As a result of the incident, he "would wake up screaming that attackers were climbing through his window." *Id.*

19. Lannie and Deithorn, *supra* note 6, at 103–104; Jorgenson, THE STATE AND THE NON-PUBLIC SCHOOL at 82–83. Many of those killed were Protestant nativists who were shot while attacking Catholic homes and churches. *Id.*

20. Jorgenson, THE STATE AND THE NON-PUBLIC SCHOOL at 81–83; Feldberg, PHILADELPHIA RIOTS.

21. Jorgenson, THE STATE AND THE NON-PUBLIC SCHOOL at 81–82.

22. *Id.* at 76–80; Hennesey, AMERICAN CATHOLICS at 122.

23. Pfeffer, GOD, CAESAR AND THE CONSTITUTION at 174–175; Hennesey, AMERICAN CATHOLICS at 116–127; *see generally* the discussion of nativism and the Know Nothing Party in Jorgenson, THE STATE AND THE NON-PUBLIC SCHOOL.

24. Jorgenson, THE STATE AND THE NON-PUBLIC SCHOOL at 28–30.

25. *Id.* at 28–30, 69–83. We see a similar phenomenon today in the push by the Christian Right to make the public schools a venue for the assertion of their values and beliefs. *See infra* Chapter Two; *see also* Matthew C. Moen, SCHOOL PRAYER AND THE POLITICS OF LIFE-STYLE CONCERN, 65 SOC. SCI. QUART. 1065 (1984)(casting the school prayer debate as a clash between a group of traditionalists trying to reinstate prayer as an affirmation of their once dominant values and modernists seeking affirmation of their contemporary values).

26. *See infra* Chapter Two.

27. *Id.;* Moen, *supra* note 25.

28. This is discussed in greater depth in Chapter Two.

29. This was also said of the public schools. Jorgenson, THE STATE AND THE NON-PUBLIC SCHOOL at 78–80.

30. Pat Robertson, THE TURNING TIDE (Word Publishing 1993). Of course, Pat Robertson is just one prominent example of those making this claim. *See* Chapter Two.

31. *See, e.g.,* Lee v. Weisman, 505 U.S. 577 (1992); *Schempp,* 374 U.S. 203; *Vitale,* 370 U.S. 421.

32. *See* Chapter Three for a more detailed discussion. It is significant that while moments of silence can sometimes be constitutional, such laws are very hard to apply in a neutral fashion in the classroom. Douglas Laycock, *Equal Access and Moments of Silence: The Equal Status of Religious Speech By Private Speakers,* 81 Nw. U.L. REV. 1, 57–58 (1986).

33. Steven B. Epstein, *Rethinking the Constitutionality of Ceremonial Deism,* 96 COLUM. L. REV. 2083, 2169–2171 (1996)(hereinafter *Ceremonial Deism*); Nadine Strossen, *How Much God in the Schools? A Discussion of Religion's*

Role in the Classroom, 4 Wм. & Mary Bill of Rights J. 607, 610–616 (1995) (hereinafter *How Much God in the Schools?*).

34. Compare *Lee*, 505 U.S. 577, and Illinois *ex rel*. McCollum v. Board of Education, 333 U.S. 203 (1948), *with* Strossen, How Much God in the Schools? at 617 and Epstein, Ceremonial Deism at 2170–2171.

35. Strossen, How Much God in the Schools? at 616.

36. Religious Liberty: Hearings before the Senate Judiciary Committee, 104th Cong., 1st Sess. S521–17 (Tuesday, September 12, 1995)(prepared testimony of Lisa Herdahl)(hereinafter Testimony of Lisa Herdahl before the Senate Judiciary Committee).

37. *60 Minutes, Profile: Lisa Herdahl v. Pontotoc County; Mother Sues Public School Over Prayer* (transcript of program aired Sunday, June 16, 1996); Gina Holland, *Judge Rules Out Prayer in School*, Cleveland Plain Dealer, June 4, 1996; Tom McNichol and Debbie Rossell, *A Town Divided by Prayer*, USA Weekend, May 21, 1995.

38. *60 Minutes, Profile: Lisa Herdahl vs. Pontotoc County; a Mother of Six Fights School Prayer in North Pontotoc County, Mississippi* (transcript of program aired Sunday, August 13, 1995).

39. *Id.; see also* Testimony of Lisa Herdahl before the Senate Judiciary Committee.

40. *Id.*

41. *Id.*

42. Testimony of Lisa Herdahl before the Senate Judiciary Committee.

43. *Id.*

44. *See* Holland, *Judge Rules Out Prayer in School*.

45. Testimony of Lisa Herdahl before the Senate Judiciary Committee.

46. Epstein, Ceremonial Deism at 2169–2171.

47. *Complaint of Paul Michael Herring, et al.*, in Paul Michael Herring v. Dr. John Key, Superintendent of Pike County Schools (filed in U.S. Dist. Ct., M.D. Ala., North. Div., on August 4, 1997); *Declaration Under Penalty of Perjury of Sue C. Willis* (filed with the complaint as Exhibit "C"); Jay Reeves, *Jewish Family Sues Public School*, Assoc. Press (August 1997). As the above citation suggests, the case was filed as Paul Michael Herring v. Dr. John Key, Superintendent of Pike County Schools. The Herring children's mother is remarried and uses the last name Willis. The children filed suit by and through their stepfather, Wayne Willis, and their mother, Sue Willis.

48. At the time of this writing, the case is still ongoing, and thus the incidents mentioned are allegations. However, several of the more significant allegations are corroborated by evidence such as school documents. *See Complaint of Paul Michael Herring, et al.*, Exhibit "A" (letter from Superintendent John R. Key to Sue Willis dated June 18, 1997).

49. *Declaration Under Penalty of Perjury of Sue C. Willis* in Paul Michael Herring v. Dr. John Key, Superintendent of Pike County Schools at 3.
50. *Id.* at 4.
51. *Id.* at 12.
52. This is compelling since everyone is essentially a religious minority somewhere in the United States and could be subject to the types of discrimination discussed in this book. Yet, when a faction that is a minority elsewhere is the majority in a particular location there is a tendency to try to impose its majoritarian norms on the religious minorities in that locale. This situation lends a certain amount of support to James Madison's words concerning factionalism, immortalized in the FEDERALIST PAPERS:

    A zeal for differing opinions concerning religion . . . and many other points . . . have, in turn, divided mankind into parties, inflamed them with mutual animosity, and rendered them much more disposed to vex and oppress each other than to co-operate for their common good.

    James Madison, "Federalist No. 10," *supra* note 15. He wrote this in the context of the innate problems that arise when a majoritarian faction has unchecked power and interests different from those of minorities. *Id.*
53. Bauchman v. West High School, 906 F.Supp. 1483 (D. Utah 1995); Bauchman by and through Bauchman v. West High School, 900 F.Supp. 248 and 900 F.Supp. 254 (D. Utah 1995), *aff'd,* 132 F.3d 532 (10th Cir. 1997).
54. *Id.*
55. *Id.*
56. *Id.*; Lisa Ness Seidman, Note, *Religious Music in the Public Schools: Music to Establishment Clause Ears?* 65 GEO. WASH. L. REV. 466, 467 (1997).
57. *Id.* Bauchman, 900 F.Supp. 254.
58. *Student Pursues Case,* FORWARD, May 31, 1996, at 2.
59. *Student Pursues Case,* FORWARD, May 31, 1996.
60. Bauchman v. West High School, 132 F.3d 542 (10th Cir. 1997); *id.* at 562 (Murphy dissenting).
61. *Bauchman,* 132 F.3d at 556.
62. Bell v. Little Axe Independent School Dist. No. 70, 766 F.2d 1391, 1396–1398 (10th Cir. 1985); *see also America's Constitutional Heritage: Religion and Our Public Schools* at 5–7 (transcript of a video presentation by the ACLU—transcript available via the Internet at <http://www.aclu.org/issues/religion/arrf.html>)(hereinafter *America's Constitutional Heritage*).
63. *Id.*
64. *America's Constitutional Heritage* at 5.

65. *Bell,* 766 F.2d at 1397; *America's Constitutional Heritage.*
66. *Bell,* 766 F.2d at 1391.
67. *Id.,* at 1397.
68. *America's Constitutional Heritage* at 6.
69. *Id.; see also Bell,* 766 F.2d at 1397.
70. *Bell,* 766 F.2d at 1397.
71. *Id.*
72. *Id.*
73. *America's Constitutional Heritage* at 6; *Bell,* 766 F.2d at 1397.
74. *Bell,* 766 F.2d at 1397; *America's Constitutional Heritage* at 5.
75. *Id.*
76. *America's Constitutional Heritage* at 5–6.
77. See *Bell,* 766 F.2d at 1398–1399; *America's Constitutional Heritage* at 5–7.
78. *America's Constitutional Heritage* at 6.
79. *Id.*
80. See *Bell,* 766 F.2d at 1408.
81. See *Bell,* 766 F.2d at 1408–1413. The court did acknowledge that these damages should not require proof of consequential harm and may necessarily require a presumption of damages. *Id.* The issue of damages in cases brought to vindicate constitutional rights is a complex one and is discussed in greater depth in Chapter Seven. The *Bell* decision is not determinative of that issue.
82. An excellent example of this is provided by the experiments described in William Peters, A CLASS DIVIDED THEN AND NOW (Yale Univ. Press 1987), and A CLASS DIVIDED (Doubleday 1971); *see also* Charles J. Russo and David L. Gregory, *The Return of School Prayer: Reflections on the Libertarian-Conservative Dilemma,* 20 J. OF LAW & EDUC. 167 (1991); Gary B. Melton, *Populism, School Prayer and the Courts: Confessions of an Expert Witness,* NEW DIRECTIONS IN CHILD DEVELOPMENT No. 33 p. 63 (1986); Brown, Clasen & Eicher, *Perceptions of Peer Pressure, Peer Conformity Dispositions, and Self Reported Behavior among Adolescents,* 22 DEVEL. PSYCH. 521 (1986); Britain, *Adolescent Choices and Parent-Peer Cross-Pressures,* 28 AM. SOCIOL. REV. 385 (1983); and *see generally* D. N. Ruble, A. K. Boggiano, N. S. Feldman, and J. H. Loebl, *Developmental Analysis of the Role of Social Comparison in Self Evaluation,* 16 DEVEL. PSYCH. 105 (1980); W. G. Stephen and C. W. Stephen, *Intergroup Anxiety,* 41 J. OF SOCIAL ISSUES 157 (1995); Stanley Coopersmith, THE ANTECEDENTS OF SELF-ESTEEM (Freeman 1967); Erving Goffman, STIGMA: NOTES ON THE MANAGEMENT OF SPOILED IDENTITY (Prentice-Hall 1963).
83. Walter v. West Virginia Board of Education, 610 F.Supp. 1169 (W.D. Va. 1985); Melton, POPULISM, SCHOOL PRAYER AND THE COURTS: CONFESSIONS OF AN EXPERT WITNESS.

84. *Walter,* 610 F.Supp. 1169.
85. *See* Melton, POPULISM, SCHOOL PRAYER AND THE COURTS: CONFESSIONS OF AN EXPERT WITNESS at 65.
86. *Id.*
87. *Walter,* 610 F. Supp. at 1172.
88. *Id.* at 1173.
89. *See* the discussion of the *Bell, Bauchman,* and *Herdahl* cases in this chapter.
90. Epstein, CEREMONIAL DEISM at 2169, 2171; Strossen, HOW MUCH GOD IN THE SCHOOLS? at 610, 616.
91. FORWARD, May 13, 1996, at 1, 12.
92. 333 U.S. 203 (1948).
93. Epstein, CEREMONIAL DEISM at 2170.
94. *Id.* (citing Vashti Cromwell McCollum, ONE WOMAN'S FIGHT 95 (Beacon Press rev. ed. 1961)).
95. *Id.*
96. 505 U.S. 577 (1992).
97. Strossen, HOW MUCH GOD IN THE SCHOOLS? at 617.
98. Doe v. Duncanville Indep. School Dist., 994 F.2d 160, 162–164 (5th Cir. 1993).
99. *Lee,* 505 U.S. at 606–607 (Blackmun concurring).
100. *Id.* at 607 (citing Engel v. Vitale, 370 U.S. at 429).
101. *Lee,* 505 U.S. at 607 fn. 10 (Blackmun concurring).
102. RELIGIOUS LIBERTY: HEARINGS BEFORE THE SENATE JUDICIARY COMMITTEE, 104th Cong., 1st Sess. S521-17 (Tuesday, September 12, 1995)(prepared testimony of Reverend James Forbes).
103. *Id.*
104. *Id.*
105. *Id.*

Chapter 2

1. Polls since the 1960s have consistently shown that a majority of Americans support public school prayer. *See* George H. Gallup, Jr., RELIGION IN AMERICA 1996 at 75 (1996)(71 percent of those responding to a 1995 poll supported a constitutional amendment allowing prayer in the schools); THE GALLUP REPORT NO. 217, at 17–19 (1983)(81 percent of respondents to a 1983 poll who were aware of a proposed constitutional amendment to permit voluntary school prayer then pending favored that amendment); 1 G. Gallup, THE GALLUP POLL: PUBLIC OPINION 1972–1977, at 503 (1978)(77 percent of respondents to a 1975 poll favored a constitutional amendment to permit public school prayer); 3 G. Gallup, THE GALLUP

POLL: PUBLIC OPINION 1935–1971, at 1779 (1972)(79 percent of respondents to a 1962 poll approved of religious exercises in the public schools). While these polls indicate that over 70 percent of the population would appear to support some form of school prayer and a constitutional amendment to allow it, many Americans do not support the Christian Right's agenda in other areas. *See generally* Ted Jelen and Clyde Wilcox, AMERICAN POLITICAL INSTITUTIONS AND PUBLIC POLICY: PUBLIC ATTITUDES TOWARD CHURCH AND STATE (M.E. Sharpe 1995).

2. Numerous quotes throughout this chapter from leading figures in these organizations demonstrate this claim. Moreover, the agenda of this movement, also addressed in this chapter, says as much quite directly.

3. For example, Jerry Falwell has written: "I hope to see the day when, as in the early days of our country, we won't have any public schools. The churches will have taken them over again, and Christians will be running them." David Cantor, THE RELIGIOUS RIGHT: THE ASSAULT ON TOLERANCE & PLURALISM IN AMERICA (Anti-Defamation League, Alan M. Schwartz ed., 1994)(hereinafter THE RELIGIOUS RIGHT) at 6 (quoting Jerry Falwell in AMERICA CAN BE SAVED (Sword of the Lord 1979)).

4. Perhaps the best way to see this effort is to read the literature distributed by Christian Right organizations. In regard to influencing school policy, of all the materials I have read, I have found the PRESIDENT'S REPORTS and other literature from Citizens for Excellence in Education to be the most instructive, primarily because their sole focus is on education.

5. James C. Schott, *Holy Wars in Education,* 47 EDUCAT. LEADERSHIP 61 (Oct. 1989)(hereinafter *Holy Wars*); Zita Arocha, *The Religious Right's into Public Schools,* 50 SCHOOL ADMINISTRATOR 8 (Oct. 1993)(hereinafter *Religious Right's*); Dan Nasman, *Combatting the Religious Right in San Diego County,* 50 SCHOOL ADMINISTRATOR 28 (Oct. 1993)(hereinafter *Combatting*).

6. Schott, *Holy Wars;* Arocha, *Religious Right's;* Nasman, *Combatting. See also* Robert L. Simonds, *Citizens for Excellence in Education,* 50 SCHOOL ADMINISTRATOR 19 (Oct. 1993)(founder of several Christian Right school action groups describes organizations and successes).

7. For example, the Christian Coalition promotes leadership training seminars and other materials on starting and maintaining a grassroots campaign. Janet L. Jones, *Targets of the Right: Public Schools—and School Boards—Are Under Attack from the Religious Right,* AMER. SCH. BD. J. (April 1993)(hereinafter *Targets*) at 22, 26.

8. *Id.*

9. Such tactics may also be disseminated to potential state and national leaders.

10. Rob Boston, *American Public Schools: Mission Field USA?,* 45 CHURCH &

STATE 8 (1994). Sekulow has also been quoted as saying, "Our public schools began as ministries of the church; now it is time to return them to the Lord." Terry Anderson, *The Religious Right Perils Our Freedoms,* BUF-FALO NEWS, Viewpoints, Sept. 7, 1995, at C3.

11. Cantor, THE RELIGIOUS RIGHT at 4.

12. Molly Ivins, *Faith Alive, Well in Public Discourse As Mohandas Gandhi Said, Those Who Believe That Religion and Politics Don't Mix Understand Neither,* FORT WORTH STAR-TELEGRAM, Sept. 14, 1993, at 21.

13. Cantor, THE RELIGIOUS RIGHT at 4.

14. Robert L. Simonds, CITIZENS FOR EXCELLENCE IN EDUCATION PRESI-DENT'S REPORT, March 1991.

15. Robert L. Simonds, HOW TO ELECT CHRISTIANS TO PUBLIC OFFICE (CEE 1985).

16. Robert L. Simonds, CITIZENS FOR EXCELLENCE IN EDUCATION PRESI-DENT'S REPORT, January 1997.

17. Robert L. Simonds, CITIZENS FOR EXCELLENCE IN EDUCATION PRESI-DENT'S REPORT, May 1997.

18. M. G. "Pat" Robertson, *Religion in the Classroom,* 4 WM. & MARY BILL OF RTS. J. 595, 601–602 (1995).

19. 1988 Concerned Women for America fundraising letter cited in Cantor, THE RELIGIOUS RIGHT at 5.

20. Susan Yoachum, *Powerhouse behind Lobbying Effort for "Traditional Values" Reverend Sheldon Says Political Clout Comes from Grass-Roots Support,* SAN FRANCISCO CHRONIC., Sept. 13, 1993, at A7.

21. *Id.*

22. John W. Whitehead, THE SEPARATION ILLUSION: A LAWYER EXAMINES THE FIRST AMENDMENT (Mott Media 1977)(hereinafter ILLUSION).

23. *See generally* John W. Whitehead, RELIGIOUS APARTHEID: THE SEPARATION OF RELIGION FROM AMERICAN PUBLIC LIFE (Moody Press 1994)(herein-after APARTHEID); John W. Whitehead, THE RIGHTS OF RELIGIOUS PER-SONS IN PUBLIC EDUCATION, rev. ed. (Crossway Books 1994). While I found the comparison between apartheid and the application of Establish-ment Clause doctrines to evangelical Christians to be offensive, the gen-eral tone of these books is more theological and legal than it is inflamma-tory—although one can certainly find disagreement with both the legal and religious positions taken.

24. Whitehead, ILLUSION at 115. Though writing from a perspective very different than Whitehead's, Stephen Feldman, in his fascinating book, PLEASE DON'T WISH ME A MERRY CHRISTMAS: A CRITICAL HISTORY OF THE SEPARATION OF CHURCH AND STATE (NYU Press 1997), suggests that the First Amendment religion clauses support Christian dominance. He suggests that the religion clauses were developed for, and reinforce, a soci-

ety that subordinates religious minorities to Christianity, that the separation of church and state was developed over time to benefit Christianity, and that in America it has historically benefited the Protestant majority. Of course, the conceptual framework underlying Feldman's position, as well as his discussion and approach to Christian dominance, is quite different from Whitehead's. The issues raised in this book, as well as some of the cases discussed in Chapter Three (particularly those upholding "voluntary, student-initiated prayer" and other religious practices in the public sphere), lend some support to Feldman's position.

25. Whitehead, APARTHEID at 146.
26. Cantor, THE RELIGIOUS RIGHT at 6.
27. Cantor, THE RELIGIOUS RIGHT at 6 (citing WASHINGTON POST); UPI, *Rulings "Not Law of the Land" Robertson Says,* LOS ANGELES TIMES, June 18, 1986 at Part 1, Page 2.
28. Statement by Reverend Donald Wildmon cited in Peggy Landers, *Preacher Blames Church for "Mess," Says Moral Decay Threatens Humanity,* MIAMI HERALD, November 16, 1993 at BR1, BR4.
29. Connie Page, *Watch the Right: The Amazing Rise of Beverly LaHaye,* Ms. MAGAZINE, Feb. 1987, at 24, 26 (citing an op-ed piece LaHaye wrote that appeared in USA TODAY).
30. Ralph Reed, executive director of the Christian Coalition, *Religious News Service* (May 15, 1990) cited in Cantor, THE RELIGIOUS RIGHT at 5.
31. Maralee Schwartz and Paul Taylor, *Ex-Candidate Robertson Creates New Christian Political Group,* WASHINGTON POST, March 14, 1990, at A6.
32. From Americans United for Separation of Church and State, *News Backgrounder, Pat Robertson's Game Plan: Sept. 13 Speech to Christian Coalition Leaders at the "Road to Victory" Conference in Atlanta* (Sept. 1997)(transcript excerpts from a tape of the address obtained by Americans United for Separation of Church and State).
33. National Committee for Responsive Philanthropy (Winter 1990) cited in People for the American Way, *Fact Sheet on the Free Congress Foundation* (July 1996).
34. Statement by Reverend Louis Sheldon on *CNN News* (Sept. 2, 1990)(also included in PFAW fact sheet on the Traditional Values Coalition).
35. Schott, *Holy Wars* at 62.
36. *Id.;* Arocha, *Religious Right's* at 19; Jones, *Targets* at 26; Kathleen Vail, *Conservatively Speaking: What Does the Christian Coalition Want for U.S. Schools? More Vouchers, More Phonics, and More Conservative School Board Members,* AM. SCHOOL BD. J. 30, 31 (Dec. 1995)(hereinafter *Conservatively Speaking*); *Religious-Right School-Board Takeovers Haven't Got a Prayer—Or Have They?* EDUC. DIGEST (March 1994)(hereinafter *Takeovers*) at 23 (from 78 AMER TEACH. 7); Nasman, *Combatting* at 28.

37. In a recent CEE PRESIDENT's REPORT Robert L. Simonds wrote:

> CEE Chapters are cooperating with all of our other Christian/conservative groups in the "common" cause. Cooperation between Concerned Women for America (CWA), Eagle Forum (EF), Focus on the Family (FOF), Family Research Council, and Christian Coalition (CC) has never been better. Christian Coalition caught up with Citizens for Excellence in Education this year, in the number of chapters (2,000) and went past us (CEE now has 1,700 chapters). Robert L. Simonds, CITIZENS FOR EXCELLENCE IN EDUCATION PRESIDENT's REPORT, November 1996.

38. *See* James Davison Hunter, CULTURE WARS (Basic Books 1991) at 141–142.

39. For example, if one looks at the literature of groups like People for the American Way or Americans United for Separation of Church and State, which frequently oppose the Christian Right agenda in the political and legal arenas with some success, it is clear that these organizations understand that they are dealing with an opponent that must be taken seriously. Likewise, the literature from the Christian Right reflects a serious belief that its opponents can affect policy.

40. The data on the organizations cited in this paragraph come from materials prepared by People for the American Way based on the literature and public tax filings of these groups. The figures for 1997–1998 may vary from those cited herein, but the figures included in this book provide a gauge for the size, resources, and sophistication of these groups as of a few years ago. Most of the groups have been growing, and current figures are probably higher. The Christian Coalition has faced a falloff in receipts recently, however, most likely due to the shuffle in leadership. Ruth Marcus, *Christian Coalition Considers Changes for Direct Political Activity*, WASHINGTON POST, Jan. 9, 1998, at A4 (noting decline in receipts from the record receipts the coalition received in 1996). One can keep abreast of the growth of these organizations (at least of their self-proclaimed figures) by writing and obtaining literature from them (this may require a fee). Funding and membership updates are sometimes provided in this literature. For example, Citizens for Excellence in Education and the National Association for Christian Educators publish the bimonthly EDUCATION NEWSLINE and regular issues of the PRESIDENT's REPORT written by Robert Simonds, CEE's president.

41. Data obtained from People for the American Way referred to in the preceding note.

42. *Id.*

43. *Id.*

44. *Id.*

45. *Id.*

46. *Id.*

47. *Id.*

48. *Id.*

49. *See, e.g.,* articles cited *supra* note 36; *infra* notes 50–54, 60–62, and accompanying text.

50. Articles cited *supra* note 36.

51. *Id.*

52. *Takeovers* at 25; Nasman, *Combatting* at 28; Josh Barbanel, *Fernandez Urges Scrutiny of Conservatives,* NEW YORK TIMES, April 22, 1993, at B1.

53. *Takeovers* at 25; Nasman, *Combatting;* Barbanel, *Fernandez Urges Scrutiny of Conservatives* at B1.

54. Vail, *Conservatively Speaking* at 32.

55. Jim Impoco, *Second Thoughts on Vista: Separating Church and School,* U.S. NEWS & WORLD REP., April 24, 1995, at 30 (hereinafter *Second Thoughts*); Seth Mydans, *A School Board in California Makes Room for Creationism,* NEW YORK TIMES, Aug. 14, 1993, at A1 (hereinafter *Makes Room*).

56. Nasman, *Combatting* at 28.

57. People for the American Way, THE RELIGIOUS RIGHT AND SCHOOL BOARDS 1992 AND 1993: EXECUTIVE SUMMARY, Nov. 1993, at 8, 10.

58. Stryker McGuire, *When Fundamentalists Run the Schools,* NEWSWEEK, Nov. 8, 1993, at 46; Impoco, *Second Thoughts* at 30; Mydans, *Makes Room* at A1; Seth Mydans, *Political Proving Ground for the Christian Right,* NEW YORK TIMES, Feb. 20, 1993, at A1 (hereinafter *Proving Ground*).

59. Impoco, *Second Thoughts* at 30; Mydans, *Proving Ground* at A1.

60. Barry M. Horstman, *Crusade for Public Office in 2nd Stage Politics: Emboldened By Victories in Low-Profile Races, Religious Fundamentalists Take Aim at Higher Posts, Intending to Govern by Biblical Principles. But Opponents Say Their Tactics are Often Anything but Christian,* LOS ANGELES TIMES, March 22, 1992, at 1 Metro, Part B1.

61. Mark O'Keefe, *Robertson's Phone Corps Boosted GOP: Local Democrats Claim Network Ambushed Them,* NORFOLK VIRGINIAN-PILOT, Nov. 9, 1991, at A1.

62. For the discovery of, and effective responses to, stealth tactics by opponents of the Christian Right, *see id.;* Impoco, *Second Thoughts;* Nasman, *Combatting;* Arocha, *Religious Right's* at 12–15. For the renouncing of stealth tactics, *see* Cantor, THE RELIGIOUS RIGHT at 20 (noting that the Christian Coalition publicly renounced stealth tactics).

63. Impoco, *Second Thoughts* at 30.

64. Vail, *Conservatively Speaking* at 30.

65. *Id.*

66. Mydans, *Proving Ground* at A1.

67. Arocha, *Religious Right's* at 11.

68. *See* Nasman, *Combatting* at 30 (regarding use of term "intelligent design theory"); CEE PRESIDENT'S REPORTS, *supra* notes 14, 16, 17 (examples of some of the other Christian Right rhetoric). Carefully watching *The 700 Club* or other Christian Right broadcasts or reading their literature in regard to public schools frequently provides excellent examples of this type of rhetoric.

69. *Pat Robertson's Perspective* (Oct.–Nov. 1992), cited in Cantor, THE RELIGIOUS RIGHT at 5.

70. Gallup polls, *supra* note 1.

71. Ruth Marcus, *Christian Coalition Considers Changes for Direct Political Activity,* WASHINGTON POST, Jan. 9, 1998, at A4 (generally dealing with the possibility that the Christian Coalition is considering creating a PAC).

72. Laurin Sellers, *Melbourne Mayor: Pray, Fast to End Abortion,* ORLANDO SENTINEL, Jan. 15, 1998, at D1.

73. *Id.*

74. Gwen Florio, *Battle Over the Bible Splits a New Mexico Community,* PHILADELPHIA INQUIRER, Feb. 28, 1998, at A1.

75. *Id.*

76. *Id.*

77. *Id.*

78. *Id.*

79. *Id.*

80. *Id.*

81. For example, despite protestations to the contrary by Jay Sekulow and others and despite attempts to resuscitate graduation prayer since the case was decided, Lee v. Weisman, 505 U.S. 577 (1992), was a significant defeat for the Christian Right legal agenda, as were the recent decisions by the Third Circuit Court of Appeals in ACLU of New Jersey v. Black Horse Pike Regional Bd. of Educ., 84 F.3d 1471 (3d Cir. 1996), and the Fifth Circuit Court of Appeals in Ingebretson v. Jackson Pub. Sch. Dist., 88 F.3d 274 (5th Cir. 1996).

82. *Lee,* 505 U.S. 577.

83. Jones v. Clear Creek Indep. School Dist., 977 F.2d 963 (5th Cir. 1992), *cert. denied,* 113 S.Ct. 2950 (1993)(*Jones II*); Adler v. Duval County School Bd., 852 F.Supp. 446 (M.D. Fla. 1994).

84. *Jones II,* 977 F.2d 963.

85. Stephen B. Pershing, *Graduation Prayer after Lee v. Weisman: A Cautionary Tale,* 46 MERCER L. REV. 1097, 1100–1101 (1995).

86. *Prayer at Public School Graduation: A Survey,* 75 PHI DELTA KAPPAN at 125 (Oct. 1993).

87. *Id.*

88. *Id.*
89. Pamela Coyle, *The Prayer Pendulum*, ABA JOURNAL (Jan. 1995) at 62, 63.
90. *Id.* at 65.
91. *Id.* at 63.
92. *Ingebretson*, 88 F.3d 274; Chandler v. James, 958 F.Supp. 1550 (M.D. Ala. 1997)(currently on appeal to the 11th Cir. Court of Appeals). These cases will be discussed in greater detail later in this book.
93. Gita M. Smith, *Alabama Nativity Scene Tests Limits: Governor Finds Room at Capitol for Manger*, ATLANTA J. CONST., Dec. 18, 1997; Kevin Sack, *In Alabama Schools, Prayer Is Protest: Students, Governor Fighting Injunction*, CINC. ENQ., Nov. 9, 1997, at A19.
94. Gita M. Smith, *Talk of the South Birmingham Governor's Bill of Rights Stand Stirs Amusement*, ATLANTA J. CONST., July 4, 1997, at A6 (hereinafter *Talk*); Kendal Weaver, *Alabama Puzzled by Its Governor: "Bizzare" View on Bill of Rights Is Latest*, ARIZ. REP., July 3, 1997, at B7 (hereinafter *Alabama Puzzled*).
95. Smith, *Talk*, at A6; Weaver, *Alabama Puzzled*, at B7.
96. John McClaslin, *Sekulow vs. Sam*, WASHINGTON TIMES, Dec. 15, 1997, at A5; Donald P. Baker, *Judge's "Prayer Police" Order Ignites Protest in Alabama Town*, WASHINGTON POST, Nov. 16, 1997, at A3.
97. *See* Robert E. Riggs, *Government Sponsored Prayer in the Classroom*, 18 DIA-LOGUE 43 (1985)(noting school prayer continues today despite being legally prohibited and that it does so in disregard of minority objections). Other demonstrations of this lack of empathy abound. In response to the situation in Truth or Consequences described earlier, Sierra County, New Mexico, Chairman Gary Whitehead was quoted as saying about his part in a proclamation encouraging the reading of the New Testament by citizens: "If I offended anyone, too bad." Steve Feldman, *Truth or Consequences: N.M. Town's "Year of the Bible" Raises 1st-Amendment Issues*, PHILA. JEWISH EXPON., Feb. 26, 1998. The quote from Pat Robertson, *supra* note 69, and accompanying text, also suggests that the feelings and concerns of those who oppose the agenda of the Christian Right are not likely to be highly regarded. The *Herdahl, Bauchman*, and *Walter* cases also reflect this likelihood.

Chapter 3

1. 20 U.S.C. §4071 *et seq.* (1984).
2. Some may also raise issues based on state constitutions and statutes. However, when a practice is challenged, the Constitution is usually at the center of the challenge.

3. School District of Abington Township v. Schempp, 374 U.S. 203, 218, 225–227 (1963); Everson v. Board of Educ. of Ewing Tp., 330 U.S. 1, 18 (1947); *See also* Rosenberger v. Rector and Visitors of the University of Virginia, 515 U.S. 819, 839–841 (1995)("A central lesson of our decisions is that a significant factor in upholding governmental programs in the face of Establishment Clause attack is their neutrality towards religion"). Of course, the concept of "neutrality" is not a simple one in its meaning, application, or relationship to the concept of church-state separation. There are several very interesting recent articles that address this, including: Douglas Laycock, *The Underlying Unity of Separation and Neutrality,* 46 EMORY L. J. 43 (1997); Carl H. Esbeck, *A Constitutional Case for Governmental Cooperation with Faith-Based Social Service Providers,* 46 EMORY L. J. 1 (1997); Ira C. Lupu, *The Lingering Death of Separationism,* 62 GEO. WASH. L. REV. 230 (1994); Douglas Laycock, *Formal, Substantive, and Disaggregated Neutrality Toward Religion,* 39 DEPAUL L. REV. 993 (1990). There are numerous other fascinating articles from a diversity of perspectives addressing the concept of "neutrality."

4. Hazelwood School District v. Kuhlmeier, 484 U.S. 260, 266–267 (1988); Tinker v. Des Moines Independent Community School Dist., 393 U.S. 503, 509–513 (1969).

5. Lemon v. Kurtzman, 403 U.S. 602 (1971).

6. *See supra* notes 3, 4, Chapter One.

7. Engel v. Vitale, 370 U.S. 421 (1962).

8. *Id.* at 422–423.

9. *Id.* at 430.

10. *Id.* at 421.

11. *Id.* at 429–430.

12. *Id.* at 430–431.

13. *Id.* at 436.

14. *Id.* at 431–433.

15. *Schempp,* 374 U.S. 203.

16. *Id.*

17. *Id.* at 222.

18. *Id.*

19. *Id.* at 223–224.

20. *Id.* at 221.

21. *Id.* at 223–225.

22. *Id.* at 224–225.

23. *Id.* at 225–226.

24. 374 U.S. at 222.

25. Lemon v. Kurtzman, 403 U.S. 602, 612–613 (1971).

26. County of Allegheny v. ACLU, 492 U.S. 573 (1989).

27. *Id.* at 594 (quoting Lynch v. Donnelly, 465 U.S. 668, 687 (1984)).
28. *Compare Lynch,* 465 U.S. at 690–691 (O'Connor concurring), and *Allegheny,* 492 U.S. at 631–632 (O'Connor concurring in part and concurring in the judgment).
29. *Allegheny,* 492 U.S. at 594 (quoting *Lynch,* 465 U.S. at 687).
30. *Allegheny,* 492 U.S. at 593; *see also* ACLU of New Jersey v. Black Horse Pike Regional Bd. of Educ., 84 F.3d 1471, 1485–1486 (3d. Cir. 1996) (hereinafter *Black Horse Pike*); Ingebretson v. Jackson Pub. Sch. Dist., 88 F.3d 274, 280 (5th Cir. 1996).
31. *Allegheny,* 492 U.S. at 632.
32. *Black Horse Pike,* 84 F.3d at 1485–1486. In *Black Horse Pike,* the court applied *Lemon,* the Coercion test, and the Endorsement test, but applied the latter test within the context of *Lemon,* acknowledging that the importance of the test is the same whether it is applied as part of the *Lemon* test or separately. *Id.*
33. Lee v. Weisman, 505 U.S. 577 (1992).
34. *Id.* at 586–587 and generally.
35. *Id.* at 586.
36. *Id.* at 581, 587.
37. *Id.* at 593–594.
38. *Id.* at 587.
39. *Id.* (quoting Lynch v. Donnelly, 465 U.S. at 678).
40. *Id.* at 588.
41. *Id.* at 591–593.
42. *Id.* at 593–594.
43. *Id.* at 594.
44. 505 U.S. 577 (1992).
45. Stephen B. Pershing, *Graduation Prayer After Lee v. Weisman: A Cautionary Tale,* 46 MERCER L. REV. 1097, 1100 (1995).
46. *Id.* at 1100–1101.
47. *Id.*
48. *Id.*
49. *Lee,* 505 U.S. at 595–596; *Everson,* 330 U.S. 1.
50. *Lee,* 505 U.S. 577.
51. 930 F.2d 416 (5th Cir. 1991)(*Jones I*), *vacated and remanded,* 505 U.S. 1215 (1992), *on remand,* 977 F.2d 963 (5th Cir. 1992)(*Jones II*), *cert. denied,* 508 U.S. 967 (1993). Unless otherwise specified in the text all references to the *Jones* case are to *Jones II.*
52. 930 F.2d 416 (5th Cir. 1991)(*Jones I*).
53. *Id.*
54. *See Jones II,* 977 F.2d at 964.
55. Jones v. Clear Creek Indep. Sch. Dist., 505 U.S. 1215 (1992); *Jones II,* 977 F.2d at 965.

56. *Jones II,* 977 F.2d 963.
57. *Id.* at 966.
58. *See, e.g., Black Horse Pike,* 84 F.3d 1471; *Harris v. Joint School District* No. 241, 41 F.3d 447 (9th Cir. 1994), *vacated as moot,* 515 U.S. 1154 (1994); Jonathan C. Drimmer, *Hear No Evil, Speak No Evil: The Duty of Public Schools to Limit Student-Proposed Graduation Prayers,* 74 NEB. L. REV. 411 (1995); E. Gregory Wallace, *When Government Speaks Religiously,* 21 FLA. ST. U. L. REV. 1186, 1261–1262 (1994).
59. *Jones II,* 977 F.2d at 966–968.
60. *Id.* at 968–969.
61. 496 U.S. 226 (1990).
62. 20 U.S.C. §4071 *et seq.*
63. *Mergens,* 496 U.S. at 250.
64. *Jones II,* 977 F.2d at 968–969.
65. *Id.* at 970.
66. *Id.* at 970–971.
67. *Id.* at 971.
68. *Id.* at 971–972.
69. *Id.* at 971.
70. *Id.* at 971.
71. *Jones II,* 911 F.2d 963.
72. *Id.*
73. Pershing, *supra* note 45, at 1100.
74. *Id.* at 1101.
75. *Gearon v. Loudoun County School Bd.,* 844 F.Supp. 1097 (E.D.Va. 1993).
76. *Id.*
77. 41 F.3d 447 (9th Cir. 1994), *vacated as moot,* 515 U.S. 1154 (1994).
78. *Black Horse Pike,* 84 F.3d 1471.
79. *Id.*
80. This means that all of the available Third Circuit Court of Appeals judges heard the case. The *Black Horse Pike* court consisted of thirteen judges. Of these, only four dissented from the majority decision. Of course, the dissent lends additional support to the holding in *Jones II. Black Horse Pike,* 84 F.3d at 1489 (Mansmann dissenting).
81. *Black Horse Pike,* 84 F.3d at 1474–1475.
82. *Id.* at 1475.
83. *Id.*
84. *Id.*
85. *Id.* at 1479.
86. *Id.* at 1480–1483.
87. *Id.* at 1478.
88. *Id.* at 1477–1478.
89. *Id.* at 1488.

90. *Id.* at 1484–1485.
91. *Id.* at 1485.
92. *Id.* at 1487.
93. *Id.*
94. *Id.* at 1487–1488.
95. *Id.* at 1488.
96. First, in *Lee,* the Supreme Court admonished that school officials should not be in the business of writing or dictating the nature of prayers. Lee v. Weisman, 505 U.S. 577 (1992). In fact, there would appear to be excessive government entanglement with religion when a school dictates the nature and substance of an allegedly student-initiated prayer. Therefore, the *Jones II* decision arguably would permit sectarian prayer, because if the students vote to have a speaker deliver a prayer at graduation the state might become too involved by censoring it. *See generally* Jay Sekulow, James Henderson, and John Tuskey, *Proposed Guidelines for Student Religious Speech and Observance in the Public Schools,* 46 MERCER L. REV. 1017 (1995).

Essentially, one could argue that *Jones II* allowed the prayer because it was not state action (since the students voted for it). Otherwise, the decision is even more ridiculous than it initially appears, because the only real dichotomy between it and *Lee* is that the majority of the senior class, as empowered by the school, voted whether or not to have a speaker and on who that speaker should be. Compare *Lee,* 505 U.S. 577 and *Jones II,* 977 F.2d 963. Thus, if it was deemed government action it would likely be unconstitutional under *Lee.*

The *Jones II* court's assertion that the situation there was different because those in the minority would understand that the prayer was the result of a democratic vote and thus representative of the will of their peers who are less able to coerce participation than an authority figure, *Jones II,* 977 F.2d at 971, is sheer folly. In fact, students in the religious minority and dissenters might find this worse, because it would seem that their peers and the school had teamed up, so to speak, to allow the prayer. In many, if not most, school districts, those students in the religious minority will never really have a vote in the process, because the majority will always remain the same. That is simply not acceptable when fundamental constitutional rights are involved.

97. Adler v. Duval County School Bd., 851 F.Supp. 446 (M.D. Fla. 1994).
98. *Id.* at 448–449.
99. *Id.*
100. *Id.* at 455–456.
101. *Id.* at 456.
102. *Id.*
103. *Id.* at 454–456.

104. *See, e.g.,* Chandler v. James, 958 F.Supp. 1550, 1560 (M.D. Ala. 1997)(acknowledging exactly this point).
105. *Adler* at 454.
106. *Black Horse Pike,* 84 F.3d at 1477–1478 (citing *Lee,* 505 U.S. at 591).
107. *Adler,* 851 F. Supp. at 452–453.
108. *Id.* at 453.
109. *Black Horse Pike,* 84 F.3d at 1478.
110. Perry Education Assn. v. Perry Local Educators' Assn., 460 U.S. 37, 45–46, 48 (1983). In this context, a policy restricting nonreligious content while allowing religious content, or allowing expression of majority views while restricting expression of minority views, could not survive strict scrutiny.
111. Assuming a public forum exists, one possible limitation might be reasonable time, place, and manner restrictions. However, this presumes a school district willing to restrict such speech and requires a fact-sensitive and detailed constitutional analysis to support those restrictions.
112. For a more detailed discussion of the "forum" issue, *See* Chapter Nine.
113. Some Religious Right leaders and attorneys have argued that the Supreme Court's denial of certiorari in *Jones II* is of some value in determining what the ultimate disposition of such arguments would be. However, this represents a fundamental misunderstanding or twisting of the precedential value of a denial of certiorari. It simply has no precedential value at all, other than to acknowledge that the circuit court's decision in that particular case will not be reviewed. *See* Pershing, *supra* note 45, at 1100 (referring to a letter from the American Center for Law and Justice, which implied this, as a "shameless distortion").
114. *See* Pershing, *supra* note 45; Robert S. Peck, *The Threat to the American Idea of Religious Liberty,* 46 MERCER L. REV. 1123 (1995); Sekulow et al., *supra* note 96.
115. American Center for Law and Justice, untitled document dated School Year 1992–1993, cited in Pershing, *supra* note 45, at 1100–1101.
116. Patricia M. Hulting, *Why Public Prayer at Graduation Is Wrong,* 16 RELIGION & PUBLIC EDUC. 39 (1989)(article written in the form of a letter to a student speaker who prayed publicly at a public school graduation in Iowa).
117. Larry W. Barber, *Prayer at Public School Graduation: A Survey,* PHI DELTA KAPPAN 125 (Oct. 1993)(providing results of survey of school superintendents regarding prayer at graduation in 1993).
118. 1994 Miss. Laws Chapt. 609 §1.
119. Ingebretson v. Jackson Public School District, 864 F.Supp. 1473 (S.D. Miss. 1994), *aff'd,* 88 F.3d 274 (5th Cir. 1996).
120. *Ingebretson,* 88 F.3d 274.

121. Ala. Code §16-1-20.3 (1995).
122. Chandler v. James, 958 F.Supp. 1550 (M.D. Ala. 1997).
123. *Id.* at 1557 fn. 4.
124. H.J.R. Res. 78, 105th Cong., 2nd Sess. (1997), as modified by House Resolution 453, 105th Cong., 2nd Sess. (1998)(amendment adopted on House floor).
125. 144 Cong. Rec. H4069–06, H4077 (daily ed. June 4, 1998)(vote on House floor); Juliet Eilperin, *School Prayer Measure Fails in House Vote,* Washington Post, June 5, 1998 at A6 (providing final vote tally and reaction to it).
126. 20 U.S.C. §4071 *et seq.* (1984). For an excellent discussion and analysis of the Act written by one of the preeminent scholars in the area of church-state law, *see* Douglas Laycock, *Equal Access and Moments of Silence: The Equal Status of Religious Speech by Private Speakers,* 81 Nw. U. L. Rev. 1 (1986).
127. *Id.*
128. 42 U.S.C. §2000bb *et seq.* (1993).
129. 494 U.S. 872 (1990).
130. 42 U.S.C. §2000bb-1 (1993).
131. City of Boerne v. P. F. Flores, Archbishop of San Antonio, 521 U.S. 507, (1997).
132. *Id.*

Chapter 4

1. *See* ACLU of New Jersey v. Black Horse Pike Regional Bd. of Educ., 84 F.3d 1471, 1488 (3d Cir. 1996).
2. Nadine Strossen, *How Much God in the Schools? A Discussion of Religion's Role in the Classroom,* 4 Wm. & Mary Bill of Rights J. 607, 616 (1995)(stating that those cases that are reported are only the "tip of the iceberg").
3. The amount of material on this subject is voluminous. Several outstanding books on the subject, but by no means the only ones, are John Duckitt, The Social Psychology of Prejudice (Praeger 1994); Gordon Allport, The Nature of Prejudice (Addison-Wesley 1954); Bruno Bettelheim and Morris Janowitz, Social Change and Prejudice (Free Press 1964).
4. Gordon Allport and J. M. Ross, *Personal Religious Orientation and Prejudice,* 5 J. of Pers. & Soc. Psych. 432 (1967)(hereinafter *Personal Orientation*); *see also* Bruce Hunsberger, *Religion and Prejudice: The Role of Religious Fundamentalism, Quest, and Right-Wing Authoritarianism,* 51 J. of Soc. Issues 113 (1995)(providing some historical information on Allport's work in this

area in the context of a broader discussion on the role of fundamentalism, quest, and authoritarianism in facilitating prejudice)(hereinafter *Religion and Prejudice*).

5. J. R. Feagin, *Prejudice and Religious Types: A Focused Study of Southern Fund-amentalists*, 4 J. FOR THE SCIEN. STUD. OF RELIGION 3 (1964); Ralph W. Hood, *A Comparison of the Allport and Feagin Scoring Procedures for Intrinsic/Extrinsic Religious Orientation*, 10 J. FOR THE SCIEN. STUD. OF RELIGION 370 (1971).

6. *See, e.g.*, Hunsburger, *Religion and Prejudice;* Lee A. Kirkpatrick, *Fundamentalism, Christian Orthodoxy, and Intrinsic Religious Orientation as Predictors of Discriminatory Attitudes*, 32 J. FOR THE SCIEN. STUD. OF RELIGION 256 (1993)(hereinafter *Christian Orthodoxy*); Bob Altemeyer and Bruce Hunsburger, *Authoritarianism, Religious Fundamentalism, Quest, and Prejudice*, 2 INTER. J. FOR THE PSYCH. OF RELIGION 113 (1992)(hereinafter *Authoritarianism*).

7. Michael J. Donahue, *Intrinsic and Extrinsic Religiousness: Review and Meta-Analysis*, 48 J. OF PERS. AND SOC. PSYCH. 400 (1985)(hereinafter *Intrinsic and Extrinsic*); *see also* Rita M. Pullium, *Cognitive Styles or Hypocrisy? An Explanation of the Religiousness-Intolerance Relationship in* SOCIAL CONSE-QUENCES OF RELIGIOUS BELIEF (William Garrett, ed., Paragon House 1989)(hereinafter *Cognitive Styles*); Sam G. McFarland, *Religious Orientations and the Targets of Discrimination*, 28 J. FOR THE SCIEN. STUD. OF RELI-GION 324 (1989)(hereinafter *Religious Orientations*).

8. Pullium, *Cognitive Styles* at 81.

9. *See* articles cited, *supra* note 6.

10. Allport and Ross, *Personal Orientation* at 434.

11. *See* Pullium, *Cognitive Styles;* McFarland, *Religious Orientations;* Donahue, *Intrinsic and Extrinsic*. The pioneering article in this regard is Allport and Ross, *Personal Orientation*. These studies, and most of the others dealing with this issue, looked at attitudes toward particular groups such as racial minorities, atheists, and Communists. Thus, they do not directly address attitudes toward religious minorities. However, the results of the studies bear on discriminatory attitudes generally.

12. *Id.* Intrinsics still scored higher on prejudice scales than nonreligious individuals. *See* Fisher *et al., infra* note 14, at 615–616.

13. *See* Kirkpatrick, *Christian Orthodoxy*. However, this phenomenon still requires more study before it can be clearly established. *Id.*

14. Randy D. Fisher *et al., Religiousness, Religious Orientation, and Attitudes towards Gays and Lesbians*, 24 J. OF APPLIED SOC. PSYCH. 614 (1994)(hereinafter *Attitudes Towards Gays and Lesbians*).

15. *Compare* Chapter One with the information contained in this section.

16. Fisher, *Attitudes towards Gays and Lesbians*. It has also been suggested that

low levels of prejudice exhibited by intrinsics toward some minorities may be "a reflection of their tendency to . . . present themselves in socially desirable ways." *Id.* at 616. Thus, they may be more prejudiced internally than externally.

17. *See generally* articles cited *supra* note 7; Hunsburger, *Religion and Prejudice.*

18. Hunsburger, *Religion and Prejudice* at 120–121; Altemeyer and Hunsburger, *Authoritarianism.*

19. C. Daniel Batson and Patricia Schoenrade, *Measuring Religion as Quest: 1) Validity Concerns,* 30 J. FOR THE SCIEN. STUD. OF RELIGION 416 (1991); C. Daniel Batson and Patricia Schoenrade, *Measuring Religion as Quest: 2) Reliability Concerns,* J. FOR THE SCIEN. STUD. OF RELIGION 430 (1991); C. Daniel Batson, Patricia Schoenrade, and W. Larry Ventis, RELIGION AND THE INDIVIDUAL: A SOCIAL PSYCHOLOGICAL PERSPECTIVE (Oxford University Press 1993). For an excellent discussion of the evolution of this concept and its relationship to fundamentalist religious orientation, *see* Hunsburger, *Religion and Prejudice.*

20. Hunsburger, *Religion and Prejudice;* Altemeyer and Hunsburger, *Authoritarianism;* Kirkpatrick, *Christian Orthodoxy;* McFarland, *Religious Orientations;* Kathleen M. Beatty and Oliver Walter, *Religious Preference and Practice: Reevaluating Their Impact on Political Tolerance,* 48 PUBLIC OPIN. QUART. 318–329 (1984)(hereinafter *Preference and Practice*). The articles by Hunsburger and by Altemeyer and Hunsburger emphasize that it is important that in this context fundamentalism should not be equated with religious orthodoxy generally, because a fundamentalist world view and tendency toward authoritarianism, in addition to strict religious doctrine, are key factors in determining the associated intolerance. *See also* Pullium, *Cognitive Styles;* Leiber, Woodrick, and Roudebush, *Religion, Discriminatory Attitudes and the Orientations of Juvenile Justice Personnel: A Research Note,* 33 CRIMINOLOGY 431–449 (1995).

21. *See* Kirkpatrick, *Christian Orthodoxy.*

22. Hunsburger, *Religion and Prejudice* at 120–123.

23. *Id.* at 121. The work of Bob Altemeyer is perhaps the most significant on right-wing authoritarianism. Some of his important works are ENEMIES OF FREEDOM: UNDERSTANDING RIGHT-WING AUTHORITARIANISM (Jossey-Bass 1988); RIGHT-WING AUTHORITARIANISM (Univ. of Manitoba Press 1981); *Authoritarianism* (with Bruce Hunsburger).

24. Fisher, *Attitudes towards Gays and Lesbians.*

25. *See* articles cited *supra* notes 11–12 and accompanying text.

26. Hunsburger, *Religion and Prejudice* at 121–122.

27. Kirkpatrick, *Christian Orthodoxy;* Fisher, *Attitudes towards Gays and Lesbians;* Beatty and Walter, *Preference and Practice;* McFarland, *Religious Orientations.*

28. Hunsburger, *Religion and Prejudice*. Some research suggests that the attitude among "quest" individuals is not one of positive association with out-groups, but rather a "don't discriminate" type of attitude. McFarland, *Religious Orientations* at 333.

29. James C. Schott, *Holy Wars in Education*, 47 EDUCAT. LEADERSHIP 61 (Oct. 1989); Zita Arocha, *The Religious Right's into Public Schools*, 50 SCHOOL ADMINISTRATOR 8 (Oct. 1993); Dan Nasman, *Combatting the Religious Right in San Diego County*, 50 SCHOOL ADMINISTRATOR 28 (Oct. 1993); Robert L. Simonds, *Citizens for Excellence in Education*, 50 SCHOOL ADMINISTRATOR 19 (Oct. 1993); *see generally* Chapter Two.

30. *Id.*

31. *See* cases discussed in Chapter One.

32. *See* William Peters, A CLASS DIVIDED THEN AND NOW (Yale Univ. Press 1987); William Peters, A CLASS DIVIDED (Doubleday 1971); NBC News Documentary: *The Eye of the Storm* (1970).

33. *Id.*

34. *See, e.g.,* Anne Locksley *et al., Social Categorization and Discriminatory Behavior: Extinguishing the Minimal Intergroup Discrimination Effect*, 39 J. OF PERS. AND SOC. PSYCH. 773 (1980); Michael Billig and Henri Tajfel, *Social Categorization and Similarity in Intergroup Behavior*, 3 EUROP. J. OF SOC. PSYCH. 27 (1973). The amount of literature addressing the relationship between ingroup-outgroup dynamics and discriminatory/prejudiced attitudes and behaviors is voluminous. Several studies of interest are Nicole Chiasson *et al., In-Group-Out-Group Similar Information as a Determinant of Attraction toward Members of Minority Groups*, 136 J. OF SOC. PSYCH. 233 (1996); Jeffrey G. Noel *et al., Peripheral Ingroup Membership Status and Public Negativity toward Outgroups*, 68 J. OF PERS. AND SOC. PSYCH. 127 (1995); Miles Hewstone *et al., Self, Ingroup, and Outgroup Achievement Attributions of German and Turkish Pupils*, 129 J. OF SOC. PSYCH. 459 (1989); Linda A. Jackson and Linda Sullivan, *The Ingroup Favorability Bias in the Minimal Groups Situation*, 127 J. OF SOC. PSYCH. 461 (1986); Leslie L. Downing and Nanci R. Monaco, *In-Group/Out-Group Bias as a Function of Differential Contact and Authoritarian Personality*, 126 J. OF SOC. PSYCH. 445 (1986); Henri Tajfel, *Social Psychology of Intergroup Relations*, 33 ANNUAL REV. OF PSYCH. 1 (1982); M. B. Brewer, *In-Group Bias in the Minimal Intergroup Situation: A Cognitive Motivational Analysis*, 86 PSYCH. BULLETIN 307 (1979); Muzafer Sherif *et al.*, INTERGROUP CONFLICT AND COOPERATION: THE ROBBER'S CAVE EXPERIMENT, (Univ. of Oklahoma Institute of Intergroup Relations 1961); *see also* Michael A. Hogg and Dominic Abrams, SOCIAL IDENTIFICATIONS: A SOCIAL PSYCHOLOGY OF INTERGROUP RELATIONS AND GROUP PROCESSES (Routledge, Chapman & Hall 1988). These, of course, are simply some examples, and there is a rich literature in this

area that addresses many of its complexities that are well beyond the scope of this book.

35. This was the case in the *Bauchman, Herdahl, Herring,* and *Bell* cases discussed in Chapter One.

36. The *Walter, Herdahl,* and *Herring* cases discussed in Chapter One provide some excellent examples of this type of situation.

37. The connection between parental/authority-figure influence and the inculcation of prejudiced or discriminatory attitudes by children has been elucidated by social scientists (frequently in the context of racial prejudice). *See generally* Mary E. Goodman, RACE AWARENESS IN YOUNG CHILDREN, rev. ed. (Collier 1964); Kenneth B. Clark, PREJUDICE AND YOUR CHILD, 2d ed. (Beacon Press 1963); Henri Tajfel, *Cognitive Aspects of Prejudice,* 25 J. SOC. ISSUES 79 (1969).

38. Peters, A CLASS DIVIDED THEN AND NOW; Peters, A CLASS DIVIDED. Additionally, the works cited in the preceding note suggests the important role authority figures can have in facilitating ideas about outgroups for children.

39. B. Bradford Brown, Donna R. Clasen, and Sue Ann Eicher, *Perceptions of Peer Pressure, Peer Conformity Dispositions, and Self-Reported Behavior among Adolescents,* 22 DEVELOPMENTAL PSYCH. 521 (1986)(hereinafter *Perceptions of Peer Pressure); see also* Charles J. Russo and David L. Gregory, *The Return of School Prayer: Reflections on the Libertarian-Conservative Dilemma,* 20 J. OF LAW & EDUC. 167 (1991)(hereinafter *Return of School Prayer);* Gary B. Melton, *Populism, School Prayer and the Courts: Confessions of an Expert Witness,* NEW DIRECTIONS IN CHILD DEVELOPMENT No. 33 p. 63 (1986)(hereinafter *Populism);* Clay V. Brittain, *Adolescent Choices and Parent-Peer Cross-Pressures,* 28 AM. SOCIOL. REV. 385 (1983).

40. Brown, Clasen, and Eicher, *Perceptions of Peer Pressure.*

41. Several of the studies cited above support this either directly or indirectly. *See* Peters, A CLASS DIVIDED THEN AND NOW; Peters, A CLASS DIVIDED; Melton, *Populism;* Russo and Gregory, *Return of School Prayer;* Brown, Clasen, and Eicher, *Perceptions of Peer Pressure.*

42. Peters, A CLASS DIVIDED THEN AND NOW; Peters, A CLASS DIVIDED; Melton, *Populism.*

43. *See* Chapter One.

44. *See* Chapter Two.

45. Many of the quotes and incidents set forth in Chapter Two, as well as some of the incidents in Chapter One, provide excellent examples of this.

46. For an interesting discussion of this in the context of western religious traditions, monotheism, and violence, *see* Regina M. Schwartz, THE CURSE OF CAIN: THE VIOLENT LEGACY OF MONOTHEISM (Univ. of Chicago Press 1997).

47. Mathew Moen, *School Prayer and the Politics of Life-Style Concern,* 65 Soc. Sci. Quart. 1065 (1985). This is a theme in many of the statements by Christian Right leaders set forth in Chapter Two.
48. Kirkpatrick, *Christian Orthodoxy* at 265–266.
49. *Id.*
50. Melton, *Populism;* Russo and Gregory, *Return of School Prayer.*
51. *See supra* note 1, Chapter Two.
52. Edward Felsenthal, *End of a Culture War? How Religion Found Its Way Back to School,* Wall Street J., March 23, 1998; Lyn Riddle, *Solving Religion in Schools: Vanderbilt Center Working to Show Common Ground,* Atlanta J. Const., Jan. 23, 1998; John Dart, *L.A. Educators Get Lessons in Handling Religious Expression Training,* Los Angeles Times, Nov. 9, 1996.
53. *Id.*
54. *Id.*
55. *Id.*
56. For example, in Alabama, where efforts are under way to mediate the ongoing school prayer dispute, governor Fob James pledged to support school prayer regardless of the efforts to mediate. Riddle, *Solving Religion in Schools: Vanderbilt Center Working to Show Common Ground.*
57. Hunsburger, *Religion and Prejudice* at 125.
58. *Id.*

Chapter 5

1. The work of Critical Race Theorists and Critical Legal Studies scholars explore this theme. For example, in Mari J. Matsuda, *Public Response to Racist Speech: Considering the Victim's Story* in Words that Wound: Critical Race Theory, Assaultive Speech, and the First Amendment (Westview Press 1993) at 17, Matsuda explores the way hate speech, as protected by the Free Speech Clause of the First Amendment, inflicts harm on minorities and perpetuates prejudice. Others have observed that antidiscrimination law may work at one level, by helping to remove symbolic barriers and indicia of oppression, but those same laws allow the material and social "subordination" of minorities. Kimberle Williams Crenshaw, *Race, Reform, and Retrenchment: Transformation and Legitimation in Antidiscrimination Law,* 101 Harv. L. Rev. 1331 (1988)(dealing with race and also pointing out the racist propensities of some "neutral" laws and norms).
2. Bauchman v. West High School, 132 F.3d 532 (10th Cir. 1997); Bell v. Little Axe Indep. School Dist. No. 70, 766 F.2d 1391 (10th Cir. 1985).
3. Walter v. West Virginia Bd. of Educ., 619 F.Supp. 1169 (W.D. Va. 1985).

4. *60 Minutes, Profile: Lisa Herdahl v. Pontotoc County; Mother Sues Public School Over Prayer* (transcript of program aired on Sunday, June 16, 1996). Another woman who was asked the question at the same time admitted that she would not like it very much.

5. Lloyd P. Jorgenson, THE STATE AND THE NON-PUBLIC SCHOOL 1825–1925 (Univ. of Missouri Press 1987) at 72–76.

6. *Id.*

7. Molly Ivins, *Faith Alive, Well in Public Discourse As Mohandas Gandhi Said, Those Who Believe That Religion and Politics Don't Mix Understand Neither,* FORT WORTH STAR-TELEGRAM, Sept. 14, 1993, at 21.

8. 1992 fundraising letter for the ACLJ, cited in David Cantor, THE RELIGIOUS RIGHT: THE ASSAULT ON TOLERANCE & PLURALISM IN AMERICA (Anti-Defamation League, Alan M. Schwartz ed., 1994), at 47.

9. *The "Ghettoizing" of the Gospel,* CHRISTIAN AMERICA, Jan. 1993 (also cited in Cantor, THE RELIGIOUS RIGHT, *supra* note 8, at 43).

10. Robert L. Simonds, CITIZENS FOR EXCELLENCE IN EDUCATION PRESIDENT'S REPORT, May 1997, at 1–2.

11. Nadine Strossen, *How Much God in the Schools? A Discussion of Religion's Role in the Classroom,* 4 WILLIAM & MARY BILL OF RTS. J. 607, 635–637 and fn. 163 (1995)(hereinafter *How Much God in the Schools?*).

12. *See* Chapter One and Herdahl v. Pontotoc County School Dist., 887 F.Supp. 902 (N.D. Miss. 1995).

13. *See, e.g.,* Doe v. Duncanville Indep. Sch. Dist., 994 F.2d 160 (5th Cir. 1993).

14. Of course, there have been some cases where a school official has behaved in a fashion that objectively appears hostile toward religion, but the actions of that official did not violate the Constitution. A good example of this is Settle v. Dickson County School Board, 53 F.3d 152 (6th Cir. 1995). In *Settle,* a teacher had prohibited a student from doing a research paper on "The Life of Jesus Christ." The student did not follow the teacher's instructions in submitting the topic. The court held that the student's free speech rights were not violated, because the teacher had the right to control the nature and content of the assignment, and that the teacher's reasons for rejecting the paper did not support the student's claim of viewpoint discrimination. *Id.* One judge wrote a concurring opinion that called the teacher's motivations into question, but found no constitutional violation because the nature of the assignment made the teacher's control over content appropriate and raised no valid free speech issues, although the concurrence stated that the situation might have been different had the assignment been an opinion paper rather than a research paper. *Id.* at 156 (Batchelder concurring).

15. M. G. "Pat" Robertson, *Religion in the Classroom,* 4 WILLIAM & MARY BILL OF RTS. J. 595, 603 and fn. 33 (1995).

16. Strossen, *How Much God in the Schools?* at 635–637 and fn. 163.
17. None of the major "school prayer" cases have precluded such activity. Lee v. Weisman, 505 U.S. 577 (1992); School District of Abington Township v. Schempp, 374 U.S. 203 (1963); Engel v. Vitale, 370 U.S. 421 (1962).

Chapter 6

1. For example, The Civil Rights Act of 1964, 42 U.S.C. §2000a *et seq.,* addresses discrimination based on race, color, gender, national origin, and religion in such diverse areas as employment, education, public accommodations, and government facilities and programs (however, religion is not included as a protected class in every area). The Americans with Disabilities Act, 42 U.S.C. §12101 *et seq.,* protects disabled individuals from discrimination in such areas as employment, public accommodations, government facilities and programs, and transportation. The Age Discrimination in Employment Act, 29 U.S.C. §621 *et seq.,* protects older Americans against age discrimination in employment. The Voting Rights Act, 42 U.S.C. §1971 *et seq.,* protects against discriminatory voting practices based on race, color, and previous condition of servitude. The Fair Housing Act Amendments of 1988, 42 U.S.C. §3604(f)(1), protect against discrimination in housing based on disability and amend the Fair Housing Act, which does the same based on race, color, religion, and national origin, 42 U.S.C. §3603 *et seq.* This list is not exhaustive and does not address state laws.

2. Examples of the former type of law are provided by two causes of action recognized under Title VII of the Civil Rights Act of 1964, "disparate treatment," which provides redress to employees who are the victims of intentional discrimination in terms or conditions of employment and "hostile work environment," which addresses severe or pervasive harassment in the workplace. *See* St. Mary's Honor Center v. Hicks, 509 U.S. 502 (1993); Harris v. Forklift Systems, Inc., 510 U.S. 17 (1993). An example of the latter is provided by the desegregation provisions of the Civil Rights Act of 1964.

3. However, a rigid holding that remedies aimed at a broad class are never appropriate in the absence of specific acts of discrimination aimed at the entire class appears to this author as horribly out of touch with social reality. When one looks at issues of racial discrimination, for example, there are any number of factors, both historical and contemporary, which may not give rise to documentable specific acts aimed at an entire class. Yet, research such as the Urban Institute Studies demonstrates that those factors have significant impact in employment and housing nonetheless. *See* Margery A. Turner *et al., Opportunities Denied, Opportunities Diminished: Racial*

Discrimination in Hiring XI, URBAN INST. REP. (1991)(overall, white job applicants fared better in the hiring process than equally qualified black applicants who applied for the same job); Margery A. Turner *et al., Housing and Urban Development, Housing Discrimination Study: Synthesis IV* (Dept. of Housing & Urban Dev. 1991)(more than 50 percent of black and Hispanic subjects seeking housing were treated less favorably than paired white subjects); *see also* Peter J. Leahy, *Are Racial Factors Important for the Allocation of Mortgage Money?,* 44 AM. J. ECON. & SOC. 185 (1985)(study controlling for socioeconomic factors between neighborhoods, which were similar in all major mortgage-lending criteria except for race, finding that mortgage lending outcomes are unequal). To divorce the remedies available under antidiscrimination laws from these factors in favor of a rigid requirement of specific verifiable acts of discrimination against those seeking redress, absent clear statutory or constitutional language requiring this, is to divorce the issue from context and history, an odd way to deal with issues that specifically arise from history and social context. Thus, antidiscrimination laws and the Constitution can be rendered powerless to deal with the aversive racism that contributes to racial inequity in our society. Two recent affirmative action cases, decided on constitutional grounds, provide excellent examples of this ahistorical and decontextualized approach. Adarand Constructors, Inc. v. Pena, 515 U.S. 200 (1995); City of Richmond v. J. A. Croson Co., 488 U.S. 469 (1989); *see also* Frank S. Ravitch, *Creating Chaos in the Name of Consistency: Affirmative Action and the Odd Legacy of Adarand Constructors, Inc. v. Pena,* 101 DICK L. REV. 281, 292–293 (1997)(criticizing the Court's ahistorical and decontextualized approach in *Adarand* and *Croson*).

4. *Harris,* 510 U.S. 17; Ellison v. Brady, 924 F.2d 872 (9th Cir. 1991); Andrews v. City of Philadelphia, 895 F.2d 1469 (3rd Cir. 1990); Department of Education Office for Civil Rights, *Sexual Harassment Guidance: Harassment of Students by School Employees, Other Students and Third Parties,* 62 FED. REG. 12034 (1997)(hereinafter *OCR Guidelines on Sexual Harassment*); Department of Education, *Racial Incidents and Harassment against Students at Educational Institutions: Investigative Guidance,* 59 FED. REG. 11448 (1994) (hereinafter *OCR Guidelines on Racial Harassment*).

5. *See, e.g.,* Title VII of the Civil Rights Act of 1964, as amended by the Civil Rights Act of 1991, 42 U.S.C. §2000e *et seq.*

6. For example, the Americans with Disabilities Act, 42 U.S.C. §12102(2), protects individuals "regarded as having" a disability, regardless of whether those individuals actually do have a disability.

7. *Cf.* Kimberle Williams Crenshaw, *Race, Reform, Retrenchment: Transformation and Legitimation in Antidiscrimination Law,* 101 HARV. L. REV. 1331 (1988); Charles R. Lawrence III, *The Id, the Ego, and Equal Protection: Reck-*

oning with Unconscious Racism, 39 STAN. L. REV. 317 (1987)(criticizing the intent standard mandated by the Supreme Court's decision in Washington v. Davis because it ignores the nature and causes of racism in the real world and precludes more effective legal avenues to address racism).

8. *See* discussion of fundamentalism and its relationship to discrimination in Chapter Four and sources cited therein.

9. Many of the statements by Christian Right leaders set forth in Chapter Two reflect this, and the research on fundamentalism discussed in Chapter Four implies this as well.

10. *See* Meritor Savings Bank v. Vinson, 477 U.S. 367 (1986)(recognizing the applicability of the hostile work environment cause of action to all classes protected under Title VII); Turner v. Barr, 811 F.Supp. 1 (D.D.C. 1993) (case involving religious and reverse racial discrimination).

11. *See, e.g., Harris,* 510 U.S. 17 (1993); *Meritor,* 477 U.S. 367 (1986). The cause of action is also applicable under other antidiscrimination laws. *See* Frank S. Ravitch, *Beyond Reasonable Accommodation: The Availability and Structure of a Cause of Action for Workplace Harassment under the Americans with Disabilities Act,* 15 CARD. L. REV. 1475 (1994)(stating that hostile work environment is an available cause of action under the Americans with Disabilities Act).

12. Most of the cases arise under Title IX of the Education Act Amendments of 1972 and involve sexual harassment. Gebser v. Lago Vista Independent School District, 66 U.S.L.W. 4501 (1998); Oona, R. S. by Kate S. v. McCaffrey, 122 F.3d 1207 (9th Cir. 1997); Kinman v. Omaha Pub. School Dist., 94 F.3d 463 (8th Cir. 1996); Doe v. Londonderry School Dist., 970 F.Supp. 64 (D.N.H. 1997); Collier By Collier v. William Penn School Dist., 956 F.Supp. 1209 (E.D. Pa. 1997); Bruneau v. South Kortright Cent. School, 953 F.Supp. 161 (N.D.N.Y. 1996); Bosley v. Kearney R-1 School Dist., 904 F.Supp. 1006 (W.D. Mo. 1995); *OCR Guidelines on Sexual Harassment,* 62 FED. REG. 12034 (1997); *see also OCR Guidelines on Racial Harassment,* 59 FED. REG. 11448 (1994)(recognizing same for racial harassment).

13. The various opinions in Davis v. Monroe County Bd. of Educ., 120 F.3d 1390 (11th Cir. 1997), reflect this. *Id.* at 1407 (Carnes concurring specially); *id.* at 1411 (Barkett dissenting).

14. *Gebser,* 66 U.S.L.W. 4501 (1998).

15. Franklin v. Gwinnett County Pub. Schs., 503 U.S. 60, 76 (1992)(Title IX case citing with approval *Meritor,* the Supreme Court case that recognized hostile work environment); *Oona, R. S.,* 122 F.3d at 1209–1211; Doe v. Claiborne County, 103 F.3d 495, 514–515 (6th Cir. 1996); *OCR Guidelines on Sexual Harassment,* 62 FED. REG. 12034 (1997).

16. 454 F.2d 234 (5th Cir. 1971).

17. *Meritor,* 477 U.S. at 64.
18. 477 U.S. 57 (1986).
19. The Court acknowledged, but did not discuss, quid pro quo sexual harassment. *Meritor,* 477 U.S. at 65. Despite the fact that the case involved only sexual harassment, the court acknowledged and approved of lower court decisions that held that harassment aimed at other classes protected under Title VII can be actionable. *Id.* at 66.
20. *Id.* at 66–68. Although *Meritor* dealt with a sexually hostile work environment, the Court implied that the standards set forth therein are equally applicable to anyone protected under Title VII. *Id.* at 66.
21. In response to the petitioner's argument that Title VII only protects against "tangible loss" of an "economic character," and not "purely psychological aspects of the workplace environment," the *Meritor* Court held:

> [T]he language of Title VII is not limited to "economic" or "tangible" discrimination. The phrase "terms, conditions, or privileges of employment" evinces a Congressional intent "to strike at the entire spectrum of disparate treatment of men and women" in employment [citation omitted].

Meritor, 477 U.S. at 64.
22. Several cases dealing with sexual harassment illustrate the variety of interpretations given the *Meritor* framework. *See* Burns v. McGregor Elec. Indus., Inc., 955 F.2d 559, 564 and fn. 3 (8th Cir. 1992)(a hostile work environment exists when the complainant can show that she belongs to a protected class and was subjected to unwelcome harassment; the harassment was based on sex (but need not be clearly sexual in nature); the harassment affected a term, condition, or privilege of employment; and the employer knew, or should have known, of the harassment and failed to take appropriate remedial action); *Ellison,* 924 F.2d 872 (a hostile work environment exists where an employee is subject to unwelcome conduct of a sexual nature that a reasonable woman would consider sufficiently severe and pervasive to alter the conditions of employment and create a hostile or abusive working environment); *Andrews,* 895 F.2d 1469 (a hostile work environment claim can be successful when the employee can show that he or she suffered intentional discrimination because of sex, the discrimination was pervasive and regular, the discrimination detrimentally affected the plaintiff, the discrimination would have detrimentally affected a reasonable person of the same sex in that position, and as to employers, the existence of respondeat superior liability); *Rabidue,* 805 F.2d 611 (to prevail on a sexually offensive work environment claim, an employee must prove she was a member of a protected class; was subject to unwelcome

sexual harassment in the form of sexual advances, requests for sexual favors, or other verbal or physical conduct of a sexual nature; and which
had the effect of unreasonably interfering with her work performance and
created an intimidating, hostile, or offensive work environment that
affected seriously her psychological well-being; and, as to employer liability, the existence of respondeat superior liability).

23. *See Ellison,* 924 F.2d 872 (severity and pervasiveness should be evaluated
from the perspective of a reasonable woman); *Andrews,* 895 F.2d 1469 (severity and pervasiveness should be evaluated from the perspective of a
reasonable person of the same sex as the victim); *Rabidue,* 805 F.2d 611
(severity and pervasiveness should be evaluated from the perspective of a
reasonable person).

24. *See Ellison,* 924 F.2d at 877–878 (no requirement that the victim show
serious effect on psychological well-being); *Rabidue,* 805 F.2d at 620 (requiring such showing); *Vance,* 863 F.2d at 1510 (same).

25. *See Ellison,* 924 F.2d 872 (no directly espoused subjective prong, although
whether the victim welcomed conduct should be considered); *Andrews,*
895 F.2d 1469 (subjective prong must be considered).

26. 510 U.S. 17 (1994).

27. *Id.*

28. 510 U.S. at 20–23.

29. *Id.*

30. *Id.*

31. *See* Frank S. Ravitch, *Beyond Reasonable Accommodation: The Availability and
Structure of a Cause of Action for Workplace Harassment under the Americans with
Disabilities Act,* 15 CARD. L. REV. 1475 at fn. 21, 24, 37, and accompanying
text (the court set forth a reasonable person standard, but implied in dicta
that it could mean a reasonable person of the alleged victim's protected
class and expressly refused to address the EEOC proposed guidelines applicable to nonsexual harassment, which applied a different standard).

32. In *Harris,* 510 U.S. at 21, the Court stated:

Conduct that is not severe or pervasive enough to create an objectively hostile or abusive work environment—an environment that
a reasonable person would find hostile or abusive—is beyond Title
VII's purview.

33. *Harris,* 510 U.S. at 22–23.

34. *Id.*

35. *Id.*

36. *See Ellison,* 924 F.2d at 878–881 (adopting the victim's perspective, because
otherwise the standard applied might simply reinforce the "prevailing level

of discrimination," and because certain classes have different life experiences and thus different perspectives on harassing conduct).

37. *See EEOC Enforcement Guidance on Harris v. Forklift Systems*, 405 FAIR EMPL. PRAC. MAN. (BNA) 7165 (discussing *Harris* and noting it is consistent with the EEOC Guidelines dealing with sexual harassment as augmented by EEOC Policy Guidance).

38. *Id.* at 7168–7170.

39. In *Ellison*, 924 F.2d 872, 878, a sexual harassment case, the court noted that a reasonable person standard could reinforce the "prevailing level of discrimination" and that "harassers could continue to harass merely because a particular discriminatory practice [is] common, and victims of harassment would have no remedy." This rationale has also been utilized in EEOC Policy Guidance regarding sexual harassment to support the conclusion that the reasonable person standard set forth by the EEOC and by the Supreme Court in *Harris* allows for consideration of the perspective of members of the alleged victim's class. *See EEOC Policy Guidance on Sexual Harassment*, 405 FAIR EMPL. PRAC. MAN. at 6690 (issued Mar. 19, 1990)(noting that the reasonable person standard should include consideration of the victim's perspective "and not stereotyped notions of acceptable behavior"); *EEOC Enforcement Guidance on Harris v. Forklift Systems*, 405 FAIR EMPL. PRAC. MAN. at 7168–7169 (approving of the EEOC policy guidance interpretation of the reasonable person standard and stating that the standard set forth in *Harris* is consistent with that interpretation).

This has significant import in the present context, because if conduct was viewed from the perspective of a "reasonable person" in Pike County, Alabama, or Ecru, Mississippi, the locales of the *Herring* and *Herdahl* cases respectively, rather than a reasonable person of a minority religion in those areas or a broader reasonable religious minority/dissenter perspective, the appropriateness of the conduct would be determined from the perspective of the perpetrators, and thus any manner of behavior in relation to these issues might be justified. However, it could also be argued that while reasonable people from these communities might disagree about the underlying school prayer issues, the harassing conduct facilitated by those issues is never reasonable. Still, looking at it from the victim's perspective, as explained above by the *Ellison* court and the EEOC, seems more in keeping with the purpose of the cause of action and certainly is a possible interpretation under *Harris*, although not the only one.

40. *See, e.g.,* Steiner, 25 F.3d at 1462–1464.

41. *Gebser*, 66 U.S.L.W. at 4503–4506. "Title IX" refers to Title IX of the Education Act Amendments of 1972, 86 Stat. 373, as amended, 20 U.S.C. §1681 *et seq.*

42. ___U.S. ___, 66 U.S.L.W. 4643 (1998).

43. ___U.S. ___, 66 U.S.L.W. 4634 (1998).

44. *Faragher,* 66 U.S.L.W. 4643; *Ellerth,* 66 U.S.L.W. 4634.

45. *Id.*

46. *Ellerth,* 66 U.S.L.W. at 4636–4637, 4640.

47. *Faragher,* 66 U.S.L.W. at 4648–4653; *Ellerth,* 66 U.S.L.W. at 4637–4638.

48. *Faragher,* 66 U.S.L.W. at 4650–4652; *Ellerth,* 66 U.S.L.W. at 4639–4640.

49. *Id.*

50. 477 U.S. 57, 69–73.

51. *Faragher,* 66 U.S.L.W. 4643; *Ellerth,* 66 U.S.L.W. 4634. Prior to these decisions other courts applied agency principles as required by *Meritor. See, eg.,* Ellison v. Brady, 924 F.2d 872, 881–883 (9th Cir. 1991); Andrews v. City of Philadelphia, 895 F.2d 1469, 1486 (3d Cir. 1991); Hall v. Gus Construction Co., 842 F.2d 1010, 1015–1016 (8th Cir. 1988).

52. *Faragher,* 66 U.S.L.W. at 4652; *See also Ellerth,* 66 U.S.L.W. at 4640.

53. *Id.*

54. *Id.*

55. *Faragher,* 66 U.S.L.W. at 4650–4652.

56. *Ellerth,* 66 U.S.L.W. at 4640.

57. *Faragher,* 66 U.S.L.W. at 4652; *Ellerth,* 66 U.S.L.W. at 4640.

58. *Faragher,* 66 U.S.L.W. at 4651.

59. *Faragher,* 66 U.S.L.W. 4643; *Ellerth,* 66 U.S.L.W. 4634.

60. Hunter v. Allis-Chalmers Corp., 797 F.2d 1417, 1422 (7th Cir. 1986); *EEOC Policy Guidance on Sexual Harassment,* 405 FAIR EMPL. PRAC. MAN. at 6695.

61. Magnuson v. Peak Technical Sevs., Inc., 808 F.Supp. 500 (E.D. Va. 1992); *EEOC Policy Guidance on Discrimination Because of Sex,* 29 C.F.R. §1604.11(e) (1993).

62. *See, e.g., EEOC Guidelines on Discrimination Because of Sex,* 29 C.F.R. §1604.11(d) and (f); *EEOC Policy Guidance on Sexual Harassment,* 405 FAIR EMPL. PRAC. MAN. at 6697–6701. Additionally, courts have addressed this issue; *see, e.g., Ellison,* 924 F.2d at 881–883; Giardano v. William Patterson College, 804 F.Supp. 637, 643–644 (D.N.J. 1992); United States v. City of Buffalo, 457 F.Supp. 612, 632–635 (W.D.N.Y. 1978), *modified in part,* 633 F.2d 643 (2d Cir. 1980).

63. *Faragher,* 66 U.S.L.W. at 4651–4652; *Ellerth,* 66 U.S.L.W. at 4640.

64. *EEOC Guidelines on Discrimination Because of Sex,* 29 C.F.R. at §1609.2(d) and (f); *EEOC Policy Guidance on Sexual Harassment,* 405 FAIR EMPL. PRAC. MAN. at 6697–6701.

65. For example, in Barrett v. Omaha Natl. Bank, 726 F.2d 424 (8th Cir. 1984), the court held that a full investigation of a complaint of harassment, followed by a reprimand and the placement of the harasser on ninety-day probation with a warning that further misconduct would result in dis-

charge, was sufficient to remedy a hostile work environment. In Katz v. Dole, 709 F.2d 251 (4th Cir. 1983), the court held that an employer's remedies for harassment should be "reasonably calculated to end the harassment," and that the employer in that case took sufficient action to avoid vicarious liability by fully investigating the allegations, issuing written warnings to stop discriminatory conduct, and telling the harasser that a subsequent act of harassment would result in suspension. *Id.* at 256.

More generalized criteria for evaluating the appropriateness of employer remedial actions were set forth in *Ellison*, 924 F.2d at 882. Despite the fact that there was insufficient evidence in Ellison's case to determine whether the employer's response was sufficient to avoid liability, the court clarified the standards for determining the appropriateness of an employer's remedial action generally. *Id.* at 882–883. First, not all harassment warrants dismissal of the harasser. *Id.* at 882. Second, employer remedial action should be assessed proportionately to the seriousness of the offense. *Id.* (citing Dornecker v. Malibu Grand Prix Corp., 828 F.2d 307, 309 (5th Cir. 1987)). Third, an employer should impose penalties sufficient "to assure a workplace free from" harassment. *Id.* Fourth, it would be inappropriate to transfer a victim of harassment out of a work environment in an attempt to stop the harassment, because that would punish the victim for the harasser's conduct. *Id.* In addition, the court noted that "Title VII requires more than a mere request" that the harasser refrain from discriminatory conduct and that unless an employer disciplines harassers, that employer sends "the wrong message to potential harassers." *Id.* The court concisely stated the essence of the criterion for determining the appropriateness of an employer's remedial action as follows:

> Employers should impose sufficient penalties to assure a workplace free from sexual harassment. In essence, then, we think that the reasonableness of an employer's remedy will depend on its ability to stop harassment by the person who engaged in harassment. In evaluating the adequacy of the remedy, the court may also take into account the remedy's ability to persuade potential harassers to refrain from unlawful conduct.

Id.

66. *See, e.g.,* Robinson v. Jacksonville Shipyards, Inc., 760 F.Supp. 1486, 1510–1512, 1517–1519, 1537–1538, 1541–1546 (M.D. Fla. 1991)(holding that sexual harassment policies implemented by the employer were inadequate and providing injunctive relief, including an order that the employer implement an appropriate sexual harassment policy as set forth by the court in an appendix to the decision).

67. *Faragher,* 66 U.S.L.W. 4651–4652; *Ellerth,* 66 U.S.L.W. at 4640.

68. *Cf. Oona, R. S.,* 122 F.3d at 1209–1211; Doe v. Londonderry School Dist., 970 F.Supp. at 72–73; *OCR Guidelines on Sexual Harassment,* 62 FED. REG. at 12042.

69. *Gebser,* 66 U.S.L.W. at 4504–4505.

70. *Id.* at 4506.

71. 441 U.S. 677 (1979).

72. 503 U.S. 60 (1992).

73. *Gebser,* 66 U.S.L.W. at 4503–4506.

74. *Id.* at 4506.

75. *Id.*

76. *Id.* at 4505.

77. 42 U.S.C. §2000d-7.

78. 20 U.S.C. §1687.

79. *Gebser,* 66 U.S.L.W. at 4507 (Stevens dissenting).

80. *Id.* at 4509 (Stevens dissenting); *Meritor,* 477 U.S. at 65 (noting that agency guidelines as "an administrative interpretation" of an Act "by the enforcing agency," while not controlling, represent experienced and informed judgments that courts may properly look to "for guidance").

81. *Gebser,* 66 U.S.L.W. at 4506.

82. *Id.* at 4508 fn. 10 (Stevens dissenting).

83. *Gebser,* 66 U.S.L.W. at 4506.

84. *OCR Guidelines on Racial Harassment,* 59 FED. REG. 11448 (1994).

85. *Franklin,* 503 U.S. 60.

86. *See supra* note 15.

87. *OCR Guidelines on Sexual Harassment,* 62 FED. REG. 12034.

88. *Id.* at 12045–12046; Brown v. Hot, Sexy and Safer Productions, Inc., 68 F.3d 525, 539–541 (1st Cir. 1995)(finding explicit AIDS awareness assembly did not constitute actionable harassment under Title IX, based in part on the educational context of the remarks and actions at the assembly).

89. *OCR Guidelines on Sexual Harassment,* 62 FED. REG. 12034; *OCR Guidelines on Racial Harassment,* 59 FED. REG. 11448.

90. *Meritor,* 477 U.S. 57; 42 U.S.C. §2000e-2(a)(1).

91. The Supreme Court recognized that harassment by a teacher aimed at a student can be actionable under Title IX in *Franklin,* 503 U.S. 60, but until *Gebser* courts disagreed about how such a claim should work and how school liability should be determined. *Compare* Smith v. Metropolitan School Dist. Perry Tp., 128 F.3d 1014 (7th Cir. 1997), *with* Oona, R. S., 122 F.3d 1207; Doe v. Claiborne County, Tenn., 103 F.3d 495 (6th Cir. 1996); *Kinman,* 94 F.3d 463.

92. Several courts have recognized the actionability of peer-on-peer harass-

ment, but there is disagreement on the exact standards which should be applied. Doe v. Londonderry, 970 F.Supp. 64; *Collier by Collier,* 956 F.Supp. 1209; *Wright,* 940 F.Supp. 1412; *Bruneau,* 935 F.Supp. 162; *Bosley,* 904 F.Supp. 106. At least one court has recognized that the conduct of third parties, such as guest speakers, could give rise to an actionable hostile environment under Title IX. Brown v. Hot, Sexy and Safer Productions, Inc., 68 F.3d 525 (1st Cir. 1995)(recognizing that conduct of guest AIDS lecturer can be considered in context of hostile environment claim, but finding that the conduct and the behavior of school officials did not create a hostile environment given the facts of the case).

93. Smith v. Metropolitan School Dist. Perry Tp., 128 F.3d 1014 (7th Cir. 1997); *Davis,* 120 F.3d 1390; Rowinsky v. Bryan Indep. School Dist., 80 F.3d 1006 (5th Cir. 1996).

94. *OCR Guidelines on Sexual Harassment,* 62 FED. REG. 12034; *OCR Guidelines on Racial Harassment,* 59 FED. REG. 11448.

95. *Gebser,* 66 U.S.L.W. 4501; *Smith,* 128 F.3d 1014; *Davis,* 120 F.3d 1390.

96. *OCR Guidelines on Sexual Harassment,* 62 FED. REG. at 12039–12040, 12042; *OCR Guidelines on Racial Harassment,* 59 FED. REG. 11450.

97. *OCR Guidelines on Sexual Harassment,* 64 FED. REG. at 12042–12043; *OCR Guidelines on Racial Harassment,* 59 FED. REG. at 11450, 11453–11454.

98. *Id.* at 64 FED. REG. 12039, 12042–12043.

99. *Ellerth,* 66 U.S.L.W. at 4638.

100. In regard to teacher-on-student harassment, *see, e.g.,* Doe v. Claiborne County Tenn., 103 F.3d 495, 514–515 (6th Cir. 1996); *Kinman,* 94 F.3d at 468–469. In regard to student-on-student harassment, several courts have modified the Title VII standard a bit by requiring knowledge as opposed to a "should have known" standard for peer-on-peer harassment, while others have applied a standard nearly identical to that of Title VII. *Compare* Doe *ex rel.* Doe v. Petaluma City School Dist., 949 F.Supp. 1415, 1427 (N.D. Cal. 1996), *with* Doe v. Londonderry School Dist., 970 F.Supp. at 72–75; *Collier By Collier,* 956 F.Supp. at 1213–1214; *Wright,* 940 F.Supp. at 1420; *Bosley,* 904 F.Supp. at 1023. Of course, other courts explicitly or implicitly reject the application of Title VII principles to determine school liability. *See* Smith v. Metropolitan School Dist. Perry Tp., 128 F.3d 1014, 1022–1028 (7th Cir. 1997); *Davis,* 120 F.3d 1390; Rowinsky v. Bryan Indep. School Dist., 80 F.3d 1006, 1016 (5th Cir. 1996).

101. *OCR Guidelines on Sexual Harassment,* 64 FED. REG. 12034; *OCR Guidelines on Racial Harassment,* 59 FED. REG. 11448.

102. *Id.* at 64 FED. REG. 12039–12040 (explicitly stating this); 59 FED. REG. 11450 (implying this).

103. *Id.* at 64 FED. REG. 12039–40, 12042; 59 FED. REG. at 11450, 11453.

104. *Id.*

105. *OCR Guidelines on Sexual Harassment,* 64 FED. REG. at 12040; *see also* Mur-

ray v. New York University College of Dentistry, 57 F.3d 243, 249 (2d Cir. 1995)(noting that an employer can be liable for harassment by co-workers if the employer failed to provide a "reasonable avenue for complaint").

106. *OCR Guidelines on Sexual Harassment,* 64 FED. REG. at 12042–12043.

107. The OCR guidelines provide some good examples of such policies and procedures, although those suggestions are not exhaustive. *Id.* at 12042–12043; *OCR Guidelines on Racial Harassment,* 59 FED. REG. at 11450, 11454.

108. Griggs v. Duke Power Co., 401 U.S. 424 (1971).

109. *Id.*

110. *Id.* at 436.

111. 42 U.S.C. §2000e-2(k)(1)(A)(§105 of the Civil Rights Act of 1991).

112. *See, e.g.,* Wards Cove Packing Company, Inc. v. Atonio, 490 U.S. 642 (1989).

113. For a post–Civil Rights Act of 1991 case pointing this out, *see* EEOC v. Steamship Clerks Union, Local 1066, 48 F.3d 594, 607 (1st Cir. 1995), *cert. denied,* 516 U.S. 814 (1995). Since that Act returned the law to the state it was in prior to the *Wards Cove* decision, the conflict between the circuits from the pre–*Wards Cove* era remains today. *Compare* United States v. Bethlehem Steel Corp., 446 F.2d 652 (2d Cir. 1971), *with* Contreras v. City of Los Angeles, 656 F.2d 1267 (9th Cir. 1981), *cert. denied,* 455 U.S. 1021 (1982).

114. This complexity is apparent from the issues discussed above in the employment context under Title VII, but is also apparent outside of the Title VII employment context. *See, e.g.,* Washington v. Davis, 426 U.S. 229 (1976)(addressing the application of this concept to a constitutional claim and demonstrating the complexity of the issue in that context); Charles R. Lawrence III, *The Id, the Ego, and Equal Protection: Reckoning with Unconscious Racism,* 39 STAN. L. REV. 317 (1987)(criticizing Washington v. Davis for not considering the way racism exists and is perpetuated in society).

115. *See* Chapter One.

116. The *OCR Guidelines on Racial Harassment* also recognize disparate treatment claims for racial and ethnic discrimination in the educational context. *OCR Guidelines on Racial Harassment,* 59 FED. REG. 11448, 11449, 11451–11452. The *OCR Guidelines on Racial Harassment* specifically refer to the key Supreme Court cases and the standards they set forth for disparate treatment under Title VII. *Id.* at 11451–11452. Thus, the guidelines cite to the standards set forth in McDonnell Douglas Corp. v. Green, 411 U.S. 792 (1973); Texas Dept. of Community Affairs v. Burdine, 450 U.S. 248 (1981); United States Postal Service Bd. of Governors v. Aikens, 460 U.S. 711 (1983); St. Mary's Honor Cent. v. Hicks, 509 U.S. 502 (1993).

117. *See* Chapters Seven and Ten.

Chapter 7

1. Bauchman v. West High School, 132 F.3d 542, 556 (10th Cir. 1997); Bell v. Little Axe Indep. School Dist. No. 70, 766 F.2d 1391, 1408–1413 (10th Cir. 1985).

2. *Bauchman,* 132 F.3d at 550–558.

3. *Id.* at 558–562 (a major facet of the appeal in this case was the efficacy of an amended complaint that alleged a long pattern of religious conduct by the teacher in question to demonstrate religious motivation; for several reasons the court rejected the idea that amended complaint could save the constitutional claims); *id.* at 562 (Murphy dissenting)(pointing out problems with the majority decision from both constitutional and procedural standpoints and implying that the majority was straining to uphold the lower court's dismissal of Bauchman's claims in that case).

4. *Id.* at 562 (Murphy dissenting).

5. Any discussion of judicial hermeneutics or the ways in which judges come to decisions in value-laden cases generally, cannot escape this issue. For an excellent discussion of this phenomenon and the ways judges sometimes use supposedly objective linguistic rules to justify decisions motivated by other factors, *see generally* Lawrence M. Solan, THE LANGUAGE OF JUDGES (Univ. of Chicago Press 1993). As Solan points out, none other than Benjamin Cardozo himself acknowledged this. B. Cardozo, THE NATURE OF THE JUDICIAL PROCESS 167–168 (1921).

6. For statistics regarding support for school prayer in the United States generally, *see supra* note 1 to Chapter Two.

7. *See* discussion of the *Bauchman* case in Chapter One.

8. *Bauchman,* 132 F.3d at 556.

9. *See* discussion of the *Bell* case in Chapter One.

10. *Bell,* 766 F.2d at 1408–1413.

11. *Id.* at 1408.

12. Monell v. Department of Social Services of the City of New York, 436 U.S. 658 (1978).

13. Parrat v. Taylor, 451 U.S. 527, 535 (1981); Chapter Ten.

14. *Bauchman,* 132 F.3d at 556; *Bell,* 766 F.2d at 1408.

15. *Id.*

16. Herdahl v. Pontotoc County School Dist., 887 F.Supp. 902 (N.D. Miss. 1995).

17. 435 U.S. 247 (1978).

18. 477 U.S. 299 (1986).

19. 461 U.S. 30 (1983).

20. 453 U.S. 247 (1981).

21. In fact, in a footnote, the *Stachura* Court recognizes the confusion courts had in applying *Carey. Stachura,* 477 U.S. at 304 fn. 5.

22. *Carey,* 435 U.S. at 264.
23. *Id.* at 254.
24. This does not mean that the *Carey* Court held that presumed damages can never be awarded in a §1983 claim. Since *Carey* focuses on tort law as a model for appropriate damages under §1983, the concept of presumed damages that exists in limited circumstances under tort law might be useful in certain situations. However, in *Stachura,* 477 U.S. at 310, the Court clarified this by explaining that presumed damages are a "substitute for ordinary compensatory damages, not a supplement for an award that fully compensates the alleged injury." Thus, *Stachura* explains that the presumed damages are only appropriate when someone seeks compensation for an "injury that is likely to have occurred but difficult to establish." *Id.* at 311. The damages should approximate the harm suffered and are meant to compensate for that harm, although it may be impossible to measure. The key is that they are still "compensatory" in such circumstances. *Id.*
25. *Carey,* 435 U.S. at 267.
26. *Id.* at 257–259.
27. *Stachura,* 477 U.S. at 308.
28. *Id.* at 309.
29. *Id.* (citing *Carey,* 435 U.S. at 265).
30. *Id.* at 314–316 (Marshall concurring in the judgment). In fact, this is exactly what the court in *Bell* held. The court found that the violation of the Establishment Clause there was compensable and to determine the most appropriate measure of damages analogized the violation to a common law action for denial of voting rights. Thus, while the Bells and McCords could not receive damages for the behavior of the third parties who caused the bulk of their actual damages, they could receive compensation for the nebulous injury flowing from the school district's Establishment Clause violation. *Bell,* 766 F.2d 1391, 1408–1413.
31. *Id.*
32. *Id.* at 1408–1413; *Bauchman,* 132 F.3d at 556.
33. *City of Newport,* 453 U.S. 247.
34. *See, e.g., Monnell,* 436 U.S. 658; *Will v. Michigan Dept. of State Police,* 491 U.S. 58 (1989)(applying Eleventh Amendment immunity to states for purposes of §1983).
35. *Smith,* 461 U.S. 30.
36. *City of Newport,* 453 U.S. 247.
37. 42 U.S.C. §2000d-7 (1986).
38. To my knowledge only two courts have directly addressed the issue. Both involved cases brought under the Rehabilitation Act of 1973, to which the Civil Rights Remedies Equalization Act also applies. In Moreno v. Consolidated Rail Corp., 99 F.3d 782 (6th Cir. 1996)(*en banc*), the court held that punitive damages were not available under §504 of the

Rehabilitation Act despite the passage of the Civil Rights Remedies Equalization Act. In Burns-Vidlak v. Chandler, 980 F.Supp. 1144 (D. Haw. 1997), the court came to the opposite conclusion, and disagreed with *Moreno*.

39. *Moreno*, 99 F.3d 782.

40. *City of Newport*, 453 U.S. 247.

41. Steven B. Epstein, *Rethinking the Constitutionality of Ceremonial Deism*, 96 COL. L. REV. 2083, 2169–2171 (1996).

42. This is the situation the Herdahls faced in regard to their case. *60 Minutes, Profile: Lisa Herdahl v. Pontotoc County: Mother Sues Public School Over Prayer* (transcript from program aired June 16, 1996); *see also* Chapters One and Two.

43. *60 Minutes; see also* newspaper articles cited in Chapter One, regarding the *Herdahl* case.

44. *Id.*

45. *See* Chapters Two and Five.

Chapter 8

1. 20 U.S.C. §4071 *et seq.* (1984).

2. 42 U.S.C. §2000bb *et seq.* (1993).

3. 494 U.S. 872 (1990).

4. Ira C. Lupu, *Statutes Revolving in Constitutional Law Orbits*, 79 VIRG. L. REV. 1, 35 (1993)(hereinafter *Statutes Revolving*).

5. *Id.* at 27–37.

6. *Id.*

7. 454 U.S. 263 (1981).

8. Lupu, *Statutes Revolving* at 27–37.

9. 496 U.S. 226 (1990).

10. Ironically, there have been a few controversies over gay and lesbian student clubs, which are also protected under the Act. Some religious conservatives in the few localities where these controversies have arisen have suggested that schools close their forums rather than allow these clubs to meet.

11. For examples of these state statutes, *see, e.g.*, Nev. Rev. Stat. §388.150; N.M. Stat. Ann. §77–11–10; Alas. Stat. Am. Title 14 §14.03.090.

12. *See* Chapters One–Three; *see also* Bruce J. Dierenfield, *Secular Schools? Religious Practices in New York and Virginia Public Schools Since World War II*, 4 J. OF POLICY HISTORY 361 (1992)(hereinafter *Secular Schools?*)(exploring some of the dynamics that can lead to noncompliance or compliance with Supreme Court mandates).

13. *See* Chapters Two and Three.
14. *See* Chapters One–Three; Dierenfield, *Secular Schools?* at 361.
15. "Conduct like that involved in *Jones*" refers to allegedly "voluntary student-initiated" conduct.
16. As the statutory language suggests, Congress could use the spending power to bind school districts and other governmental entities. What is less clear from the statutory language is what power Congress could use to legislate for private actors in this area. My suggestion would be to utilize the Commerce Clause (which might also be used in regard to the governmental entities). As discussed in Chapter Five, public school religious exercises and the discrimination they can facilitate may cause people to be less willing to move or travel to areas they perceive as potentially hostile to their faiths. This could affect the abilities of companies to recruit top employees or relocate operations, and it could prevent employees from taking a job in an area perceived as hostile even when unemployment would be the result. Congress has based other civil rights legislation on the Commerce Clause with similar bases, and the Supreme Court has upheld those exercises of power. *See, e.g.,* Heart of Atlanta Motel, Inc. v. United States, 379 U.S. 241 (1964)(upholding public accommodations section of the Civil Rights Act of 1964, which was enacted by Congress pursuant to its powers under the Commerce Clause); Katzenbach v. McClung, 379 U.S. 294 (1964)(same for section as applied to restaurants). By suggesting this, I do not mean to exclude other potential bases for legislation in this area. Moreover, should states choose to enact legislation of this type, state legislatures would naturally need to derive their power to do so from appropriate state powers.

   If Congress used the Spending Clause as the basis for implementing the proposed statute in regard to governmental entities, it is of course possible that school districts may decide to forego federal funding to avoid being bound by the statute. A similar option is available under the Equal Access Act, 20 U.S.C. §4071 *et seq.,* and other federal legislation. However, few school districts would be willing to give up federal financial assistance, and even if some are, it would be politically sensitive to do so to avoid antidiscrimination provisions such as these. Essentially, a school district that does so would be saying that it would rather forego federal financial assistance than stop engaging in conduct that facilitates discrimination, or attempt to engage in such conduct in a more sensitive fashion so as to avoid liability under the proposed statute. Still, it is possible that some school districts might choose this route. Those districts might be "back doored" into the statute through the "other entity" language set forth in §1(a)(i), although I am wary of that approach, because it could create interpretive and boundary problems for the proposed statute. If legislation were passed based on the spending clause in this area, this issue would need to be addressed. For now, however, the key is beginning discourse about these issues and demonstrating the feasibility of a civil rights based remedy, in the hope that such legislation will be considered. Thus, these largely speculative issues are best left to be resolved at a later date, placing the current focus on the problem itself and on the substantive issues raised by attempting to address it.

17. Robert Simonds, HOW TO ELECT CHRISTIANS TO PUBLIC OFFICE (CEE 1985)(hereinafter HOW TO ELECT CHRISTIANS); James C. Schott, *Holy Wars in Education,* 47 EDUC. LEADERSHIP 61 (Oct. 1989); Dan Nasman, *Combatting the Religious Right in San Diego County,* 50 SCHOOL ADMIN. 28, 29–30 (Oct. 1993)(hereinafter *Combatting*).

18. David Cantor, THE RELIGIOUS RIGHT: THE ASSAULT ON TOLERANCE & PLURALISM IN AMERICA (Anti-Defamation League, Alan M. Schwartz ed., 1994) at 53; Simonds, HOW TO ELECT CHRISTIANS. For a discussion of the humanism movement and its relation to religion, *see infra.* notes 20–21 and sources cited therein.

19. *See, e.g.,* Schott, *Holy Wars in Education* at 64; Nasman, *Combatting* at 29–30; Zita Arocha, *The Religious Right's into Public Schools,* 50 SCHOOL ADMIN. 8, 9–10; *See also* Stanley Ingber, *Religion or Ideology: A Needed Clarification of the Religion Clauses,* 41 STAN. L. REV. 233, 315–319 (1989)(noting this in regard to moral relativism, evolution, and other topics).

20. That is not to say that legal scholars cannot, or should not, address this issue. Stanley Ingber's article, *Religion or Ideology: A Needed Clarification of the Religion Clauses,* 41 STAN. L. REV. 233, provides an excellent discussion of the legal problems inherent in treating secularism as a religion for Establishment Clause purposes in cases involving public school curricula. He explains why, in that context, "secular humanism" is not a religion. *Id.*

21. Judge Brevard Hand's opinion in Smith v. Board of School Commissioners, 655 F.Supp. 939 (S.D. Ala. 1987), *rev'd,* 827 F.2d 684 (11th Cir. 1987), did hold that "secular humanism" as embodied in the public school curriculum constitutes a religion, but that holding was reversed on appeal and has also been the subject of scholarly criticism. *See, e.g.,* Ingber, *Religion or Ideology: A Needed Clarification of the Religion Clauses,* 41 STAN. L. REV. 233 (1989). Additionally, in a footnote in Torcaso v. Watkins, 367 U.S. 488 (1961), a case that invalidated a provision in the Maryland Constitution requiring state officials to declare they believed in the existence of God, Justice Black did include secular humanism in a list of "religions in this country which do not teach what would generally be considered a belief in the existence of God." *Id.* at 495 n.11. That case had nothing to do with public school curricula.

Moreover, what those in the Christian Right characterize as "secular humanism" is far broader than the humanism as faith that Justice Black was referring to. He was likely referring to the Humanism movement, which has embodied its edicts in two manifestos, the first of which characterized the ideology as religion (and that was the one in effect when *Torcaso* was written). HUMANIST MANIFESTOS I AND II (Paul Kurtz ed., 1973). However, the second manifesto, drafted in the early 1970s, denounced the idea that "humanism" is a religion. Of course, if a school held organized religious exercises based on a religious faith in secular humanism and those exercises facilitated discrimination against religious minorities or dissenters as defined in the statute, the statute would be triggered as discussed in the text accompanying this note.

22. If, however, a school district were to try to insert identifiable religious content into a regular subject, such as attempts to teach the bible as literal history, any discrimination facilitated by those attempts could be actionable. Significantly, this would not be the case if the bible were discussed in its historical context, such as its significance to western culture and history. In that case, religious doctrine is not being taught, and the statute would not be triggered, nor, for that matter, would the Constitution. School District of Abington Tp. v. Schempp, 374 U.S. 203, 225 (1963)(noting that objective study of the historic and literary qualities of the bible as part of a "secular program of education" would not violate the Establishment Clause).

23. *See* Chapter One.

24. *See* Chapter Four; Gary B. Melton, *Populism, School Prayer and the Courts: Confessions of an Expert Witness,* NEW DIRECTIONS IN CHILD DEVELOPMENT No. 33 p. 63, 68 (1986); W. G. Stephen and C. W. Stephen, *Intergroup Anxiety,* 41 J. OF SOCIAL ISSUES 157 (1995).

25. *See* Chapters One–Three.

26. *See, e.g.,* Harris v. Forklift Systems, Inc., 114 S.Ct. 367 (1993)(explaining this in the hostile work environment context). However, as in cases of hostile work environment, it is possible that a single incident would be actionable if sufficiently severe. *See generally* Ellison v. Brady, 924 F.2d 872 (9th Cir. 1991).

27. 42 U.S.C. §12101 *et seq.*

28. The Supreme Court has held that renting school space to religious organizations on an equal access basis is constitutional. Lamb's Chapel v. Center Moriches Union Free School Dist., 508 U.S. 384 (1993).

29. *See* the discussion of those cases in Chapter One.

30. This is similar to the requirement that an employer must take immediate and appropriate corrective action in order to avoid liability for a hostile work environment. 29 C.F.R. §1604.11(c)(d). However, unlike the hostile work environment doctrine, which is a single cause of action, the pro-

posed statute can be implicated both through a pattern of harassment and the other practices set forth above. Significantly, even in regard to those other practices, immediate and appropriate corrective action by a school might shield it from liability if the practices it engaged in are not violative of the Constitution.

31. One final note regarding discrimination as defined under this provision: if a school district has in place policies to prevent religious speeches at a graduation exercise or other school events and a student or speaker engages in such an exercise, the school would not be liable unless it fails to take appropriate corrective action to avoid a recurrence of the situation and any discrimination that might be facilitated.

32. Steven B. Epstein, *Rethinking the Constitutionality of Ceremonial Deism*, 96 Col. L. Rev. 2083, 2169–2171 (1996)(hereinafter *Ceremonial Deism*).

33. *See* Chapters One, Two, and Four.

34. *See* discussion of incidents in Melbourne, Florida, San Diego and Vista, California, in Chapter Two, and the discussion of the school board policy in the *Black Horse Pike* case in Chapter Three.

35. *See, e.g.,* Chapter One; Epstein, *Ceremonial Deism* at 2169–2171.

36. *See* Nadine Strossen, *How Much God in the Schools? A Discussion of Religion's Role in the Classroom*, 4 Wm. & Mary Bill of Rights J. 607, 616 (1995)(stating that such cases are "only the tip of the iceberg").

37. Epstein, *Ceremonial Deism* at 2171.

38. Epstein focuses primarily on the "dismal prospect" that given the current state of constitutional law, a dissenter might obtain no relief. *Id.* This book acknowledges this in contexts beyond ceremonial deism and moreover recognizes that constitutional mechanisms are not really designed to address the pernicious discrimination that dissenters face and thus may not be the best incentive for such people to come forward.

39. *See* Chapter Seven; *Bauchman*, 132 F.3d at 556; *Bell*, 766 F.2d at 1408.

40. *See* Chapter Six; *OCR Guidelines on Sexual Harassment*, 64 Fed. Reg. 12034 (1997).

41. *Id.*

42. *OCR Guidelines on Racial Harassment*, 59 Fed. Reg. 11448–11449 (1994); *cf.* Title VII, 42 U.S.C. §2000e(a)–(b)(defining "person" and "employer" under Title VII).

43. *OCR Guidelines on Racial Harassment*, 59 Fed. Reg. at 11448–11449.

44. Alabama is an excellent example of this. The behavior of the former governor, other politicians, and civil servants within the state have increased tensions over school prayer and called negative attention to those who oppose it. *See* the discussion of the recent actions of Governor Fob James in Chapter Two.

45. 42 U.S.C. §2000d-7 (1986).

46. Kentucky v. Graham, 473 U.S. 159 (1985); *see also* Hafer v. Melo, 502 U.S. 21 (1991)(addressing the personal-official capacity distinction and noting that state officials may be held liable in their individual capacities, but not their official capacities).

Chapter 9

1. The United States Constitution, Amendment 1.
2. Ira C. Lupu, *Statutes Revolving in Constitutional Law Orbits,* 79 VIRG. L. REV. 1 (1993)(hereinafter *Statutes Revolving*).
3. *Id.* at 1–2.
4. *Id.* at 2.
5. Equal Access Act, 20 U.S.C. §4071 *et seq.;* Religious Freedom Restoration Act, enacted as 42 U.S.C. §2000bb *et seq.* (1993), and found unconstitutional in City of Boerne v. P. F. Flores, Archbishop of San Antonio, _U.S._, 117 S.Ct. 2157 (1997); Freedom of Choice Act, S. 25, 102d Cong., 2d Sess. (1992)(neither this bill nor its virtually identical House version passed).
6. Lupu, *Statutes Revolving* at 35–36, 70.
7. As explained earlier in this book, the Equal Access Act extended to secondary schools the basic holding of a Supreme Court case granting religious clubs equal access to a public university since the university allowed a broad array of other clubs and organizations access, but the Act did so in a modified way that considered the differing context of the high school environment. *Id.* at 27–37.
8. Lupu, *Statutes Revolving* at 2.
9. Lupu, *Statutes Revolving,* generally.
10. Eric M. Freedman, *A Lot More Comes into Focus When You Remove the Lens Cap: Why Proliferating New Communications Technologies Makes it Particularly Urgent for the Supreme Court to Abandon Its Inside-Out Approach to Freedom of Speech,* 81 IOWA L. REV. 883, 884–886 (1996); Alan E. Brownstein, *Rules of Engagement for Cultural Wars: Regulating Conduct, Unprotected Speech, and Protected Expression in Anti-Abortion Protests,* 29 U.C. DAVIS L. REV. 553 (1996); Keith Werhan, *The Supreme Court's Public Forum Doctrine and the Return to Formalism,* 7 CARDOZO L. REV. 335, 341 (1986); C. Thomas Dienes, *The Trashing of the Public Forum: Problems in First Amendment Analysis,* 55 GEO. WASH. L. REV. 109, 110 (1986); John Hart Ely, *Flag Desecration: A Case Study in the Roles of Categorization and Balancing in First Amendment Analysis,* 88 HARV. L. REV. 1482, 1490–1493 (1975).
11. *See* Chapter Eight.
12. This is because a fundamental aspect of the hostile environment cause of

action is that conduct, which can include expressive activity, be severe or pervasive enough to create a hostile environment for member(s) of a protected class, Harris v. Forklift Systems, Inc., 510 U.S. 17, 114 S.Ct. 367 (1993); Ellison v. Brady, 924 F.2d 872 (9th Cir. 1991); Burns v. McGregor Elec. Indus., Inc., 955 F.2d 559 (8th Cir. 1992), *rev'd,* 989 F.2d 959 (8th Cir. 1993); Brooms v. Regal Tube Co., 881 F.2d 412 (7th Cir. 1989); Hall v. Gus Construction Co., Inc., 842 F.2d 1010 (8th Cir. 1988).

13. For hostile work environment cases involving public employees, *see Ellison,* 924 F.2d 872; Andrews v. City of Philadelphia, 895 F.2d 1469 (3d Cir. 1990); Delgado v. Lehman, 665 F.Supp. 460 (E.D. Va. 1987). For a discussion of hostile educational environment cases, *see* Chapter Six. The *Gebser* case, which significantly limited this liability in the Title IX context, was not based on free speech issues. See discussion of *Gebser,* 66 U.S.L.W. 4501 (1998), in Chapter Six.

14. 484 U.S. 260 (1988).

15. 393 U.S. 503 (1969).

16. 478 U.S. 675 (1986).

17. *Tinker,* 393 U.S. 503.

18. *Id.* at 506.

19. *Tinker,* 393 U.S. 503.

20. *Id.* at 508–509; *Hazelwood,* 484 U.S. at 266.

21. *Hazelwood,* 484 U.S. 260.

22. *Id.*

23. *Id.* at 272–273.

24. Stuart L. Levitan, *Is Anyone Listening to Our Students? A Plea for Respect and Inclusion,* 21 FLA. ST. U. L. REV. 35, 51–53 (1993)(hereinafter *Is Anyone Listening?*).

25. *Hazelwood,* 484 U.S. at 266 (citation omitted).

26. *Id.* at 267 (citing Perry Education Assn. v. Perry Local Educators' Assn., 460 U.S. 37, 47 (1983)).

27. *Id.* (citing *Perry,* 460 U.S. at 46, n. 7).

28. *Id.* (citing Cornelius v. NAACP Legal Defense & Education Fund, Inc., 473 U.S. 788, 802 (1985)).

29. *Id.* at 273.

30. *Id.* at 270–271.

31. *Fraser,* 478 U.S. 675.

32. *Id.* at 682–686; *Hazelwood,* 484 U.S. at 266–267.

33. Levitan, *Is Anyone Listening?* at 53–54.

34. *Hazelwood,* 484 U.S. at 270–273.

35. *Id.* at 273.

36. *Id.* at 271.

37. *Tinker,* 393 U.S. at 508.

38. *Hazelwood,* 484 U.S. at 267; *Perry,* 460 U.S. at 45–46.
39. *See* Rendell-Baker v. Kohn, 457 U.S. 831, 840 (1982)(receipt of federal funds by private schools does not directly bind those schools to constitutional standards).
40. *Perry,* 460 U.S. at 37.
41. *Id.* at 45. How *Gebser,* 66 U.S.L.W. 4501 (1998), discussed in Chapter Six, might affect this is unclear, but as was pointed out, for present purposes the OCR guidelines are more germane than *Gebser.*
42. Hague v. CIO, 307 U.S. 496 (1939).
43. *Perry,* 460 U.S. at 47.
44. *Id.* at 45–46.
45. *Id.*
46. *Id.* at 46.
47. *Hazelwood,* 484 U.S. at 267–268; *see also Perry,* 460 U.S. 37.
48. *Hazelwood,* 484 U.S. at 273 (school officials can exercise "control over the style and content of student speech in school-sponsored expressive activities" if their actions are "reasonably related to legitimate pedagogical concerns); *see generally* Eugene C. Bjorklun, *Show and Tell, the Establishment of Religion, and Freedom of Speech,* 84 WEST's EDUC. L. REV. 601 (1993).
49. *Hazelwood,* 484 U.S. at 267–268.
50. Duran v. Nitsche, 780 F.Supp. 1048 (E.D. Pa. 1991), *aff'd,* 972 F.2d 133 (3d Cir. 1992); DeNoyer v. Livonia Public Schools, 799 F.Supp. 744 (E.D. Mich. 1992).
51. *Hazelwood,* 484 U.S. at 270–273.
52. ACLU of New Jersey v. Black Horse Pike Regional Bd. of Educ., 84 F.3d 1471, 1478 (3d Cir. 1996).
53. *See* Chapter Three.
54. *Cf. Hazelwood,* 484 U.S. at 267–273; *Duran,* 780 F.Supp. 1048; *DeNoyer,* 799 F.Supp. 744.
55. *Perry,* 460 U.S. at 45–46.
56. *See Perry,* 460 U.S. 37; *Hague,* 307 U.S. 496. For purposes of this paragraph, I am not drawing a distinction between "limited" and "traditional" public forums. As *Perry* demonstrates, once a limited public forum is created, it creates similar expressive rights to those of a traditional public forum, although there is a legal distinction. *Perry,* 460 U.S. at 45–46; *Hazelwood,* 484 U.S. at 267; *see also* discussion of this issue in Chapter Three.
57. Capitol Square Review and Advisory Bd. v. Pinette, 515 U.S. 753, 761–762 (1995)(Compliance with the Establishment Clause is a compelling state interest); EEOC v. Mississippi College, 626 F.2d 477, 488–489 (5th Cir. 1980)(preventing discrimination as compelling interest); *Denoyer,* 799 F.Supp. at 751 (avoiding an Establishment Clause violation could be a compelling governmental interest).

58. Of course, any such limitation would be based on the Constitution and not the proposed statute.

59. *Pinette*, 515 U.S. at 761–762; *Black Horse Pike*, 84 F.3d at 1477–1478.

60. *See* Cynthia L. Estlund, *Freedom of Expression in the Workplace and the Problem of Discriminatory Harassment*, 75 Tex. L. Rev. 687 (1997)(pointing out the complexities involved and proposing a test that balances some of the concerns on both sides of the issue). Additionally, in R. A. V. v. City of St. Paul, 505 U.S. 377 (1992), the Supreme Court suggested in dicta that hostile work environment claims under Title VII do not automatically violate free speech rights. That case, however, did not involve a hostile work environment claim.

61. *See* Chapter Six. Some courts, however, have not recognized student-on-student harassment, while other courts and the OCR specifically have. *Id.*

62. OCR Guidelines on Sexual Harassment, 62 Fed. Reg. 12034, 12045–12046 (1997).

63. *Id.* at 12046.

64. *See* Chapter One.

65. OCR Guidelines on Sexual Harassment, 62 Fed. Reg. at 12046.

66. There are differences, however, as discussed in Chapter Eight.

67. *See* Chapters Six and Eight.

68. This is because individual comments that might themselves be offensive do not become actionable as a hostile work environment unless they are severe or pervasive enough to alter a term or condition of employment and create a hostile or abusive working environment. *See* Chapter Six. Thus, the expression by itself is not subject to sanction, rather the pattern of conduct to which that expression might contribute can become actionable, but only if it rises to the level of discrimination described above. It is the discrimination and not the expression that is the focus in hostile work environment claims and under the proposed statute. Although, as discussed in this chapter, this issue can become quite complex, depending on the situation and actors involved.

69. Robert S. Peck, *The Threat to the American Idea of Religious Liberty*, 46 Mercer L. Rev. 1123 (1995).

70. *See* Chapter Eight, at proposed statute §I(a).

Chapter 10

1. *See* Nev. Rev. Stat. §388.150; N. M. Stat. Ann. §77-11-10; Alaska Stat. Ann. Title 14, §14.03.090.

2. *See* Chapter Seven.

3. Hafer v. Melo, 502 U.S. 21 (1991); Monell v. Department of Social Services of the City of New York, 436 U.S. 658 (1978).

4. For examples of some of these limitations, *see* Will v. Michigan Dept. of State Police, 491 U.S. 58 (1989)(Eleventh Amendment immunity applies to states under §1983); DeShaney v. Winnebago County Dept. of Social Services, 489 U.S. 189 (1989)(no affirmative duty for state to protect citizens from abuse by others); City of Oklahoma v. Tuttle, 471 U.S. 808 (1985)(no *respondeat superior* liability under §1983); Harry A. Blackmun, *§1983 and Federal Protection of Individual Rights—Will the Statute Remain Alive or Fade Away*, 60 N.Y.U. L. REV. 1 (1985); Susan N. Herman, *Beyond Parity: §1983 and the State Courts*, 54 BROOK. L. REV. 1057 (1989).

5. *See* Charles F. Abernathy, *Section 1983 and Constitutional Torts*, 77 GEORGETOWN L. J. 1441 (1989)(noting as part of a much broader discussion that §1983 concepts are often couched in tort-like terms and that the availability of §1983 has also affected the development of constitutional standards).

6. *Monnell*, 436 U.S. 658; *see also* Maine v. Thiboutot, 448 U.S. 1 (1980)(regarding other federally protected rights).

7. *Monnell*, 436 U.S. 658; *Hafer*, 502 U.S. 21.

8. *See Will*, 491 U.S. 58 (states are immune based on Eleventh Amendment immunity); *Hafer*, 502 U.S. 21 (state government officials are immune for actions taken in their official capacities, but not for those taken in their individual capacities).

9. Flagg Bros., Inc. v. Brooks, 436 U.S. 149 (1978). *Flagg Bros.* involved "public function doctrine," which is not relevant to the type of private actor discussed in this book, and which as *Flagg Bros.* demonstrates, is quite hard for plaintiffs to prevail on anyway. *Id.*

10. Sheldon Nahmod, *Section 1983 Discourse: The Move from Constitution to Tort*, 77 GEORGETOWN L. J. 1719 (1989); *cf.* Abernathy, *Section 1983 and Constitutional Torts*, 77 GEORGETOWN L. J. 1441.

11. *Monell*, 436 U.S. 658; Pembaur v. City of Cincinnati, 475 U.S. 469 (1986).

12. *Tuttle*, 471 U.S. 808; *Monell*, 436 U.S. 658.

13. *See* Forrester v. White, 484 U.S. 219 (1988)(regarding absolute immunity); Harlow v. Fitzgerald, 457 U.S. 800 (1982)(regarding qualified immunity).

14. Corporation of Presiding Bishop of the Church of Jesus Christ of Latter-Day Saints v. Amos, 483 U.S. 327, 339 (1987).

15. Bauchman v. West High School, 132 F.3d 542 (10th Cir. 1997); Bell v. Little Axe Indep. School Dist. No. 70, 766 F.2d 1391 (10th Cir. 1985).

16. *Bauchman*, 132 F.3d at 556.

17. *Id.*

18. *Bell*, 766 F.2d at 1408.

19. *See supra* note 9 and accompanying text. Regarding liability based on private actors acting in "conspiracy" with government actors, *see* Dennis v.

Sparks, 449 U.S. 24 (1980); Adickes v. S. H. Kress & Co., 398 U.S. 144 (1970).

20. *Id.*

21. *See* the discussion of the *Herring* case in Chapter One.

22. *Id.*

23. Pursuant to Harlow v. Fitzgerald, 457 U.S. 800 (1982), state officials can have qualified immunity when their official actions do not contravene "clearly established law."

24. Several of the "classic" Establishment Clause cases involving the public schools as well as other such cases have been accompanied by incidents of harassment or discrimination, but the courts have all but ignored those incidents. *See* Chapters One and Three.

25. *Bauchman,* 132 F.3d at 556.

26. *See* 42 U.S.C. §2000c *et seq.*

27. *See* 42 U.S.C. §2000a *et seq.*

28. *See* 42 U.S.C. §2000a.

29. 42 U.S.C. §2000a(a).

30. 42 U.S.C. §2000a(d).

31. *See* Small v. Hudson, 322 F.Supp. 519 (D.C. Fla. 1970)(finding racial segregation in a home for the aged and a nursing home owned by a county to be actionable).

32. Runyon v. McCrary, 427 U.S. 160 (1976).

33. *See* 42 U.S.C. §2000a *et seq.*

34. *See* Chapter Nine.

35. 42 U.S.C. §2000c *et seq.*

36. *Id.*

37. 42 U.S.C. §2000c(6)(a).

38. 42 U.S.C. §2000c–8.

39. *See* 42 U.S.C. §2000c(b)(definition of desegregation for purposes of the public education provisions of the Civil Rights Act of 1964).

40. 42 U.S.C. §2000d *et seq.* (Title VI); 20 U.S.C. §1681 *et seq.* (Title IX).

41. *See, e.g.,* Nev. Rev. Stat. §388.150.

42. *See, e.g.,* N.M. Stat. Ann. §77–11–10.

43. Alaska Stat. Ann. Title 14 §14.03.090.

44. *See, e.g.,* Conn. Gen. Stat. Ann. §10–15c (West 1988); N.J. Stat. Ann. §18A:36–20 (West 1989). To my knowledge, no state antidiscrimination law has been utilized to address this problem, but the Connecticut and New Jersey laws cited above demonstrate that the language contained in some of these statutes may be readily usable or amendable for this purpose if a court or the state legislature were to so recognize. There are also numerous state constitutions that protect against religious discrimination, but they vary in scope, language, level of enforcement, and applicability

to various situations. As is explained later in this chapter, I chose not to address state constitutions because few, if any, would cover the discrimination that is the focus of this book and they raise a large number of peripheral issues. Their utility in the present context does not justify the space needed to address them.

45. Hsu v. Roslyn Union Free School Dist., 876 F.Supp. 445 (E.D.N.Y. 1995)(school board antidiscrimination policies are valid and enforceable, but the case involved a very different fact situation from those discussed in this book).

46. For example, Mississippi, a state in which some of the most egregious violations have occurred (*see* discussion of *Herdahl* case and local reaction to it in Chapter One), has no such statute, and I could not find local policies providing protections in this regard either.

47. For a general description of these torts, *see Restatement (Second) of Torts* (1965). For IIED, *see id.* at §46; NIED, *id.* at §436A (not as separate tort); battery, *id.* at §13-§20; assault, *id.* at §22. Of course, not every state recognizes all of these torts, and not all states follow the Restatement definition for each of these torts.

48. *Id.* at §46 cmt. d.; Frank S. Ravitch, *Hostile Work Environment and the Objective Reasonableness Conundrum: Deriving a Workable Framework from Tort Law for Addressing Knowing Harassment of Hypersensitive Employees,* 36 Bos. Col. L. Rev. 257, 267–268 (1995).

49. *Id.* at §46 cmt. J.

50. *See supra* notes 43–46.

Chapter 11

1. Nadine Strossen, *How Much God in the Public Schools? A Discussion of Religion's Role in the Classroom,* 4 William & Mary Bill of Rts. J. 607, 616 (1995).

2. *See supra* note 1, Chapter Two.

3. Strossen, *How Much God in the Public Schools?,* 4 William & Mary Bill of Rts. J. 607; Steven B. Epstein, *Rethinking the Constitutionality of Ceremonial Deism,* 96 Colum. L. Rev. 2083, 2169–71 (1996).

4. *Id.*

5. *See* Chapters One and Two.

6. *See supra* note 105, Chapter One and accompanying text.

7. Jerome Lawrence and Robert E. Lee, *Inherit the Wind: New Two-Act Edition with Production Notes by the Playwrights* (Dramatists Play Services 1986).

8. *Id.* at 55–56.

Index

KF 4162 .R38 1999

Ravitch, Frank S., 1966-

School prayer and
 discrimination